The Martha Cook Building's First 100 Years

The Story of a Women's Residence Hall and Its Community
at the University of Michigan

Catherine Walsh Davis
Oct 24, 2015

Catherine Walsh Davis
Kathy Graneggen Moberg

Kathy Graneggen Moberg
Oct. 24, 2015

Ann Arbor, Michigan

Copyright © 2015 **Catherine Walsh Davis and Kathy Graneggen Moberg**

All rights reserved. No part of this publication may be reproduced, distributed or transmitted in any form or by any means, without prior written permission.

Cover Art © 2014 Bill Shurtliff Studios (www.gallery242.com)

Book layout by Bert Moberg from template © 2014 BookDesignTemplates.com

**The Martha Cook Building's First 100 Years/
Catherine Walsh Davis and Kathy Graneggen Moberg** –First Edition
ISBN-13: 978-1512143454

We dedicate this book to the memory of those who have gone
before, in appreciation of the heritage they left us;
to the young women now living at Martha Cook who carry on
the fine traditions of many years;
and to those yet to come, in the hope they may find the same
fulfillment while living at Martha Cook as we did.

CONTENTS

Preface i
Introduction v
1   William W. Cook: Friend and Benefactor 1
2   The Vision Takes Shape 13
3   The Furnishings: Comfort with Elegance 29
4   The Art of Martha Cook: Ornaments of Gracious Living 37
5   The Garden 61
6   The Structure Adapts 69
7   Financial Well-Being: Income, Expenses, and Stewardship 91
8   Fundraising: Ensuring the Future 103
9   A Board of Women 113
10 The Staff: Providing the Comforts of Home 125
11 The Residents: Choicest Spirits of the University 139
12 Alumnae: Beyond Graduation 155
13 The Quest for Diversity 169
14 In Loco Parentis: Rules and Rebellion 185
15 Scholarships: Room, Board, and Encouragement 205
16 Food and Fellowship 219
17 "Our Innumerable Cups of Tea" 231
18 Tradition: Songs, Goals, and a "Ghost" 243
19 Tradition: Parties and More 257
20 Tradition: Phantoms of the Past 289
21 Coming Home: Alumnae Reunions 301
Postscript: The Future 315
Appendix A Deed of Gift 319

Appendix B Architecture and Furnishings..321
Appendix C Martha Cook Building Directors....................................325
Appendix D Martha Cook Building Governors..................................333
Appendix E Martha Cook Building Associate Directors...................335
Appendix F Martha Cook Building House Presidents.......................339
Appendix G Martha Cook Building Outstanding Resident Award ..343
Appendix H Martha Cook Women Who Served as U-M Regents ...345
Notes...347
Photo Credits..373
Index..377
About the Authors...382

Frequently Used Acronyms and Abbreviations

AESS	Anne E. Shipman Stevens (as in AESS Scholarship)
Annual	*Martha Cook Annual*, the student yearbook
ARD	Assistant Resident Director
The Building	Martha Cook Building
Cookie	A resident or alumna of the Martha Cook Building
DPE	Diversity Peer Educator
FC	Martha Cook Building Fundraising Committee
Housing	University Housing, University of Michigan
MCAA	Martha Cook Alumnae Association
MCAAD	Martha Cook Alumnae Association of Detroit
MCB	Martha Cook Building
MCPA	Multi-Cultural Peer Advisor
RA	Resident Advisor
RHA	Residence Hall Association
U-M	University of Michigan

The Photo Credit section lists abbreviations used in the captions.

Preface

Back in the early 2000s, while trying to document the history of the Martha Cook Building's scholarship fund for a Board of Governors meeting, we ventured into the Bentley Historical Library at the University of Michigan. We were awed by the amount of primary material about the Building and the women who have lived there. We commented, "Someone should write a book about all this." In 2010, we decided we'd take on the task and set ourselves a goal of publishing a history of the Building's first 100 years to coincide with its 100th Anniversary Gala in October 2015.

We spent one day a week for three years, either at the Bentley or the Martha Cook Building, reading through every scrap of MCB documentation we could find. Our search took us through not only files, articles, and books labeled "Martha Cook" but also led us to other documents such as the correspondences of William Cook, Harry Hutchins, and Walter Sawyer; Law School and University Housing records; various photo files; and scrapbooks of individual Cookies. In our spare time, we pored over relevant internet documents.

While writing this volume, we also condensed and shared some of what we learned via a series of articles on change at Martha Cook, published in the seven issues of *The Martha Cook Building Alumnae Newsletter* between spring 2012 and spring 2015.

Over the past 100 years, the names of some rooms at Martha Cook and buildings of the University of Michigan have altered.

Within this book, we used the term that was in mode at the time period being discussed. For instance, we refer to the main parlor as the Blue Room when discussing times prior to 1962 and as the Gold Room for dates after that.

All photos were printed with permission of the photographer or, in the case of off-copyright material, of the repository where we located the photograph.

We could not have written this book without the support and assistance of others but all opinions and conclusions expressed are strictly those of the authors and do not necessarily reflect the views of any other person or group. Kathy's former MCB roommate, Debra Ball Johnson, a historic preservation architect, was the first to encourage us, reminding us that documenting our community's history is as important as preserving the Building. Our friend and fellow Cookie, Pam Sameck Wiedenbeck, volunteered to edit a companion book of memoirs written by many Cookies. Her volume, *With Portia O'er the Door,* was co-published with our book. The Board of Governors approved our proposals for the two books, gave us access to Building information, permitted the inclusion in this volume of photographs and other materials from the MCB collections housed at the Building and at the Bentley Historical Library. Similarly, the Martha Cook Alumnae Association allowed us to use their materials. MCB Building Director Marion Law and the Building's staff members not only welcomed us, answered questions and helped shift boxes of documents but provided us with ice water and fans while we worked on the fourth floor during sweltering summer days. The staff at the Bentley Historical Library provided valuable service in locating materials and photocopying what seemed like zillions of documents and allowed us to publish photographs under their control. Nanci Young and Elizabeth Carron, College Archivists at Smith College, Northampton, Massachusetts found and provided us with information on Mary Gleason, MCB's Social Director of 1936–39. Artist Bill Shurtliff kindly permitted us to use his watercolor on our book cover.

Margaret A. Leary, the biographer of William Cook (*Giving It All Away: The Story of William W. Cook & His Michigan Law Quadrangle)*, reviewed our material for consistency with her understanding of MCB's benefactor. Dorothea Coleman, Debra Magolan Holt, Deborah Day Jensen, Debra Ball Johnson, Mabelle Kirk, Janet Kreger, Marion Law and Pamela Wiedenbeck proofread this volume for content, format, and grammar. Any errors remaining are strictly ours.

Those who purchased our books deserve special mention and an assurance that after publication costs are paid, all proceeds from the sale of this and Pam's book will be deposited in the Martha Cook Annual Fund to benefit the Building and its programs.

Finally, our husbands, Bill Davis and Bert Moberg, each deserve the spouse of the century award for putting up with all things Martha Cook for many years but especially during the last two years as we frantically wrote text. Bert also gets special thanks for assembling the chapters and getting them ready for publication. He also prepared the pictures for publication, created the cover layout, and completed the final version in CreateSpace.

Catherine Walsh Davis
Kathy Graneggen Moberg
October 2015

Introduction

In memory of my mother, Martha Cook, I will build a Woman's Dormitory Building for the use of women exclusively ....

With these words, William Wilson Cook sent a deed of gift to the Regents of the University of Michigan on February 10, 1914, formally putting into motion the creation of a building that was "quite generally conceded to be one of the most artistic structures of its kind in the country"[1] and would later be called "the gem in the University's crown."[2] The deed of gift for the Building that would open to residents in fall 1915 was the result of three years of negotiation between Cook and University President Harry Burns Hutchins, ably aided by the inspired efforts of a young University graduate, Myrtle White. Cook's gift of the Martha Cook Building is notable for several reasons, not the least of which is the fact that it was his "starter gift" to the University, a gift that paved the way for his later decision to build the Michigan Law Quadrangle and, in his will, to bequeath the bulk of his fortune to the Michigan Law School.

Cook wanted the Martha Cook Building to be built and furnished with the best materials and, to this end, he hired architects York and Sawyer and interior design firm The Hayden Company to ensure that it was done. Even though he never saw the Building, either during construction or after it was built, he was deeply interested in it and personally met and corresponded with the leaders of both firms and was most definite in his choices and demands for the Building's grandeur.

But more than anything, Cook wanted Martha Cook to be a home. In 1936, describing the first twenty years of the Building's history, Marion Slemons wrote of Cook's vision:[3]

> But mere size and elegance of structure could not, he believed, accomplish his purpose. It must be a college home, inspiring cultured courtesy, sincere friendship, devoted service, integrity of character, industry, self-reliance, sound scholarship, and an appreciation of the finer things of life.

Cook's dream was fulfilled. If he were alive today, he would be pleased to discover that the women who have lived there call themselves Cookies long after graduation and refer to returning to the Building as "coming home." They still think of their residence hall in the same words set to song in the very first years, *Martha Cook, our Building, our Dormitory Dear*. It is a testament to the community that has developed over the last 100 years that the residents of the Building formed the Martha Cook Alumnae Association in 1918 and the group still meets at least twice yearly. The group is the only alumni/ae association affiliated specifically with a residence hall at Michigan, and may be the only such group in the world.

While the ambience certainly played a role in making the residence hall a home, it is the women who lived in the Building, those who managed the Building, and the staff who have maintained the Building that are the true creators of the Building's traditions and the sense of community that pervades this unique, historic building. A history of the first 100 years of the Martha Cook Building must account for all these things—the donor, the designers, the furnishings, the staff, and the women of the Building and their actions. This volume is our attempt to do just that.

CHAPTER ONE

William W. Cook: Friend and Benefactor

...a strange composite of the urbane and the tyrannical, the generous and the suspicious, the dreamer and the dictator.
Shirley Wheeler Smith, U-M Vice President [1]

Until Margaret A. Leary published her meticulously researched biography of him in 2011,[2] William Wilson Cook was an enigma to those who did not know him and even to some who did. His writings and his actions pointed to a man of contradictions. He was a small town boy from Hillsdale, Michigan, who "made it big" in the financial world of New York City and wrote a book that for many years was *the* textbook on corporations. He was a very private person yet socialized with the elite of New York. He believed that home was the nation's safety, but he built a dormitory for women and encouraged their leadership in areas beyond home and the residence hall. He was extremely prejudiced against those who were not white, Anglo-Saxon Protestants but did not prohibit the Social Directors of the Martha Cook Building from seeking residents from around the globe nor did he ever impose his racial prejudices on any other part of the University.[3] His writings pinpoint him as irascible yet his niece Florentine Cook Heath remembered him as a kind man and generations of Cookies have affectionately referred to him as "Uncle William." He was a prudent business man who amassed a fortune but, in the end, gave it all away.

1. (mcb) William W. Cook

The very privacy that Cook demanded created a certain mystery about him and urban legends, most of them totally untrue, developed in Ann Arbor and some have been passed down from Cookie to Cookie. Generations of Martha Cook residents have believed that Cook was a misogynist who never married and that the piano in Martha Cook's Gold Room was purchased for his opera singer mistress. They've also thought he built the Martha Cook Building to provide wives for lawyers, required the Building to serve ice cream twice a week, and left an endowment for the upkeep of the Martha Cook Building. They have also believed he never saw the Building. Only the last is true!

A Brief Biography[4]

William Cook, born on April 16, 1858, was the fourth of nine children of John Potter Cook (1812–84) and his second wife, Martha Wolford (1828–1909). John and his first wife, Martha's sister Betsey, had five children, three of whom were living when John married Martha. John and Martha were born in or near Cato, New York. John, the descendent of distinguished ancestors, including Governor William Bradford of Plymouth Colony,[5] went to Detroit in 1832 and moved in 1836 to Hillsdale where he founded the first bank in the town. John was an active businessman and land speculator and served in the Michigan legislature. Martha was not highly educated but she was known to have been a warm, generous and virtuous woman, highly influential in William's early life.[6] Of his siblings, Will was closest to his brother Chauncey who often acted as his proxy during the negotiations for and building of MCB. Chauncey's wife was one

2. (fty) Martha Wolford Cook

of the first Governors of the Martha Cook Building and others of his female descendants have also served as Governors; two descendants lived at MCB while attending U-M.[*] Chauncey's family maintains an interest in the Building to this day.

---

[*] See Chapter 9, A Board of Women.

As a youth, William attended the Hillsdale Academy, a college-preparatory school. He attended the University of Michigan for six years, graduating from the literary college in 1880 and earning a Bachelor of Laws degree in 1882. He then moved to Manhattan, working first for private law firms. By 1895, Cook was general counsel for John W. Mackay's company, Postal Telegraph and Commercial Cable, and for twenty-five years effectively served the various companies owned by Mackay and his son, Clarence. "Most significantly, he excel[ed] ... at helping them stand up to Western Union and stave off a threatened government takeover of the communications industry[7] .... His work for the Mackays would make him fabulously wealthy."[8]

William Cook was a prolific writer on corporate law. His first and most famous book contained 900 pages and was published in 1887. *A Treatise on the Law of Stock and Stockholders** (sometimes referred to as *Cook on Corporations*) would become the leading work on corporations and would have eight editions, the last of which, published in 1923, contained 5,936 pages over six volumes.[9]

Cook married Ida Olmstead in New York City on February 20, 1889, but it was a troubled relationship. They separated in 1892, reunited in 1894, and divorced on June 8, 1898. Ida filed for divorce in Wahpeton, North Dakota, and claimed desertion on Cook's part. Cook countersued, claiming that Ida had deserted him. The judge found Cook's claim to be more compelling and granted him the divorce.[10] After the divorce, Cook referred to himself as single; no one at U-M knew he had been married until after his death. In

---

* The complete title of the first edition was *A Treatise on Stocks and Stockholders as Applicable to Railroad, Banking, Insurance, Manufacturing, Commercial, Business Turnpike, Bridge, Canal and Other Private Corporations*. By the second edition, the title was shortened to *A Treatise on Stocks and Stockholders and General Corporation Law*. The fourth through the eighth editions were all titled *A Treatise on the Law of Corporations Having a Capital Stock*.

February 1931, John Creighton, trustee of Cook's estate, informed Henry Bates, Dean of the Michigan Law School, that Ida was threatening to file a suit claiming the divorce invalid and seeking half of Cook's estate, the bulk of which he had left to the Michigan Law School. The University was concerned about two issues: 1) the potential legitimacy of Ida's claim which could cause them to lose half the bequest and 2) the potential for the gift to decrease in value if the Depression continued and the case significantly delayed the receipt of the gift. To avoid both eventualities, the University, on January 28, 1932, settled with Ida for $160,000. The Martha Cook Building was not a party in the lawsuit.[11]

According to his niece Florentine Cook Heath,[12] William and Ida had a child with mental problems who predeceased Cook but other sources show different information. Their divorce decree stated they had no children[13] and the 1900 US census, which recorded the number of children a woman had had and the number still living, shows a zero in both columns for Ida.[14]

Contrary to the misogynist rumor, William Cook provided allowances for his nieces (but not his nephews, who were expected to earn their spending money) and was friendly with several women, notably Cornelia Otis Skinner, the first Mrs. Clarence Mackay, Mrs. John Creighton, and Mrs. Irving Berlin.[15]

In 1901, he began acquiring real estate. He first leased a site, on which he built a cottage, at the Blooming Grove Hunting and Fishing Club in Pike County, Pennsylvania, and in 1910, along with a friend, buying 900 acres adjacent to the club. In 1903, Cook began acquiring the land that would become a sprawling estate in Port Chester, New York, and, in 1908, he purchased a town house at 327 West 75th Street in New York City. He sold that house in 1913 and built a new town house at 14 East 71st Street where his neighbors included Henry Frick and Cornelius Vanderbilt. To design this house, Cook chose the architecture firm York and Sawyer and the interior design firm

The Hayden Company, businesses he would also choose to design the Martha Cook Building and the Michigan Law Quadrangle.

In 1920, Cook was diagnosed with tuberculosis. Between then and his death, the disease would limit his mobility. This may be part of the reason he never ventured to Ann Arbor to see either the finished MCB or the work-in-progress Law Quad (begun 1924, completed 1933), although U-M Vice President Smith told a sweeter story, later contradicted by Cook's niece, Florentine Cook Heath:[*]

> Regent Sawyer, on the occasion of Mr. Cook's visit to his old home town of Hillsdale, asked him to go along on a drive to Ann Arbor and there see the buildings which he had constructed. Mr. Cook's reply was, "No, Doctor, you cannot persuade me. You want to spoil my dream. I shall never go to Ann Arbor."[16]

As his disease worsened, he lived primarily at his Port Chester estate where he died on June 4, 1930.[17] His ashes were buried at his request on the Port Chester property. The Governors and residents of the Martha Cook Building sent a wreath of yellow roses and blue larkspur with a card inscribed "In Memoriam, William Cook – Friend and Benefactor."[18] They also sent a telegram to his family:

> The Governors and all the residents of the Martha Cook Building University of Michigan send a message of deepest sympathy in the death today of Mr. William Cook, friend and generous benefactor whose memorial will ever be a living testimony of his wise provision for present and future usefulness.[19]

Cook's remains were removed in 1972 to the Oakgrove Cemetery in Hillsdale.

---

[*] According to Florentine Heath, Cook made annual visits to Hillsdale and had planned to visit Ann Arbor in 1918 but his plans did not work out. Concerning Regent Sawyer's story, she said, "While I do not believe Mr. Cook actively contributed to the rumor ... I am sure he would have let any rumor stand rather than let anyone think he was ill." Source: Elizabeth Gaspar Brown, *Memorandum to the Law Faculty,* September 29, 1959. Bentley Historical Library, Elizabeth Gaspar Brown Papers, Box 1.

The Why and What of Cook's Gift of MCB

The Martha Cook Building owes its existence to the convergence of three points: the need of the University, Cook's realization that a great University cannot exist without the financial assistance of her alumni, and the skillful negotiations of University President Harry Burns Hutchins and alumna Myrtle White (later Myrtle White Godwin).

The University's need was simple. It required residence halls to house the increasing number of women attending U-M. First accepted as U-M students in 1870, women, like their male counterparts, lived primarily in local boarding houses. The rooming houses were often dirty and unsafe and many landlords would not rent to women. The first Dean of Women was Eliza Mosher, appointed in 1895. She was an 1874 alumna of the medical school. Among her accomplishments were the establishment of the Michigan League, an organization to foster the health and development of women, and the creation of a registry of safe, clean rooming houses for women. She called these abodes League Houses. Her 1903 successor as Dean, Myra Beach Jordan, an 1893 alumna, further refined Mosher's system and required rooming houses to be inspected, supervised, and approved by her office. However, by 1910, Jordan and the Regents recognized that the system was ineffective. Only 350 of the University's female students were accommodated in League Houses or sororities; four hundred were still required to find their own housing.[20] The Michigan League hired recent graduate Myrtle White '10 as financial secretary and set her the task of raising funds for four women's dormitories, each to house 100 women. The original plan called for each dorm to be built and furnished for a cost between $100,000-150,000.[21]

At the same time that plans for the women's dormitories were being made in Ann Arbor, William Cook was re-engaging with his alma mater. In 1909, he took an active interest in U-M's search for a new president and corresponded with Regent Walter Sawyer, a family friend from Hillsdale, about the possibilities.[22] He was also recognizing the need for alumni to play a part in the development of the University and wrote to Sawyer on May 12, 1909, "The university has become too great for one state to support."[23] As Leary wrote, he had learned via earlier donations to Hillsdale College "that a gift could offer him some control over a project and that the more money he gave, the more control he would have."[24] In its turn, U-M was beginning to recognize that it might benefit from "wooing" wealthy alumni. On May 25, 1910, the Regents voted to confer an honorary Doctor of Laws degree on Cook, provided he received the degree in person at commencement.[25] Cook declined the honor.[26]

In the meantime, White traveled and met with University alumni and alumnae in the attempt to raise funds. Her original attempts raised only small amounts and Hutchins advised her to instead "reach a few wealthy persons, from whom we may perhaps get something."[27]

One of the wealthy men White was advised to seek out was William Cook. She met with him at his office in January 1911. In 1930, she reported in an article in the *Michigan Alumnus*[28] that Cook was happy to see her and to learn about "conditions for girls in Ann Arbor" from one who had student experience. She reported in the same article,

> the suggestion was made that some alumnus might find a hall of residence a worthy memorial to his mother. Mr. Cook mused for several seconds and said, "Little girl, that idea strikes a sympathetic chord in my heart. I'll tell you now that I'll give $10,000 toward the project and it may be a great deal more. Tell your president to come see me."

White's memories, however, did not quite match the reality of what she earlier reported to Hutchins. Her letter to Hutchins on January 16, 1911,[29] describing the meeting did not mention anyone's mother and she did not obtain a gift of any size at that first meeting. She wrote:

> He expressed a great interest in the University but did not approve of the "indirect" way we are attempting to raise the funds for the Residence Halls. He said "If the President should say to me 'We need Halls of Residence for our girls at the University and want $150,000 to build the first Hall—I expect you to give so and so toward this fund'—why I'd be a stick of an alumnus if I didn't do it." Then he continued "If the president is in sympathy with this movement, why doesn't the appeal come direct from him instead of through a Women's League which is simply a name to me." I met the situation to the best of my ability and before I left he said "You come in again, and bring your list of subscriptions, and I'll put my name down for something."

Hutchins met with Cook on February 3. The combined efforts of White and President Hutchins were successful and Cook donated $10,000 in February[30] with the request that the donor's name remain anonymous.[31]

By summer, the Michigan League administrators were getting discouraged at how little they had collected toward dormitories and, when an opportunity arose to purchase for $17,000 the home of Professor Richard Hudson as a residential cottage to house sixteen to twenty women, Hutchins contacted Cook on their behalf. He asked if Cook would be willing to use his $10,000 for this, with the other $7,000 to be mortgaged.[32] Cook responded,

> The plan of purchasing a private residence for the accommodation of sixteen to twenty of your four hundred and fifty students does not appeal to me from any point of view. A little later I may increase my subscription and help you to do something worthwhile.[33]

Hutchins replied that this is what he thought Cook would say and asked to set up a time when the two men could meet.[34]

It is not known how negotiations progressed or exactly when Cook agreed to finance an entire building, but in February 1912, when declining a request from Hillsdale College to build a women's dormitory there in honor of his mother, he replied, "… the president of the University of Michigan has called upon me to build a similar building at Ann Arbor at an expense of $150,000."[35] The request from Hillsdale may have been, as Leary postulates,[36] the first time Cook was presented with the idea to name a building for his mother, Myrtle White's article notwithstanding. The idea did not appear in any extant correspondence with the University of Michigan until Cook sent his formal commitment, the deed of gift, on February 10, 1914, which began, "In memory of my mother, Martha Cook." The deed also first revealed Cook as the donor who had been dubbed "anonymous" in previous announcements.

By 1920, the University had built three of the four proposed residence halls. The Martha Cook Building was begun in 1914 and was credited by U-M VP Shirley Smith as "the beginning of the University's system of residence halls."[37] It opened its doors to residents for the fall semester 1915. Helen Newberry Residence, the gift of the children of the building's namesake, was not begun until 1915[38] but the much smaller building was completed by summer term 1915,[39] one semester ahead of MCB. Betsy Barbour Residence, a gift of Regent Levi Barbour in honor of his mother, welcomed its first residents in 1920.[40] Two smaller houses were opened in 1921 and 1925 as cooperatives where students earned part of their expenses. The movement to build larger dormitories began in 1930 with Mosher Jordan[41] and in 1933 all women's dormitories except the Martha Cook Building were united under one business management.[42] MCB's deed of gift stipulated that the Building remain an independent operating unit under the supervision of its own Board of Governors and that requirement has been honored by the University through the present day.

Cook's Later Gifts

William Cook was not done giving to the Martha Cook Building or to the University of Michigan in 1915. Throughout his lifetime, he continued to gift MCB with items ranging from books to terrace furniture to art. In 1917, he purchased land for the Garden and the tennis court. Cook also built the entire U-M Law Quadrangle, with construction taking place from 1924–1933. The Law Quad stands on State Street between South University Avenue and Monroe Street. Its back end on Tappan Street faces the side of the Martha Cook Building, but providing husbands for the women living there was not part of Cook's decision to purchase the State Street land. Rather, he liked that the buildings of the Quad "would be away from heavy traffic, near the literary college, the General Library, the Clements Library of Americana, the Alumni Memorial Hall, and the Michigan Union" and away from the "factory construction" of the science buildings.[43] Cook also donated to U-M a wedge-shaped piece of land on Washtenaw Avenue at North University. The Ruthven Museums Building now stands on it.

Cook's will left relatively small bequests to family members, the Bar Association of New York City, the Law Institute in New York City, the superintendent of his Port Chester estate, his housekeeper, physician, nurse, and two secretaries. It left his Port Chester estate to the New York Presbyterian Hospital with the proviso that if the hospital could no longer use the estate for hospital business, the property would become an asset of the U-M Law School. (This happened in 1972 and the Law School sold the property.) To the Martha Cook Building he left "the piano and the needlework on standards in my city house."[44] The piano, a pole fireplace screen, now in the Red Room, and a piano scarf were shipped to MCB in November 1930.[45] The Martha Cook Building did not receive an endowment from Cook, either before his death or via his will.

The rest of Cook's estate, including $770 paid to the estate by the Martha Cook Building for some of Cook's personal items which were then given to the family, was left as an endowment to the U-M Law School for legal education and the completion of the quadrangle's buildings, including dormitories. As in the case of MCB, it did not include any endowment for the operation of the quad's residence halls. *The Washington Star* of June 11, 1930, estimated that the Law School received $12 million via the will and had already received $8 million for the construction of the Quad.[46] Cook's total gifts to the Law School are the equivalent of $260 million in today's dollars.[47]

Leary premises that Cook's primary motivation for giving to the University of Michigan was his desire to preserve American institutions, whether it be the family and home or the law. She noted that he also wanted to demonstrate the value of philanthropy. Though his donations to the Law School greatly surpassed his earlier contributions, it would be a mistake to downplay the importance of his gift of the Martha Cook Building. It was the beginning of a twenty-year span of donating to the University, where his gifts grew over time. As one of the first major gifts ever received by U-M, it demonstrated a way in which an alumnus or alumna can benefit the greater good at Michigan. It helped the University fulfill a need, and, significantly, it provided a home that has become a closely knit community of women, empowering them to seek new goals and achieve their aspirations.

CHAPTER TWO

The Vision Takes Shape

I suppose it is bad form for architects to tell their clients how good their own work is, but we want you to know that we consider this one of our most successful buildings and one that we are going to be more and more proud of as it is softened by time and good honest wear and tear.

Edward P. York, Architect[1]

Even before Cook formalized his commitment to build a residence hall in February 1914, both he and the University were busy planning the Building. On July 30, 1912,[2] U-M President Hutchins notified William's brother Chauncey that the Regents had approved the purchase, not to exceed $30,000, of land on South University Avenue that Chauncey, Regent Sawyer, and Hutchins had examined. Then, on March 6, 1913,[3] Hutchins informed Chauncey that four city lots with a frontage of 132 feet on South University and 264 feet running south on South Thayer Street (now called Tappan) had been purchased by the University for $28,840. Cook had clearly contracted with the architecture firm of York and Sawyer of New York City prior to any formal declaration because Edward York arrived in Ann Arbor on May 27, 1913, to "look over the ground purchased for the new residential hall and to submit a tentative plan that he has sketched."[4] At the University's commencement exercises in June, Hutchins announced that a women's dormitory would be built by an anonymous donor.[5]

Cook placed his project in the hands of people he trusted and knew well. His brother and sister-in-law, Chauncey and Louise Cook, from nearby Hillsdale helped oversee the process. He had already worked closely with York and Sawyer and The Hayden Company, a design firm, on his New York townhouse which was completed in 1913. Their working relationships were so good that Cook employed these two companies again for the massive Law School project, which began the following decade. The two firms also continued to advise the Martha Cook Building until their demises. Letters between Cook and Edward York and especially I. Elbert Scrantom of The Hayden Company reveal comfortable and effective communications. With both firms based in New York, Scrantom and York often met in Cook's office or home to discuss plans. They stayed in touch with their client through letters while in the city and when they were on location in Ann Arbor.

The Architects and their Architecture

Edward Palmer York (1865–1929) and Philip Sawyer (1868–1949) were prominent architects who specialized in college buildings, banks, and hospitals. They met originally as associates at the firm of McKim, Mead, and White. However, they left to form their own company in 1898 after winning a design competition for Rockefeller Hall at Vassar College, where they eventually designed six buildings.[6] In their first few years as a new firm, they won eleven of fourteen competitions they entered when the norm was one in four.[7] Before York's death in 1929, they had built "fifty bank buildings, most of them on a monumental scale, and as many hospitals."[8]

There are no descriptions of how the firm carried out the tasks of designing the Martha Cook Building. But, in a small book written as a memento for York's children after his death and later published by York's wife Muriel, Sawyer described the usual working relationship between the two principals. It is logical to assume that MCB was designed according to their usual modus operandi, that is, York designed the Building in his head and Sawyer translated the cerebrations into architectural plans. Sawyer described York as the thinker "who got his stuff drawn by others, let the contracts, built it satisfactorily without noise, working so intangibly that no one ever caught him at it."[9] Sawyer described himself as a draftsman whose "interest was in rounding out the building on paper to the last detail."[10] York and Sawyer both visited Ann Arbor several times during MCB's construction as did other partners from their firm.

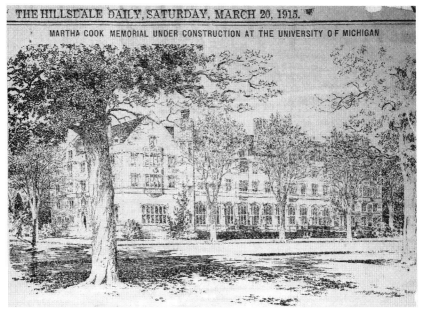

3. (bh1) Architects' sketch of the proposed Martha Cook Building, from the garden

16 · The Vision Takes Shape

4. (bhi) The bricks were laid in the Flemish Diagonal Bond pattern.

5. (cjd) Arched windows and buttresses, shown here along the Terrace, reflect the medieval influence on the Building's architecture.

In designing their college buildings, York and Sawyer turned regularly to the Collegiate Gothic style, which had been popular in the United States since the late nineteenth century. Secular in character, the style evoked the gravitas of Oxford and Cambridge Universities. To distinguish this campus home for women from the solemnness sought in an academic building, however, the architects drew richly from English Domestic Gothic design. For example, the substantial qualities of stone and masonry were hallmarks of the Collegiate Gothic style, but for MCB, a warm maroon brick was chosen and laid with the diamond patterning of a light and elegant Flemish Diagonal Bond.[11] The slate roof was gabled as a means to continue the residential feeling. And a long terrace on the east side of the Building faced a setting that would in 1921 become an informal and domestically-scaled garden created by New York-based landscape architect Samuel Parsons. Residents could easily access this terrace, welcomed by comfortable furniture, spots perfect for studying, and a large open lawn. York and Sawyer successfully incorporated a domestic sensibility that masterfully anticipated the more formal and public Law School buildings the firm would later design for Cook while making clear that MCB's purpose was quite different.

6. (kgm) Turrets and crenellations are among the Building's medieval features.

Other Gothic features represented in MCB are brick buttresses, crenelated turrets, and gabled dormers. The tall, narrow windows, framed in stone and with small leaded glass panes, are also typical features. The front portal is arguably the grand focal point of the Building, however, with its substantial double doors of oak, stone arch, ornate carvings, tracery windows, and elaborate Gothic niche that since 1918 has held a statue of Portia, heroine of Shakespeare's *The Merchant of Venice*. While this portal is reminiscent of medieval cathedrals, it is purely secular. It includes MCB's name carved in relief, and is repeated in decorative carvings both inside and outside the Building.

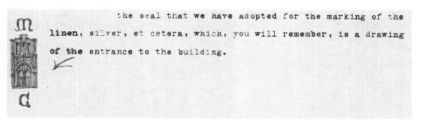

7. (mcb) Marginalia from a letter to Cook from Scrantom, June 21, 1915

Scrantom recognized its value as the Building's definitive icon and included a sketch of it in the margin of a letter to Cook in June 1915.[12] With Cook apparently in agreement, a detailed line drawing of the portal was used from the beginning to mark silverware, china, linens, and stationery.

Stone chimeras (similar to gargoyles except that they do not function as downspouts) adorn all levels of the Building. The carved heads, some grotesque, others comic or natural, are repeated and none are known to represent particular individuals. Additional ornamental designs and carvings,

8. (kgm) Chimera

9. (mcb) The Flemish Bond pattern of the brick is easily discernable in this photo of the portal, ca 1915–1917, before the installation of the statue of *Portia*.

including lamps of knowledge, appear in the stone and complete the medieval effect. Particularly notable are the charming figures of female students carved in relief on either side of the oak doors. The Scholar wears a graduation gown and mortar board. She holds a book, but props up her head, fighting off sleep. The Athlete is a college woman at play with her hair tied with a bow and holding a tennis racquet. Between them, they humorously represent a balanced ideal for the women living within.

The firm of York and Sawyer was employed by Cook, not the University, and so was beholden primarily to him. Nonetheless, the architects tried to design the Building to also fulfill desires of U-M. When they attempted to meet the University's requirement for large parlors on the first floor, the estimated costs of the Building soon exceeded Cook's willingness to pay. He wrote to the architects on December 1, 1913,

> I wish $250,000 to cover the entire expense, including your fees. Originally, you will recollect, the University people figured the building would cost $150,000. You thought it would cost ... $200,000, but later you stated it would cost more than that, and I raised the limit to $250,000. We will stop at that, because any money beyond that sum might better be used elsewhere, I think.[13]

By reducing the size of the Building from 1,000,000 to 800,000 square feet, simplifying the interiors of the public rooms, and omitting the plantings, Edward York was able to reduce the cost to $280,000, but he warned Cook,

> I am mentioning this [i.e., the reductions], so if I have to show you later on the designs of the corridors and large rooms with a very simple high base and the rest of the work in accordance, in order to get the building within the prices I have given you, you will know the reason.[14]

The four-and-a-half story Building was designed as an L, with the short leg facing South University Avenue and the long leg running along Tappan Street. As visitors come through the entry portal into the first floor level, their attention is immediately captured by the grand vaulted gallery that dramatically runs the length of the Building. It is lit by eleven arched windows facing onto the terrace and garden and has been visually anchored since 1917 at its far end by a marble replica of the *Venus de Milo*. An elegantly paneled foyer primarily serves as the anteroom to this impressive corridor. It also

10. (bgm) The corridor with *Venus*

efficiently provides access to the office, the Building Director's apartment, a guest room that now serves as a meeting room, and the original cloak room that is now the Director's office. From this foyer, a short flight of marble steps leads to the progression of splendidly decorated public spaces filling the long leg of the L, all of which open off the gallery and have windows facing Tappan Street.

Student bedrooms fill both segments of the L on the upper floors and two mezzanines.

By the time MCB opened in September 1915, Cook had paid for the entire building, including design, materials, labor, and furnishings, at a cost to him of $400,000. His gift is the equivalent of $9,720,000 of purchasing power in 2014 dollars.[15] The labor cost alone to construct a similar building today, using unskilled wage scales and excluding benefits and other additional compensation, would be $40,500,000.[16]

Construction Phase

Just as he had throughout the planning stages, Cook continued to correspond frequently with York and Sawyer while the Building was under construction. On June 10, 1914, he made a serious request of them but with humorous wordplay that reflected their familiarity with one another,

> I wish you would let me hear from you once a month as to the progress at Ann Arbor. I realize that I am only a deadhead in the enterprise, but I would like to have a glimmering of an idea occasionally as to whether it has collapsed.[17]

The general contractor for the Martha Cook Building was the New York-based George A. Fuller Company. Fuller's crew broke ground in summer of 1914. On July 1, Louis Ayres, a partner of York and Sawyer, noted that the footings were complete and that the steel girders would be delivered on the first of August. He also reported,

> A more or less curious thing happened during the excavation; five or six skeletons or parts of skeletons were discovered in various portions of the basement. Fuller Company's superintendent said that as near as he could find out they were probably put there by medical students who in the older days had to do their dissection secretly in their rooms and dispose of the remains in the same way where they could.[18]

The architects had purposely chosen an architectural style for the Martha Cook Building that evoked tradition and home, but they were fully up-to-date in the construction techniques they chose. The Building was thus completely fabricated of reinforced concrete in an effort to make it fire-safe but was covered on the exterior with decoratively laid brick and on the interior with walls faced with decorative wood and plaster. A photo taken in October 1914 shows

11. (bhc) By October 1914, the walls were beginning to rise.

that the outer walls had begun to rise but Cook was already concerned the contractor would miss the 1915 opening deadline. He wrote to Fuller that he was "very much dissatisfied with the slow progress .... Cold weather is likely to set in next month and if it stops the brick laying that might throw the completion of the building over into 1916."[19]

By summer of 1915, Cook was expressing with ever-greater frequency his concerns about completing the project on time, perhaps with good reason. A late June correspondence between Cook and Elbert Scrantom of The Hayden Company indicates that the shields and motto to be carved in the marble of the Dining Room fireplace had not yet been chosen. On June 23, Cook chose "Home the Nation's Safety" as the inscription because "As I pass along Wall Street and hear the strident voices of women suffragettes, declaiming in open automobiles, I feel that we are drifting from our ancient moorings. Hence a 'recall' inscription on the Ann Arbor Building might be appropriate."[20] A July 13 letter from Scrantom, apparently in response to concerns of Cook, reported that "it will be a pretty close connection" but he believed the Building would be completed on or before September 15.[21] A week later, Cook responded, "You know that if it is not ready somebody is liable to be clapped in the County Jail, and it looks to me as though that would be between you and York and Sawyer and the contractor."[22]

12. (a23) Sketch of the Dining Room fireplace motto by Catherine Heller '22

On August 19, only one month before the scheduled turnover date, Scrantom assured Cook that all the woodwork, except for that for the large parlor, was in place and being finished. Painters were at work and "floor layers" had started laying the floor tile. Marble for the facings and hearths had been shipped and was anticipated to arrive the next week as was the woodwork for the large parlor.[23] But on September 2, the room's woodwork, though now in Ann Arbor, still had not been erected.[24] Nonetheless, the bulk of the work was completed on time, while tweaks and repairs to the dining room floor and some of the pipes[25] were made after the Building opened.

Business Manager Frances Mack moved into the Building during the week of September 2 and MCB opened for residents sometime after September 18.[26] Completed, MCB attracted the attention of

Michiganensian as well as the more widely read *Detroit Saturday Night* that described it as "the most magnificent building of its kind ... to be found in this or any foreign university.[27] It also garnered praise in the January 1916 editions of *Architecture and Building* and *The Brickbuilder,* nationally-recognized architectural journals. According to the latter, "The whole effort in the somewhat free spending of money on this building was to create an atmosphere of solid substantiality, in the realization that such surroundings must have a healthy influence on the minds of the students at a time when such an influence is most necessary."[28]

Others also showered praise on the Building's design. Edward York related to Cook in a letter of November 4[29] that a U-M Professor of Architectural Design had said that he could now show his students both "a standard of excellency" and "the highest type of construction." In the same letter, he also reported that Charles Moore, Director of the Detroit Museum of Art (the forerunner of the Detroit Institute of Arts) and a member of the President's National Fine Arts Commission, "told Mr. Sawyer that he considers the Martha Cook to be the best building in the State, and that it sets a standard which will have its influence in improving their building plan and design for a long while to come."

It is unlikely that MCB has remained the best building in the state. Innovations in architecture and technology have created whole new classes of buildings and established requirements unheard of in 1915. But that Cook insisted on, and York and Sawyer and George Fuller adhered to, a standard of excellence that would be recognized for years cannot be denied. It is that fineness, representative of the best of its era, and the sheer architectural beauty of the Building that makes it a contributing building in U-M's listing on the National Register of Historical Places, acquired in 1978. It was also the basis for MCB's 1989 inclusion in the Michigan State Register of Historic Sites.

Dedication of the Building

MCB's Board of Governors planned an elaborate dedication dinner and reception for November 2, 1915, to introduce the Building to a variety of dignitaries and to the University community in general. Cook was opposed to the whole idea. He wrote to U-M President Hutchins,

> I do not think that a dedication is appropriate to a building of that kind. It is merely a home. My idea is that it should be opened simply, and conducted simply, without formality, gratulation or exploitation. In order that the faculty may see it fully occupied, there is no objection to a reception, but beyond that I would not go.[30]

Hutchins responded that he noted Cook's comments but "The whole matter ... is in the hands of the Board of Governors. Your desires will certainly be observed by the Board."[31]

Woodbridge N. Ferris, Governor of Michigan, must have shared some of Cook's feelings. He chose to express them, however, not in the formal words of the State's Chief Executive but as the husband of a woman perhaps intent upon participating in this splendid confirmation that women belonged in Ann Arbor. He informed Hutchins,

> The fact that I am coming to Ann Arbor on Tuesday is due to the persistency of Mrs. Ferris. I can't tell you now when I will reach Ann Arbor. You can rest assured that it will be at the latest moment before 6 PM .... Mrs. Ferris says that she is going to be present. Mrs. Ferris is exceedingly grateful for your kind invitation.[32]

Despite the negativity of the Building's benefactor and the state's highest official, the Governors chose to carry on with their elaborate plans. The festivities began with a dinner for eighty friends of the Building, held in the main floor corridor.

Marion Slemons described the dinner in *A Booklet of the Martha Cook Building at the University of Michigan*. Guests were served an old-fashioned Thanksgiving dinner, with many of the dishes made from favorite recipes of the Building's namesake, Martha Wolford

Cook. The Regents of the University of Michigan carved the turkeys. The guests took their places while a hidden group of residents sang U-M's alma mater, *The Yellow and Blue.* Speakers included Ferris; Hutchins; James B. Angell, U-M President Emeritus; Louise Stock Cook, President of the MCB Board of Governors and sister-in-law of William Cook; and Emilie Sargent, President of the Martha Cook Student Organization. Other guests included architects Edward York and Philip Sawyer and landscape architect Samuel Parsons.[33]

Following the meal, the diners adjourned to the Blue Room for a reception to which 800 guests had been invited. (York commented in a letter to Cook "that almost everyone in Ann Arbor was there."[34]) Residents led the guests on tours of the Building. Refreshments were served in the second and third floor sitting rooms.

Dedication ceremonies did not end with the dinner and reception. Slemons describes two other events, the second of which was a simple ceremony held November 11, 1917, to dedicate the Blue Room's south fireplace to the Board of Governors. The earlier event, on January 16, 1916, was much more poignant. In celebration of the eighty-seventh birthday of President Emeritus Angell, the north fire place in the same room was named the Angell Fireplace. The ceremony began with a presentation of a birthday cake with eighty-seven candles, missing the traditional eighty-eighth "to grow on" candle. Instead, President Angell was asked to be the first to light the fireplace as the growth symbol. He did so and expressed a few words of hope that the "fire thus started might burn always bright, always cheerful, and that it might warm the hearts and inspire the lives of the girls before him and the hundreds of girls who should follow." These, his last public words before his death, were prophetic as the warmth of the Martha Cook community continues to inspire its residents today.

CHAPTER THREE

The Furnishings: Comfort with Elegance

The Long Gallery ... is certainly a noble sight.
I. Elbert Scrantom[1]

William Cook's continuing hands-on interest in the Building's construction extended to an active role in choosing the furnishings, both built in, such as fireplaces and woodwork, and stand-alone furniture and art. His guiding principal was to "buy the best, but without waste or extravagance."[2] He corresponded frequently with I. Elbert Scrantom of The Hayden Company. Correspondence from Scrantom to Cook regarding dining room chairs is indicative of the level of Cook's interest:

> We are submitting to you an alternate design for the Dining Room Chair, which is approved by Mr. Hayden, and is submitted for your consideration. We hope that this type of chair will more fully meet with your approval. There is a slight difference in cost between this chair and the one originally proposed; the original chair being at $8.25 a piece, and the present design at $9.50.[3]

Cook thought the new chair so much a better choice that he approved paying the fifteen percent increase.[4]

William Cook continued to purchase furnishings for the Building for several years beyond the Building's opening. His purchases imply that he did not want a plain, bare-bones dormitory, but rather a haven in which a resident could be comfortable amid some elegance, a place where the rooms, although sophisticated, would not sit idle but be used for activities (e.g., under the rugs in the Gold Room is a wooden ballroom floor). In short, he wanted it to be a home similar to his own and he was not amenable to ideas that would vary from his ideal. A letter from him to Scrantom on October 4, 1915, when the Building had been open for only a couple of weeks, indicated that the women in Ann Arbor had ideas for changes and Cook wanted Scrantom to nip them in the bud. He wrote,

> When you go out there they will probably talk with you about a lot of changes and additions, and I wish that you and Mssrs. York & Sawyer would set a face of adamant against any changes whatsoever, and especially against spoiling the effects of the first floor by littering it with a lot of tables, chairs, and other truck.[5]

13. (mcb) Corridor with the grandfather clock, before *Venus*

In 1916, he commissioned a portrait of his mother from French painter Henri Caro-Delvaille to be hung in MCB's Red Room. That same year, he ordered six antique Chinese porcelain vases for the Building and donated teakwood tables and chairs for the terrace. In 1917 and 1918 he purchased two statues, *Portia* to be placed over the front door and an exact replica of the *Venus de Milo* for the gallery hallway on the main floor. For several years, Cook funded the purchase of smaller items, such as window screens, bookcases, and books. There came a time, however, when the Building's Board of Governors tried his patience with their numerous requests. He continued to make purchases for the Building, but it is likely that the Governors were more selective in what they requested after Cook wrote on October 29, 1918, to Scrantom,

> These Ann Arbor people never seem to get through asking for things. The latest is a case of drawers for filing cards giving the title, author, etc. of books. I enclose an explanation. They think you should make it in order that the drawers may match the present woodwork. I wish you would send them an estimate of the cost and tell them that Mr. Cook looks upon this as one of the current expenses, and so they will have to pay for it themselves. I think this will help to shut them off.[6]

Scrantom wrote an article about the furnishings of the main floor that is still their best description. In it, he pointed out the ceilings and furniture that were replicated from manor houses in England.[*] Minor

14. (kgm) The decorative plaster work of the Red Room ceiling, with its barrel vault or "wagon head" shape, is a replica of a ceiling in the early seventeenth century Chastleton Manor House in Oxfordshire, England.

---

[*] His essay was included in the 1921 *Martha Cook Annual* and is incorporated into this book as Appendix B.

changes to the décor have occurred over the years and the large and small parlors to which Scrantom referred were relabeled the Blue Room and Red Room by the residents. Upholstery and rugs have been replaced multiple times. The largest alteration was the 1961 conversion of the Blue Room to the Gold Room.

Even the plaster ceilings which Scrantom didn't mention—in the foyer, Sparking Room and elevator vestibule—are decorative. It is unknown whether these were also taken from historic British casts or if they were designed specifically for MCB. Anyone raising their eyes upward in the Building will be richly rewarded.

15. (kgm) Foyer ceiling

Two items of decoration that Scrantom did not discuss in his article are also worthy of mention, the architectural carvings throughout the first floor and the stained glass medallions of the Red Room windows. In the latter device, a lamp of knowledge embedded in the window facing South University Avenue and the seals of the United States and the State of Michigan in the window facing Tappan Street, were formally listed in the Michigan Stained Glass Census in 2000[7].

Ornately carved wood paneling extends from the entry to the long corridor and into the Red and Gold Rooms. The lamp is represented multiple times on shields, as are the MCB and U-M logos. Carvings of gryphons, winged cupids, lions, and a head in profile appear atop carved columns in the Red Room paneling and the marble fireplace sports cupids, fruits, and other designs. The Dining Room's marble

16. (kgm) Stained-glass lamp of knowledge in the Red Room

fireplace also features the lamp, and MCB and U-M logos in the relief.

Phonographs and radios were not included in the original furnishings and residents were at first prohibited from bringing their own because Cook did not like canned music.[8] Radios were first allowed in the Building in 1933[9] and by the end of the year seventeen residents owned one. The next year the total number of radios in-house rose to twenty-nine.[10] In January 1944, the Governors approved the purchase of a Capehart, a combination radio and phonograph, and designated $50 to be spent on phonograph records.[11] At least one other phonograph was purchased by House Board[12] and, in August 1973, Nancy Kovacs Mehta '55 and her husband, Conductor Zubin Mehta, gave stereo components to the residents as a thank you gift for hostessing a reception following a performance at Hill Auditorium by the Israeli Philharmonic.[13] The Martha Cook Student Organization agreed to pay for a cabinet to house the components in the Gold Room. Resident Marguerite Munson arranged with Rudolph and Susan Fink of The Tree House Cabinet Shop to design and build the cabinet.[14] The first house television, a black and white model, was purchased by the students and installed in the basement on April 18, 1955.[15] The first color TV was purchased for the house by the residents in 1967.[16]

In 2007, the Law School donated to MCB a cabinet which came originally from William Cook's study and then stood in the Law School Faculty Lounge.[17] It now resides in Martha Cook's rec room next to the Knabe grand piano, the Building's first piano,[18] and serves as a repository for sheet music. Although there is no documented evidence, it is possible that the Law School has also donated other items acquired as part of its inheritance of Cook's estate. For instance, the library table in the MCB's main hallway and the Gold Room's art carved table that closely resembles MCB's piano are reputed to have been Cook's.

Both the architectural details and furnishings are more elaborate in the public rooms than on the upper floors but even here the hall floors are terrazzo, the bathroom stalls are marble with oak doors, bedroom closets include built-in storage drawers, and bedroom carpeting was woven especially for MCB. The majority of bedrooms on the mezzanines and second and third floors are arranged in suites; each suite or stand-alone room has its own sink. The fourth floor, in contrast, is basically an attic with dormers defining the bedroom spaces. All student bedrooms were furnished with a bed, desk and chair, arm chair, tea table, and full-length mirror; the woodwork of all was gumwood.[19] The mirrors were not included in the original plans but were suggested by U-M Dean Myra Jordan while going over plans with the architects.[20] Bookcases were added in 1936.[21] Much of the original furniture is still in place today.

17. (bh6) The elegance of the architectural details and furnishings are evident in this early picture of the Blue Room.

Through the years, the Building's Governors and Directors have done their best to maintain the Building and its furnishings in a way that retains the original vision of William Cook. For example, the addition of the two major statues, *Eve* in 1967 and *Edwina* in 2005, carry on Cook's desire to "get away from conventional art"[22] and the new dining room chairs of 2009 replicate the originals.

36 · The Furnishings: Comfort with Elegance

18. (kgm) Carving from the Red Room wall paneling

CHAPTER FOUR

The Art of Martha Cook: Ornaments of Gracious Living

> *[MCB] reveals an extraordinary perfection in detail as well as comfort in its appointments and a richness in decoration which cannot but have its happy influence on the ... fortunate women who live there.*
> Wilfred Shaw[1]

Cook prized art and great architecture and thought they had the capacity to improve society. His 1914 deed of gift includes the purchase of art as one of his approved uses for potential profits the new women's dormitory might raise. Cook personally commissioned and selected art for the Martha Cook Building and later bequeathed his custom-made Steinway piano to the Building. Since that time, alumnae have followed in his footsteps and gifted MCB with significant artworks. These are all integral to making MCB not a museum or showplace but a college home that conveys the ideal of gracious living.

Chinese Vases – Spring 1916

Cookies have long been proud and somewhat awed to live in a home with Ming vases. Two Ming vases (c. 1600) and four eighteenth century vases were among Cook's first gifts to the

Building. Their story provides a window into the relationship between Cook and Elbert Scrantom, who was always on the lookout for objects that would please his client. Scrantom wrote to Cook on April 6, 1916, detailing six Chinese vases and two incense burners that he obtained for $200. He charged Cook an additional $25 to cover the packaging. He seemed to realize that incense burners were not quite appropriate for a residence hall at a public University for he wrote,

> I might say in connection with the two incense burners that these pieces are not common, being considered rather sacred family relics in which joss sticks are burned before the family gods. These are not large pieces and would be very nice for you to have in your own house.[2]

As for the vases Scrantom intended for Martha Cook, he continued, "These pieces would give them a very good start on good ornaments and distributed in the two parlours will help very much on the decoration."

Scrantom included lovely colored pencil drawings of each object. Cook responded the next day, approving the purchase of the "Chinese ware" for Martha Cook and two small pieces for his own home.[3] He asked for directions for proper placement in both residences, demonstrating his lively interest in interior decoration as well as his trust in Scrantom's esthetic sense.

Four of the vases were lost in the 1970s. Three were stolen while Thelma Duffell was Building Director and she arranged to have MCB etched on the bottom of the remaining three. One more disappeared during Olive Chernow's final year as director. In September 1992, Director Gloria Picasso contacted the U-M Art Museum for assistance in devising a safer presentation for the vases.[4] A display case for the Director's office was first considered, but the next fall, the cabinetmaker suggested converting the bookcase in the Sparking Room. The project moved slowly. In December 1995 the Martha Cook Alumnae Association agreed to contribute $300 toward the planned $650 case, but after running into problems with the woodworker, that contract was canceled. A new proposal was put forward in December 1996 for a case designed to sit on top of the bookcase. The cost was $1200 and MCAA contributed $300. The case was finally completed for $1300 in June 1997.[5]

Portrait of Martha Wolford Cook – January 1917
Henri Caro-Delvaille (1876–1928)

The portrait of Cook's mother, Martha Wolford Cook, hangs in the Red Room location personally chosen by the artist when he visited the Building in December 1916.[6] Born in Bayonne, France, Caro-Delvaille studied at the School of Fine Arts of Bayonne and the School of Fine Arts in Paris; he was a member of the French National Society of Fine Arts. He won the great gold medal of the International Exhibition in Munich in 1905 and was knighted in the Legion of Honor in 1910. He was living in the US, recovering from wounds suffered in World War I, when he received the commission from Cook.

19. (bh1) Sketch drawn by the artist while visiting MCB in 1916. The finished portrait can be seen in Chapter 18.

Scrantom originally suggested hiring Irving R. Wiles (1861-1948), a successful portrait painter from New York. Architect Philip Sawyer felt, however, that Caro-Delvaille had the greater reputation and was surprised when both artists quoted the same price. The sculptor Theodore Spicer-Simpson (whose name will come up again in relation to *Portia*), also assisted with negotiations, writing to Scrantom on October 5, 1916, "I spoke to him [Caro-Delvaille] of your friend and he said '*on pourrait s'arranger!*' and would be ready to do a three-quarter length portrait for $2500 as like myself, the old-fashioned costume interests him a great deal."[7] Scrantom wrote to Cook on November 18, 1916 and reported that Caro-Delvaille "was most enthusiastic over the commission …. It will probably take him in the neighborhood of a month or six weeks to complete the portrait."[8]

The project developed into full-length, companion paintings of Cook's parents, and the artist worked from daguerreotypes. Each painting also includes a miniature of the subject's spouse. The completed painting of Martha was mounted in January 1917. The painting of Cook's father is now displayed in the John Potter Cook Dormitory at the University of Michigan Law Quadrangle.

It was the artist's desire

> to bring back to life a past, with all the impressions which cling to our memories like unseen spirits. Martha Cook represents our great grandparents, a glimpse of whom we caught in childhood. I remember these ancestors full of dignity and abnegation. I have tried to portray an epoch in which the mother was queen in her home, living respected for the simplicity of her manners and the greatness of her virtues. I wish to make this portrait a symbol."[9]

The May 1917 *Michigan Alumnus* included a photograph and glowing description of the new artwork and remarked that it was one of the three best portraits then owned by the University.[10] The artist's wife, Aline Caro-Delvaille, visited the Martha Cook Building on March 15, 1938, ten years after his death, and wrote in the guest book, "So happy to have been able to see my husband's painting of Mrs. Cook, painted in 1916."[11]

An alumna's poem written on the occasion the MCB's Twentieth Anniversary includes amusing verses about the painting and its place in the Building's lore:[12]

> Though she graces the Red Room where young men in hordes
> Sit and fuss with the fringes and wear out the cords,
> 'Tis her spirit that fills every room in the place
> 'Tis her ideals we feel as we gaze at her face.
> She embodies the character, womanly grace
> That the donor would fain have us all to embrace
> She is regal and splendid – and now, if you'll look
> We will see that famed painting of our Martha Cook.

After hanging undisturbed for more than ninety years, except as the backdrop for many resident photos, the painting became the object of thieves in 2008. Out-of-state fraternity brothers visiting their U-M counterparts for the weekend broke into the Martha Cook Building in the early hours of March 8, stealing a lamp and the Outstanding Resident Award plaques; the burglary was not immediately detected. They returned the following night and stole the Martha Cook portrait. A trail of broken antique glass led police to the Ann Arbor chapter's door a few hours after the theft was discovered. Evidence, including the broken picture frame, was found and the lamp recovered, but not before the painting was roughly handled and taken to Wisconsin. The plaques were never located. Security cameras, installed earlier that year, captured images of the perpetrators, and they were formally charged and punished. The painting was professionally restored, placed in a new custom frame with solid support, and reinstalled in April 2009.

Venus – May 14, 1917

The Carrara marble replica of the *Venus de Milo*, sculpted in Italy, stands in state at the end of the corridor, facing the front entrance. The difficulties of long distance communication in the early twentieth century were exacerbated by World War I and obtaining this statue was not simple. The project began in April 1916 at Cook's behest and was coordinated by The Hayden Company. In an August letter to Cook,[13] Scrantom said that while his company's

Italian contact, Mr. Girard of Florence, would procure the desired Venus statue, a cost estimate was difficult,

> owing to present war conditions. I would judge that the statue would cost between $1300 and $1600 delivered .... His [Girard's] letter states that he can procure the services of one of the best sculptors of Florence and would have the statue executed in strict accordance to the original in statuary marble of Carrara. This would be slightly antiqued in order to give it the mellow atmosphere of the original.

The matter dragged on. Scrantom wrote again February 6, 1917, and explained in great detail that the original sculptor had been called to the war front and was no longer available. However, Girard had located an unnamed sculptor who had an already completed *Venus* statue,

> an exact size and copy of the original, which is about one foot higher than that ordered. He writes that if we could use this Statue we could reduce the base to about fifteen inches (15") in height which would be in good proportion and could be shipped at once ....
> If it is your wish we can cable Mr. Girard to ship this .... Otherwise, we can order him to proceed to reproduce the Statue as per our original instructions and wait the time for delivery .... Mr. Girard further writes in his letter that fine Carrara Marble has become quite scarce as most of the miners are at the War.[14]

A May 8 letter by Scrantom indicates that not only did Cook choose to purchase the already completed statue, but he actually viewed the statue when it finally arrived in New York on its journey to Ann Arbor.[15]

Venus was positioned in her place of honor May 14, 1917, under Scrantom's supervision[16] and immediately became a beloved symbol of the Building. Photographs of the statue regularly appear in MCB annuals, *Venus* is mentioned in resident poetry and songs, and she has been featured on resident-designed T-shirts.

York and Sawyer evidently would not have chosen *Venus* for the main hallway had the choice been theirs. Cook wrote to them on June 29, 1917, giving an opinion shared by Cookies of all generations:

20. (bgm) The Martha Cook *Venus*

I have your letter criticizing my selection of a statue of Venus for the medieval building at Ann Arbor. I am somewhat surprised at this. I was under the impression that the statue of Venus knows no age, no nationality and no locality. I thought it was cosmopolitan, belonging to all ages, all nations and all localities. Venus, you know, according to the Greeks, was born of the foam of the wave, and hence was a child of nature. Her statue a finished product of nature, touched by the hand of man, is, like the hills, always new, however old. You would not dare to say that she is not as young now as she was in the days of Troy. You dare not.[17]

Portia – June 1918
Attilio Piccirilli (1866–1945) and Furio Piccirilli (1868–1949)

Martha Cook's elaborate, Gothic portal is a work of art itself and was conceived to be iconic. It was selected as the Building's logo early in the design phase, carved in woodwork and marble, and reproduced on the letterhead, dishes, and silverware. However, for the first two years, the niche above the door remained empty. How to fill that important space was a serious decision, not to be rushed.

In May 1917 Cook suggested a bust for the niche, but York and Sawyer responded, "This niche is high and narrow, being designed to hold a full-length figure, like those Gothic buildings by which the design of Martha Cook was originally suggested."[18] Cook also considered Minerva, goddess of wisdom and the arts, an image he came back to again a few years later when contemplating a statue for a garden gazebo that was never constructed. Minerva was discouraged by the architects, too. York and Sawyer wrote back, very diplomatically, on June 20 to discuss the project further.

Their letter also reveals that Theodore Spicer-Simson, a sculptor known today primarily for his metal relief portraits of famous men, had been hired to create the statue and that he suggested a medieval statue as an appropriate middle point between the historic *Venus* and the modern-woman residents.

> It is not as easy to find the right thing for this position as it was to select a place for Venus. She is a separate object and needs only a pedestal and a background for she is like an easel picture or an important piece of moveable furniture.
> This exterior figure is a very different proposition. It is fixed in position and in its height above the eye. It must be proportioned to the niche, already built for it, and in harmony with the architecture which surrounds it so that it will form, if properly done, an integral part of the building. If it is right in composition and in its pose everyone will feel that it is the thing to put there and could not be otherwise ....[19]

A week later, on June 29, Cook responded to his architects with a new and final choice:

> You ask me to select a medieval statue for the niche on the outside of the building. That is easily done. Let us have no statue of any medieval saint, nor any statue of a medieval angel. But let us take Shakespeare's greatest lawyer, Portia, who exposed 'quaint lies' and brought to book the bloodthirsty Jew – a full throated woman of vivacity, poise and feminine charm.[20]

The decision finally made, the next step was to produce an original work of art to both fit the existing niche and please Cook. The latter proved to be the most difficult as Cook was dissatisfied with Spicer-Simpson's statue mockup and his price. He wrote to York and Sawyer on August 1:

> Frankly the miniature plaster cast of the proposed statue of Portia by Spicer-Simson disappoints me. It has no force or originality or representative spirit. It might well be taken for the statue of a sweet girl graduate .... Sweetness is all very good, but is hardly appropriate to this particular statue in this particular place and representing this particular character of Portia, facing the judges and unfolding startling propositions of law ....
>
> I enclose some pictures which the Professor of Art at Ann Arbor has sent to my people at Hillsdale, giving suggestions as to a proper statue. You will notice they are all angels or saints, and not a lawyer or sinner among them .... I wish to get away from conventional art in this particular instance.[21]

Following what appears to have been a prolonged stalemate, the situation took an interesting turn in December 1917 when landscape architect Samuel Parsons wrote to Cook and recommended hiring Attilio and Furio Piccirilli, well-known marble carvers and sculptors. They had already modeled the bronze doors of Cook's New York house, and would later, in 1920, carve Daniel Chester French's Abraham Lincoln for the Lincoln Memorial.[22] Cook agreed and after further discussion as to whether the statue should be made in bronze or stone, the Piccirilli brothers completed the work in Napoleon gray marble.[23] The statue was set in place in June 1918.[24]

21. (bgm) *Portia*

The dedication on Commencement Day 1918 was covered with a full page in the November 1918 issue of *The Michigan Alumnus*, illustrated with a photograph of the statue taken pre-installation.[25] Margaret Yerkes Holden '18, House Board President and later a Martha Cook Governor, was involved in dedicating *Portia* that June. (She also rededicated the statue at the Seventy-fifth Anniversary Gala Weekend in October 1990.) The June 1918 *Annual* included the same photograph, Portia's Quality of Mercy Speech (*The Merchant of Venice, Act IV, Scene I*), and the following message:

> It seems very appropriate that a representation of the most intellectual woman created by the master English poet should have a place in this Building – this masterpiece of the early English style of architecture and a residence for women during their college years.

Clearly, this gift was appreciated by the residents, particularly for the character's perceived learning and wisdom. By 1922, both *Portia* and *Venus* appeared together in what would become a traditional house song, *Martha Cook Our Building*.* The two statues were

---

* See Chapter 18, Tradition: Songs, Goals, and a "Ghost."

beloved and immediately became part of the fabric of Martha Cook life.

The *Portia* statue has sometimes raised controversy due to anti-Semitic overtones in *The Merchant of Venice* as well as Cook's choice of words when describing how the character "brought to book the bloodthirsty Jew,"[26] and his published anti-Semitic writings.[27] None of this appears to have been Cook's intention when choosing a subject for the all-important portal niche. Rather, it was Portia's status as an educated woman and attorney that brought her to Cook's mind and struck him as an appropriate figurehead for a women's university residence hall. The character's controversial aspects in fact, make it an ideal subject for public art at an educational facility. The University of Michigan's Commission on Public Art states on their website that the goal is to relate "individual works of public art to the educational, cultural, historical, social, or political dimensions of its environment, however complex those dimensions may be."

Red Room Tapestry – Fall 1919

Scrantom came across the Red Room tapestry in the summer of 1919, and wrote to Cook on July 16,

> Mr. Hayden has procured, through a trade deal, a small Flemish tapestry. In my opinion it would be most appropriate and the right size for the small parlor of the Martha Cook Building ....
>
> The tapestry is what is known as a Flemish Verdure Tapestry and should, I would say, date [from] the latter part of the 17th century. Its quality is not unusual, but very fair. The figures are very pleasing and the coloring extremely nice ....[28]

Cook responded two days later, having seen the tapestry that morning, with questions about the size and how well it would fit the ambiance:

48 · The Art of Martha Cook: Ornaments of Gracious Living

22. (sfa) MCB's seventeenth century Flemish verdure tapestry

The tapestry is a hunting scene and I don't know whether such a scene would fit in with that building, unless they call it 'Uncle William hunting duck in the 17th Century'. I am not sure whether it is a duck or a goose. Judging from most of the people I run across I guess it is a goose.[29]

The $800 purchase was made and Scrantom wrote to Social Director Grace Greenwood September 27, 1919, notifying her and explaining exactly where to hang it.[30]

Cook's 1913 Art Case Steinway Piano – November 1930

The art case Steinway piano in the Gold Room is as much a work of art as any statue or painting. Cook commissioned the Model A Steinway in 1913 at a cost of $1300 for the piano and $300 for the handwork,[31] probably for professional pianist Isabel Hauser who may have been the love of his life.[32] The rumor for decades among Cookies was that Cook had it built for an opera diva mistress, but Leary makes a convincing case that there was no diva and Hauser, who died tragically of peritonitis on December 11, 1915, was at the very least Cook's dear friend and the woman family members later reported he mourned deeply.

The piano is unique and took a year to complete. Steinway built the piano and then sent it to The Hayden Company which designed the decorative elements, oversaw the painstaking work and applied the veneer. Approximately 400 people were involved in the piano's creation. It is made of Italian walnut with rosewood and mahogany inlays and hand-inked, intricate designs. According to Robert Grijalva, U-M's Director of Keyboard Maintenance and Assistant Professor of Piano Technology,

> "Every single piece of wood in there, every sliver, is a separate piece of wood. The inlay on this is utterly seamless and unbelievable. Also, all the little figures that you see throughout the panel, whether angels or little animals, has its own expression because each one was hand inked."[33]

The piano has forty-two species of wood from seventeen countries, and there are twelve thousand moving parts. Centered above the keyboard is the Latin phrase meaning, "Music is medicine to the troubled soul." The piano remained in Cook's New York townhouse until his death, and it was shipped to MCB November 8, 1930,[34] prior to the probate inventory; it arrived three days later with the Red Room fire screen tapestry and a red velvet piano scarf.[35]

23. (a41) Art Case Steinway piano, 1941

The Steinway is one of two art case pianos owned by the University; the second is a 1930 Model B Steinway at the U-M Museum of Art.[36] The Cook piano was meant to be played and has been a well-used and much loved instrument. The piano was once played by Vladimir Horowitz. Olive Chernow related the story:

> On April 19, 1975 Vladimir Horowitz paid an unexpected call at MCB. He was in Ann Arbor to give a concert the next day. Luckily, I was in the lobby of MCB when Mr. Gail Rector, president of the

University Musical Society, brought Mr. and Mrs. Horowitz to see the piano in the Gold Room.

As we walked into the Gold Room, we saw one of the residents, Elizabeth Munson, playing the piano softly. She didn't see us because she was absorbed in her playing. She was a classic figure with her hair done up neatly. Mr. Horowitz stood quietly and listened to her play until she finished. He told her that the piece was very nice and asked her what it was. She said she had composed it. Imagine how thrilled she must have been to have played her original composition for him!

Then Mr. Horowitz sat down and played vigorously for a few minutes. He said the piano played well. One of the residents slipped in with a camera and asked if she could take his photograph, but he refused. We were all so disappointed that we did not have a record of that memorable event.[37]

Professor Grijalva was invited to a Board of Governors meeting in 1993 to discuss internal and external repairs to the piano, much needed due to age, use, and accidents. Significant damage to the keyboard occurred two years later after someone sat on it. Some repairs were made.[38] Considerably more work was still required for the case and mechanisms: $40,000-worth of highly skilled restoration to bring the piano back to its original glory.

It was unclear how this would ever be achieved until MCB alumna Helen Lightfoot Panchuk '29 donated $20,000 in spring 2001 for the purpose of restoring the piano which she had such fond memories of playing as a student. A special fund drive began, with the final donations raised through a matching grant from the Martha Cook Alumnae Association with money from its Memorial Fund. The piano was transported to Pianocrafters in Plymouth, Michigan, on June 28, 2002, where Patrick DeBeliso, in close association with Professor Grijalva, began the restoration project.*

---

* Grijalva and DeBeliso worked together again in 2013-14 to restore another Model A Steinway for the University—one of George Gershwin's pianos. Source: University Record, Sep 23, 2014, <http://record.umich.edu/articles/u-m-unveil-historic-george-gershwin-piano-free-concert>, (Oct. 6, 2014).

The piano returned to the Gold Room eighteen months later in time for the grand rededication at the 2004 Spring Tea.

Bust of William W. Cook – 1930
Georg J. Lober (1892–1961)

The bronze bust of William W. Cook was created by sculptor Georg J. Lober in 1930 using a cast of Cook's death mask, thirty-year-old photographs and descriptions by people who knew him. Lober is well known as the creator of the bronze sculpture of Hans Christian Andersen (1956) located in New York City's Central Park. The U-M Regents gave the Board of Governors permission to purchase the bust in 1930.[39]

The bust was mounted in the place of honor on the Blue Room's Angell fireplace mantle. It has not always remained

24. (bgm) Bust of William W. Cook

there, however. The bust was stolen by a campus fraternity in the late 1960s. The Board of Governors' March 24, 1969, minutes state that, "the Board is grateful to campus security for the return of the bust of Mr. Cook." It was firmly attached to the mantle, but again went missing the night of March 25, 2006, causing damage to the mantle. After two years with no leads and advertisements in *The Michigan Daily* for his return, the Governors' Minutes of June 13, 2008, described its sudden reappearance:

Mr. Cook's bust is back at home in the Building after being anonymously dropped off at the Student Legal Services Office in the Michigan Union. The bust shows no visible damage. The bust will have additional security added to the mounting when it returns to its original spot above the north fireplace in the Gold Room.

Eve – Dedicated October 21, 1967
Paul Suttman (1933–1993)

The bronze sculpture of a young woman in the Martha Cook garden was commissioned by the Martha Cook Alumnae Association after receiving donations in honor of the Building's Fiftieth Anniversary. Adele Huebner '54, chairwoman of the event, wrote in a thank you note to alumnae:

> After careful consideration of many possibilities and in accordance with William W. Cook's belief that the Building should be a source of beauty and inspiration for its residents, it has been decided that a statue placed in a proper setting in the Garden would be the most appropriate Alumnae gift to commemorate the Fiftieth Anniversary.[40]

The sculptor, Paul Suttman, received a Bachelor of Fine Arts degree from the University of New Mexico in 1956 and a Master of Arts from the Cranbrook Academy of Art in 1958. He designed and built race cars, worked as a draftsman for the Atomic Energy Commission, and worked for architect Eero Saarinen prior to becoming an established artist. He was an instructor at the University of Michigan from 1958 to 1962 where he received a Rackham Foundation Grant and a Fulbright Grant. He was the Winner of the Prix de Rome in 1965. His U-M background made him an obvious candidate for the commission when Governor Elizabeth Black Ross '29 and Elizabeth Payne '21 (a curator at the Detroit Institute of Arts) spearheaded the search. According to Olive Chernow, Elizabeth Payne proposed to the ten-member MCB Gift Committee the concept of a statue of a young woman and, "we agreed that the idea was appropriate and that Mr. Cook would have agreed, since he already had commissioned the statue of *Portia* over the doorway and

Venus down the hall."[41] Payne also recommended Suttman, and after examining his work at a nearby gallery, the committee agreed.

The statue was created in Rome during the summer of 1967 and the artist's wife, Elisse, was the model. Progress reports and photographs were periodically mailed to the committee. At one point, Olive Chernow and Adele Huebner "felt that the statue's mood was downtrodden and depressing,"[42] and Huebner phoned Suttman with their concerns. "He was delighted that she had called. He had had the same feeling and so had modified the statue after sending the last batch of photographs."[43]

The statue was paid for in three $1700 installments to the Donald Morris Gallery on July 25, August 15, and November 6, 1967. The Board of Governors had decided to use all gift money (approximately $3500) received in the fiftieth anniversary year for the statue. At their final meeting of the fiscal year, they also chose to include profits from the vending machine, which had previously gone into the Anne E. Shipman Stevens Scholarship Fund, into this gift fund until enough was raised to pay for the statue, saying that the scholarship fund was now self-sufficient.[44]

A security guard was hired to patrol the garden October 19, 20, and 21, while the sculpture was installed, and the formal dedication was held on October 21, 1967. This was the University's Sesquicentennial Year and the University had dedicated October to celebrating culture and the arts, making this a perfect time to unveil the new public sculpture.[45] Suttman and his wife were on hand for the event and stayed in the guest room.[46] He did not name the statue, saying that he hoped the Building's residents would do so.[47] Sometimes referred to as *The Girl in the Garden*, *The Lady in the Garden*, and even *Galatea* in the early years, *Eve*, referring to the three bronze apples at her feet, is the name that has truly stood the test of time among MCB's residents and alumnae.

25. (bgm) *Eve* in the garden

Eve was Suttman's final free-standing human statue, as still life became his new focus[48].

MCB Façade, Pen and Ink – Summer 1974
Milt Kemnitz (1911–2005)

Milt Kemnitz was a 1933 U-M graduate, social activist, and artist, principally known for his depictions of Ann Arbor buildings and scenes.

Olive Chernow, who was Building Director at the time this piece of art was created, tells the story of the print's acquisition best in her book, *My Years at the Martha Cook Building*:

> On Sunday morning, May 19, 1974, at 10: a. m. I looked out my window and recognized the well-known Ann Arbor artist, Milt Kemnitz, leaning against his stationwagon and sketching the entrance of MCB. I went out and introduced myself. His story was that he graduated from the University of Michigan .... One of his classmates was Jessie Winchell Forsythe, also an artist and an MCB alumna. Eventually, she opened the Forsythe Gallery where Milt exhibited many of his paintings. He had painted just about every historical building in Ann Arbor but not MCB. Mrs. Forsythe had asked him for years to do it. Finally, he was going to exhibit it in his show scheduled for June 1974 in the Forsythe Gallery in connection with the sesquicentennial celebration in Ann Arbor. He said he had never been in MCB. Well, I couldn't believe that so I promptly invited him in and gave him a tour. He was a delightfully droll character.
>
> I asked him if we could purchase his painting for the Building. He was willing, with the understanding that it would hang in the Forsythe Gallery until July 1974. I went to the gallery to see the painting as soon as it was finished, before it was framed. I loved it. I took Marilyn Hoag and Martha Nash to see it and get their opinion. They loved it. I called the Board of Governors and persuaded them to buy it on our recommendation. I'm so glad they approved the purchase.[49]

The picture has hung in the Sparking Room and the Director's Office. It is currently in storage.

Edwina – Dedicated September 25, 2005
Edwina Jaques BFA '70, MFA '75

The multi-media sculpture of a woman in the Martha Cook foyer is the work of artist and MCB alumna Edwina Jaques, a native of Saginaw, Michigan, who has long resided in England. It is the Building's first piece of twenty-first century art as well as the first created by a woman and an alumna. She wrote,

> I envisioned a statue which would represent the diverse nature of a Martha Cook woman who challenges the University world and brings a modern outlook to education but would also celebrate the gentle heart of such a woman and recognize the womanly arts that bind our past and future. I also wanted all Cookies to be a part of it and to

continue to interact with MCB by adding hearts over the years, making this an ever-evolving work.⁵⁰

The statue is constructed of polymer clay, Italian mosaic, semi-precious gems (some donated by Building Director Marion Law, keepsakes from her years in Zambia), gold leaf and an overskirt and headdress of elaborately knotted linen cord. The skirt provides the base for attaching ivory and gold leaf hearts in three sizes which may be signed or inked with short messages by anyone wishing to make

26. (bgrn) *Edwina*

the requisite donation to the MCB Annual Fund. In this way, the statue helps to preserve the Building while also connecting alumnae and friends in individual ways. Messages range from celebrations of friendship, commemorations of deceased friends and parents, anniversaries, and simply names of donors. The statue's welcoming arms have outstretched palms imprinted with the lines on the artist's own hands.

The inspiration came in the fall of 2003 when the sculptor reconnected with MCB and stayed overnight in the guest room. Her idea for donating an interactive work of art that could generate further monetary donations was presented to the Board of Governors who accepted the gift. By April 2004, the project was moving forward with the goal of unveiling the statue at the Building's Ninetieth Anniversary Gala Weekend, scheduled for September 23–25, 2005.[51] U-M's Office of Student Life (known then as the Office of Student Affairs), under the direction of Vice President E. Royster Harper, assisted with the expenses of transporting the statue from England and providing a custom-designed, lighted oak case to be housed in the foyer.

The statue is dedicated to "All Cookies, past, present and future." The artist asked the Board of Governors to name it, and they chose *Edwina*, both to honor the sculptor and because of her name's meaning, "rich or valuable friend," which represents relationships among all Martha Cook alumnae.

MCB's Art is Part of Everyday Life

Martha Cook's art collection is a source of pride, but it is more than that. The Steinway is played regularly. *Venus* is a friend, sometimes dressed for Halloween, Valentine's Day, or other occasions. William Cook's bust, known to occasionally sport a party hat or holiday greenery, is treated with affection. The painting of his mother is beloved. The art is never pretentious and melds into the residents' daily lives, creating a gracious ambiance, much as Cook probably hoped it would.

The Building's four statues, *Venus, Portia, Eve,* and *Edwina* were dubbed Our Silent Sisters by the Building's 2006–07 residents. The *2007 Annual Report* wrote of them:

> they have been described as representing traits of MCB women – wisdom, beauty, independence and friendship. To those of us who lived at Martha Cook, these mute ladies speak of significant events. Once new to MCB, each settled into her place in Building history and lore, as we all did. Just as each MCB woman is unique, the sisters are in different mediums, from different time periods, with different body types and shades of meaning. Yet, they, as we, are all Martha Cook women. Each silent sister reminds us of stories and memories, as do our Cookie Friends, old and new.[52]

CHAPTER FIVE

The Garden

The Martha Cook Building now has a proper setting, a garden nestling under its eaves forever.
Samuel Parsons, Landscape Architect[1]

Working through his brother Chauncey, Cook purchased the Condon property next door to the Building in 1917. He sold it to the University for $1 in a contract deed dated December 31 and accepted by the Regents at their meeting on February 21, 1918. In that contract, U-M agreed to "remove the present buildings on said premises" within four years and to

> preserve and maintain said premises as an open space adjunct, recreation grounds and park for the benefit and use of the occupants of said Martha Cook Building exclusively, and will not allow any building on said premises hereby conveyed, except such peristyle or building in the nature thereof as the party of the first part [Cook] may himself desire to erect thereon.[2]

The contract also stipulated that it would be null and void if the Regents or their successors "failed to perform, fulfill and keep the trust." At that same meeting, the Regents also agreed to the same stipulations regarding use and purposes for the lot directly behind the Martha Cook Building, destined to become its tennis court. That land was deeded to the University in July 1917 and accepted by the

Regents at their November 16, 1917, meeting.[3] Maintenance of the tennis court was not spelled out. The tennis court was completed in 1918.[4]

27. (a30) Tennis court by Dorothy Wilson '31

Cook commissioned Samuel Parsons, the landscape architect for New York City from 1895–1911, to create an appropriate garden for the Martha Cook Building. Parsons was involved as early as August 1915 with designing the plantings around the Building.[5] A November 4th letter from architect Edward P. York to Cook mentioned that he and Philip Sawyer, while traveling to Ann Arbor for the Building's dedication, "went over the planting very carefully with Mr. Parsons, who was on the same train with us."[6] It's not clear if this referred to immediate plantings or if Cook was already planning the reconstruction of the Condon lands two years before he purchased it. He may have had an inkling that the land would be for sale as the Condons were known to be in serious financial difficulty.[7]

Cook's use of the word "peristyle" in his contract with U-M indicated that he had already begun to think of ways to landscape the newly acquired property and he began urging I. Elbert Scrantom of

The Hayden Company to locate a statue of Minerva to be housed in a "little stone temple which I contemplate putting on the Condon property."[8] Scrantom recommended[9] that the statue not be made of bronze as it would blacken and not be as distinctive as marble and that it not be of "heroic size" as the statue of *Venus* is. Rather, he suggested, it should be an exact replica of one of the authentic *Minervas*, which he estimated would not be over four feet, six inches tall. He further suggested that the statue be acquired first and the temple then created to fit. He consulted with an expert in Florence, Italy who could not find any *Minerva*[10] casts and also with Gisela M. A. Richter, Assistant Curator of the Metropolitan Museum of Art, who noted, "the 'Lemnian' Statue of Athena is considered the best extant statue of that Goddess. We have cast of it in our museum."[11]

28. (bhi) The Condon garden. 1915

Scrantom informed Cook that the *Minerva* statue, although smaller than *Venus*, would cost considerably more to reproduce because the cost of marble had increased.[12] Whether the anticipated cost of $2500 to $3000 for the statue alone was more than Cook wanted to spend, or for some other reason, neither the peristyle nor a statue were included in Parsons' plan for the garden. As Margaret A. Leary wrote in her biography of Cook,

> The Condon property already had attractive and extensive gardens, and Parsons kept some of the best: three maples, three blue spruces, a rare Japanese locust, and some magnolia trees. He added to these a variety of plantings on the north, east, and south sides of the property, leaving a central greensward as a canvas on which the trees, shrubs, and perennials stood out. Martha Cook residents could sit on the terrace on the east side of the building on teak chairs, benches, and tables supplied by Cook and look out at the garden.[13]

Parsons' blueprint of the garden indicates he added 150 shrubs, eight trees, nine evergreens, and 2500 perennials.[14] The Condon property was cleared and work begun on the garden in 1921. Parsons continued to provide gardening maintenance advice to MCB until his death in 1923.[15] Cook took as much of a hands-on interest in the development and maintenance of the garden as one could from more than 600 miles away. While the garden was being planned and created, he corresponded many times with Parsons, MCB Social Director Grace Greenwood, and U-M Superintendent of Grounds E. C. Pardon over details as small as the procurement of topsoil and

29. (bhi) Parson's garden, June 1921

removing the fence from the Condon property.[16] After Parsons' death, he provided information regarding the proper way to prune shrubs gleaned from the gardener at his Port Chester estate.[17]

Maintaining the garden to the standard set in the original plan has been difficult over the years. Plants grew and what was once attractive became raggedy and overgrown. Maturing trees added shade but in the process many of the original perennial beds disappeared. Minutes of their meetings relate that the Governors approved major restorations of the Garden in 1933 and in 1963, while the death of the magnolias in the mid-1970s caused another change in the Garden's appearance. The magnolias were replaced in 1983 with ornamental cherry trees as part of a larger landscaping project paid with gifts received in memory of Lenore Libby Sahn '69. In each restoration, the plantings, while still beautiful, became simpler. A significant change in the Garden's vista occurred when the Building's alumnae commissioned the statue of Eve in 1965 for the Building's Fiftieth Anniversary. The statue was erected in 1967.*

30. (a33) Parsons' garden, ca 1930

---

* See Chapter 4, The Art of Martha Cook: Ornaments of Gracious Living.

From the beginning, U-M did not completely live up to the maintenance stipulations of Cook's contract deed, at least as Cook and the Governors defined maintenance. As the Governors' Minutes at the time of the 1963 restoration put it, "The University has a different interpretation of upkeep" and this apparently was true even in Cook's day. In November 1918, nine months after the Regents had accepted his contract deed, Cook complained to his brother Chauncey about a bill for shrubs and a gardener when the deed had a covenant that U-M would maintain the park. "I think if I give a park to the University it can well afford to keep it up year by year, and not expect the Building to pay the expense."[18] In a letter of July 19, 1927, to Superintendent Pardon, he again noted that the Board of Governors paid for the maintenance.[19] At various times in later years, U-M has paid, or not, for the upkeep. MCB paid for both the 1933 and 1963 restorations and in 1983, the aforementioned Sahn Memorial provided the ornamental cherry trees and landscaping of the Terrace plantings and gardens at the front and side of the Building. Today, U-M fully complies with the Cook deed and covers all the costs associated with garden upkeep.

The real issue of Cook's 1927 letter to Pardon, a very irate three-page document, however, was not the cost of upkeep but rather an effort on the part of the Architecture Department[*] to remove some of the MCB garden plantings. Its newly erected building was directly behind Martha Cook and was considered to be remote from campus.[20] Cook's letter makes it clear that the authorities of the Architecture Department were insisting that plants be removed so that the Architecture Building would be more visible for those on campus and that the campus be visible to the students in the new

---

[*] The Architecture Department was originally part of the College of Engineering. It became the College of Architecture in 1931. The college's first building behind Martha Cook is now Lorch Hall and is the home of various departments of the College of Literature, Science, and Arts.

Building. Cook was incensed that the privacy of MCB residents would be violated. He wrote,

> The trees and shrubs were planted where they now are for the very purpose of shielding the park and securing its privacy .... If publicity was desired for the architects' building, they should have built elsewhere; if the young architects want the satisfaction of seeing what their neighbors are doing and how they look, let them gaze to the west where the young lawyers won't mind. The young women should not be subjected to the espionage and curiosity of students architectural. What really should be done is to erect a high wall on the dividing line and on top of that wall should be placed broken glass bottles ....

The wall was never built, and relations between MCB, the School of Architecture, and the current inhabitants of Lorch Hall have been and are very cordial, but the two buildings have been separated by a twelve-foot chain link fence for many years. The remainder of the Garden is surrounded by a low, decorative iron fence and the garden remains a haven for MCB residents and their guests.

31. (cjd) Softball in the garden, spring 1969

Parsons prophesized in an essay in the 1921 *Annual* that the garden "is well for the great University. Soon a green space will be a novelty, a cause for wonder, a refreshing relief to the eye, in and around campus."[21] While not the only green space on U-M's main campus, MCB's Garden today is one of only a handful of open spaces in a well built-up area and it has been and still is more than just a spot of beauty. As the locale for intermural sports practices, pickup softball games, sunbathing, May Day parties, and even the location for a bounce-house and inflatable water-slide during fall 2013 welcome week, it is indeed the private park and recreation grounds Cook envisioned.

CHAPTER SIX

The Structure Adapts

The history of Martha Cook is in the process of making.
                          Martha Cook Annual, 1926[1]

The Martha Cook Building looks the same today as it did when it was built but the beauty and functionality of MCB have continued to the present through careful and necessary changes which are a facet of good stewardship. When the Building opened in fall 1915, it was called the "most magnificent building of its kind ... to be found at this or any foreign University."[2] It was built of the finest materials and was intended to meet the needs of the modern University woman. But needs change over time and the Martha Cook Building has adapted physically to meet the demands of social change, technology, and safety standards. Change at MCB has often been subtle or even invisible to the eye, but it has kept the Building's residents safe and it has enhanced the tradition of gracious living.

Room Use

The first post-construction decision to adapt portions of the Building occurred even before the first residents arrived when the Building increased the number of women it planned to house and needed space to hold them. Early letters between Cook and his architects York and Sawyer,[3] and between then U-M President Harry Hutchins and others,[4] indicate that the Martha Cook Building would house 100 women. In November 1914, however, after construction had started, Hutchins wrote to Robert Kelly, President of Earlham College, "We are building two dormitories for women, one to accommodate one hundred and twelve girls ... the other to accommodate fifty girls."[5]

The Building accommodated the additional twelve girls by changing the designated use of the rooms at the back half of the fourth floor which were marked in the original architectural drawings as "servant rooms."[6] The floor was created and remains today exactly as defined in the drawings—terrazzo floor in the front half, cement floor in the back, and the two halves separated by a door—indicating that throughout the construction phase, staff was intended to live there. An MCB urban legend claims that servants did actually live here* but room rosters document that from the beginning through today, students, not employees, have been housed in the rooms of the back as well as the front half of the floor. In the first year, twelve women lived in the back half, exactly the number of additional women included in President Hutchin's statement.

In actuality, 115 students were domiciled at MCB during 1915–16, according to room lists. At least two of the women were probably

---

* The urban legend further claims that the first residents brought their personal maids and the bedrooms on the lower floors are divided into suites so that student and maid would have connected but separate rooms. Three room suites are defined by this legend as being the abodes of the more wealthy residents, each of whom had a bedroom, sitting room, and maid's room. Later, still according to the legend, these three-room suites were set up so that each of two women would have separate rooms with a sitting room between them. Extant room lists, however, prove that, from the opening of the Building to the present day, all of these rooms housed only students. Any bedroom/sitting room arrangements that existed—and women are still living who claim they or someone they knew lived in such an arrangement—were not officially created and most likely were the result of suitemates pooling their furniture between rooms.

accommodated in rooms that had been designed to be large singles but became doubles. The third woman may have also lived in such a room, or she may have been assigned to the room in which Frances C. Mack, the House Director, was originally slated to live. There are no notes that have come down through posterity to tell us where Mack was supposed to live, but the room list for that year indicates she lived in room 401,[7] one of three bedrooms on the front transept on the fourth floor not designed for regular student use but, along with a small kitchenette and private bath, were meant, according to the architects' drawings, to be a suite of quiet rooms for residents to recover from illness. Later,[8] these three rooms were designated guest rooms.

For the first few years, the total number of women in the Building hovered near the 112 that President Hutchins specified and this number was held as the ideal as late as August 20, 1945, when MCB Governor Florentine Cook Heath wrote to U-M President Alexander G. Ruthven, "It is our considered opinion that ... the capacity of the building is 112 and all kitchen and serving facilities are keyed to that number ...."[9] Nonetheless, it was rare when occupancy was only 112 women. University housing did not keep pace with the increasing number of women admitted to U-M[10] so the Martha Cook Building slowly accepted more applicants. In 1936, "The Building opened with 124 students ...,"[11] a rise which required the fourth floor guest rooms to become student rooms.[12] That number held steady until fall 1943, when Social Director Leona Diekema noted in her report to the Governors that MCB had accepted extra students so there were 134 women in residence.

Then in fall 1945, the Building housed 150 women and a dining table was added to the hall to accommodate a full house at the evening meal.[13] In a letter to Heath, President Ruthven requested that MCB increase its numbers to 180-185 women to assist with the post-World War II housing shortage.[14] Florentine replied, "... we cannot possibly go over 150 without abandoning all semblance of decent living."[15] The Building was now housing thirty percent more women than it did when it opened.

In fall 1946, the number housed shrunk to 137 and the dining table in the hall was removed.[16] In February 1949, perhaps in anticipation of an employee strike and subsequent pay raise of five cents per hour for hourly employees and $8.33 per month for non-hourly personnel,[17] the Governors directed Diekema to fill vacancies for the next fall to the number of 150.[18] In May 1956, the Governors announced that the rooms behind the pantry, which had been reserved for live-in staff,[19] would become student rooms,[20] raising the total capacity to a potential 155 women, where it remained until 1993. All the increases over the years were accomplished by converting the larger singles at both ends of the Building to doubles (leaving the center sections of the second and third floors as single suites) and occasionally converting a few doubles to triples, sometimes requiring bunk beds in the triple rooms.[21] In 1993, several of the smaller doubles were reconverted to singles and occupancy since then has remained at 144 women.

To create an apartment for House Director Sara Rowe in 1934,[22] a bathroom was added to the suite composed of rooms 231 and 232. Except for the time between fall 1952 and fall 1958, when it was a student triple, this apartment has remained the home for MCB's second-in-command. In 1952, when dietician Shirley Remquist married Roger Buslee, a door was inserted to connect two rooms on the first floor, creating a suite for the married couple. When they moved out just a few months later, the suite continued as the dietician's apartment until fall 1958, when her accommodations moved back to the second floor apartment. The first floor suite was later reconverted to two unconnected single rooms. Roger was the first of only two men to live at MCB. The second is David Law PhD

(BS'67), who became a resident when he married Building Director Marion Scher in 2008.[23]

Other spaces at Martha Cook also adapted to new uses. The basement chamber at the foot of the front stairway, which has a washroom attached, was earmarked in York and Sawyer's drawings as a men's retiring room. A report written by Diekema gives the history of this area through 1955.[24] "Several years ago, the room was done over and used as a card room. Men callers used the men's staff toilet further down the corridor …. For large parties (dances for instance), the room again became the men's room." The space could also be used for studying, as a place for typing after hours or as a spot for private parties. In 1955, the chamber changed into a television room. It remained that until 1989 when a computer room was a more pressing need and the television was moved down the hall to the recreation room.

The recreation room, in turn, was first proposed by the residents in 1941 when, according to Diekema, the main desire was to have a place where male guests[25] could smoke.[*] In 1956, the residents suggested converting the trunk room to a coed study hall.[26] But it was not until 1969 that a rec room was created in part of the space originally designed to hold trunks.[27] The piano from the third floor music room was moved to the new recreation area and the music room was converted to a second library. In 1974, a second portion of the trunk room became a bike holding area that could accommodate twenty bicycles.[28]

---

[*] MCB has complied with U-M smoking rules, banning smoking in the public rooms in 1998 and becoming completely smoke-free in 2003.
Source: http://www.ur.umich.edu/update/archives/100419/smokefree (Aug 4, 2015)

The Red Room, the smaller parlor on the main floor, was often used as a meeting place for the Board of Governors, Martha Cook Alumnae Association, and other groups conducting MCB business. This necessitated moving furniture and setting up folding tables and chairs. In 2011, the Governors considered the purchase of a furniture grade conference table to be kept permanently in the Red Room, but instead decided to convert the first floor guest room to a conference room.[29] A table and chairs that fit the room was purchased.

32. (a40) Fourth floor sewing room, 1940

Part of the fourth floor attic space was used as a sewing room and was also used for years as a second television room. It later became a study room and in 1979 new curtains, a large round table, and four of the terrace tables and matching chairs were placed there.[30] Today, the room is used only for storage.

The most intriguing mention of building change found in all the documents about Martha Cook was a note in the June 10, 1946, minutes of the Board of Governors stating that they showed a sketch to President Ruthven of a possible addition to the Building and a rearrangement of the kitchen and dining room facilities. The Building paid $1,092.88 to York and Sawyer for consultation and sketches. In November 1956, the Governors again discussed the "architectural drawings developed some years ago to extend the Martha Cook Building on the present tennis court area," but no action was taken and the plans' location, if they still exist, is a mystery.

Dining Facilities

The kitchen in the basement and the first floor serving area (called the pantry in MCB parlance) on the first floor have remained in their places but changes to the equipment have occurred within them. In November 1915, Frances Mack, MCB's House Director, complained of inadequacies in the kitchen and dining room[31] and House Director Alta Atkinson requested a reconstruction of the pantry in 1930.[32] In 1937 the kitchen was modernized but the pantry remained as it was.[33]

In 1946, Cook's niece and MCB Governor, Florentine Cook Heath, wrote to Ralph Sawyer at York and Sawyer, "The eternal question is of enlarging the serving pantry and I feel this is a must. At the same time, the matter of refrigeration of food should be reviewed ...." She requested that a representative of York and Sawyer visit the Building and this may have been the instigation for the plans for the building addition mentioned above. Just as the discussion on expanding the Building seemed to die with new drawings, nothing seems to have come of the suggestions for the pantry. It remains today much as it was in the beginning, although equipment has been added or replaced over the years.

The U-M Department of Environmental Health and Safety surveyed the kitchen and pantry in 1971 and reported,

> At Martha Cook the antiquated facilities hinder any small scale attempts to modernize the food service operations. Although food-handling and housekeeping techniques are more than adequate, the predominance of ancient, non-approved equipment nullifies the effects of these techniques.[34]

Although a complete renovation of the kitchen and serving area was recommended, it was not undertaken. Individual pieces of equipment have been replaced over the years, however. The original oak walk-in refrigerator, for instance, was replaced in 1984.[35] That newer refrigerator was renovated in 2005[36] to lower the maximum temperature to 42 degrees to meet new health standards. A convection oven was added to the kitchen in 2005.[37] One recommendation of the 1971 survey was easily met—to store the silver flatware in plastic cylinders that are used for both sanitation and storage. As the report said, "Although the velvet-lined silverware drawers lend a gracious air to the dining room, they are not considered sanitary in a food service establishment."

The continuing need for a complete renovation of the kitchen and the "eternal question of enlarging the serving pantry" make them primary concerns in the planned renovation of the Building described in the postscript.

Telephones

The Martha Cook Building's telephone system has changed with the times, too. When the Building opened, there were seven phones: one each on the second, third, and fourth floors, one in the office, one in the Social Director's bedroom, one in the cloak room, and one in the kitchen.[38] Each had its own number and the women on the floors took turns on phone duty, answering the telephone and locating the person being called. In 1928–29 there were eight phones. The cloak room instrument was removed while new phones were installed on each mezzanine.[39] By the following fall, two phones were added to each of the second and third floors and specific rooms assigned to each of the

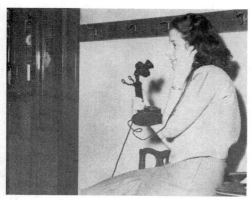

33. (a40) Phone in the cloak room, 1940

instruments.⁴⁰ There were now for the first time only three numbers listed for the entire house, one each for the Social Director, House Director, and "the House," so this is probably the first time that a switchboard with trunk lines was installed at Martha Cook.

All calls coming to the Building were now made to a single number and a student office assistant routed the calls to the telephone nearest the room of the woman being called. Phone duty was no longer necessary as each woman was assigned a ring tone made up of a combination of long and short rings. Long distance calls were marked at the switchboard with a binder clip and could not be interrupted. The switchboard operator could interrupt a non-long distance phone call for three specified reasons:

> 1. A call was waiting for another woman assigned to the same phone. In this case, the switchboard operator would ask the first woman to send the second woman to the next nearest telephone.
> 2. A second call came in for the woman already on the phone. In 1960, Night Chaperone Janice Bird announced that a code system would be used to help a speaker determine whether or not she wanted to limit her current call. "Do you want to limit your call?" would warn that the incoming message was from a female while "Would you like to limit your call?" would be the signal that a male was waiting. The operative words were "want" and "like," W for woman and L for lad.⁴¹
> 3. Because residents were informed by the office assistant at the front desk when they had a guest, an operator might break in to a call to announce the woman had a visitor or to ask her to relay the message if the guest was for another woman assigned to the same telephone. In any case, guests were announced in a similar code as multiple phone calls. "You have a visitor" indicated a female, "You have a caller," the old-fashioned term for date, meant a man was waiting,

and "You have guests" meant a mixed group was in the front lobby.

The phones were shut off when the front desk closed and all after-hours calls were routed to the room of the night chaperone.[42] In 1963, the rest of the University adopted a Centrex phone system with phones in individual rooms in residence halls. Because conduit and installation would be expensive and because there would be monthly rental fees charged to the residents, The Board of Governors, after consulting with House Board,[43] elected to opt out of the system, subject to reconsideration after it was determined how well the system worked.[44] It was not until June 1975 that Centrex system phones were installed in rooms or single suites. The switchboard* was carted off to "star" as a prop in a University Players production of *Hot'l Baltimore!*[45] In 1996, the wall-mounted phones were changed to desk phones, and each room in a single suite now had its own.[46]

Computers

Although computers had been on U-M's campus for specialized use since 1953, the first major computational facility for research and education, housing a mainframe computer, was established in 1959 at the North University Building (colloquially called NUBS by students). A larger computing center was built on North Campus in 1971 and the mainframe computer was moved there. NUBS became a "faculty/student computing site with remote terminal connections to the mainframe on North Campus. Other computing sites were later established at the Michigan Union and other campus locations."[47] U-

---

*An article in the *Ann Arbor News* (July 4, 1975) claimed the switchboard was installed in 1957, but this is untrue as other information indicates a switchboard was probably in existence as early as 1929. It may have been replaced in 1957, but this was not the switchboard removed in 1975 as the Governors' Minutes of March 14, 1970, state a new switchboard had been installed over the Christmas holidays.

M students, including Cookies, soon became used to trudging to one of these sites to complete class assignments. But, "by the 1980s, the introduction of personal computers led to a movement away from centralized, mainframe computing towards a more distributed computing environment" and in January 1986 the Martha Cook Building adapted by installing two computers, provided by the U-M Computing Center, in the cloak room.[48]

In September 1989, the residents won a MacSE computer with a twenty megabyte hard drive and Laser Writer for having the greatest attendance of all dorms at the Tour de Mac (a set of education sessions on using Microsoft computers run by University Housing). The Governors must have been impressed because Building Director Rosalie Moore reported to the residents via the House Board Minutes on October 2, "The Governors have requested that I explore possibilities for a NICE computer room. I'm open to suggestions ...."

The TV room in the basement was determined to be the best space for the new computer room and the television was moved to the Recreation Room down the hall. During summer 1996, five new Macintosh computers and monitors were installed there.[49] One computer/monitor combination was a gift of the Martha Cook Alumnae Association. Today, there are seven computers, a combination of Macs and PCs, supplied by University Housing as part of its Residential Computing (Rescomp) Network.

In summer 1996, Ethernet was installed in student rooms so that residents could use their own computers.[50] Hubs were installed during the summer of 2010 to provide wireless access.[51] Now residents and their guests or study groups can conveniently use laptops anywhere in the Building. A serendipitous result has been greater use of the public rooms.

Main Elevator

For most of MCB's history, one of the unofficial traditions was the ever-surprising elevator experience. In 1919, a cartoon in the *Annual* made fun of the foibles of riding the elevator. Cookies of all generations can sympathize with overcrowding or just missing the elevator. But, until the installation of the current elevator in 1999, Cookies also dealt with the likelihood of the elevator landing not quite in line with the floor on which it was to stop.

34. (a19) Drawing by Juliet Peddle '22

The elevator has been replaced twice, after also having had its driving unit completely replaced in September 1927. The car, the rails, and machine were kept.[52] In 1931, the brake was replaced. By 1955, the Building was in need of a new elevator. Service was inconsistent and students were clamoring for a self-serve elevator instead of the existing lift that required an operator and was only usable from 7:30 AM to 9 PM.[53] In 1956, an estimate was obtained from Otis Elevator for an elevator that could be operated either with or without an attendant and which would retain the old cab frame and safety system but replace everything else.[54] The possibility of replacing the cab and doors was considered[55] but apparently not acted upon. When repairs where done in 1976, it was found that the wooden cab was sixty years old while the electrical components were approximately fifteen years old.[56]

But time and use take their tolls on any piece of equipment and this new elevator was no exception. By the end of the 1960s, the elevator would cease running for days at a time and would often stop between floors on the days that it did run. In November 1970, House Board "unanimously recommended to the Board of Governors and Directors that the elevator be permanently overhauled or permanently replaced with a more modern one." House Board attended "an 'elevator workshop'… with our maintenance man … so that any one of them will be able to help rescue stranded elevator passengers."[57] Permanent repairs were not made, however, until 1976.

In June 1997, a report by Jim Vibbart, foreman of the U-M Plant Department Elevator Shop,[58] stated that repair problems had escalated dramatically over the previous two years. He added the life expectancy of an elevator in the US was twenty-three years, but, through U-M's attention to maintenance and repair, most University elevators lasted forty years. Martha Cook's elevator was now fifty years old and parts were no longer manufactured. The Elevator Shop consulted Millar Elevator Company which reported that to retain any part of the elevator for historical preservation purposes would require special waivers from the state of Michigan. In addition, new controls, as required by code, would not fit in the same place as the old cab's controls and the resulting "patch" would be unsightly. Final plans called for a completely new elevator to be housed in the old shaft.

The original cost estimate for replacement was $425,000. Procuring these funds was problematic since the Building had only recently begun to consider its historic preservation and was in its infancy in terms of fundraising. The Governors decided they needed to seek assistance from the University. The residents, via House Board, agreed to send a supporting letter.[59] In the meantime, construction plans went on. It was determined that the elevator would take six months to construct and four months to install. On June 11, 1998, Paul Courant, then Assistant Provost of the University of Michigan, notified Elaine Macklin Didier '70, MA'71, PhD'82, Chair of MCB's Board of Governors, that the University would provide the full costs of the elevator, now expected to be $500,000, but also warned that the Governors needed to determine a long-range plan for funding the Building's needs.[60]* On May 1, 1999, installation of MCB's all-new elevator began and was completed in time for fall move in.[61] The wood-lined cab was modeled after the one it replaced, to the point that the decorative rosettes were made from a mold of the original.[62]

Barrier-Free Access

Although women with physical challenges have lived at Martha Cook at various times, they did so by making their own concessions, sometimes aided by temporary ramps. This situation improved markedly with the 1995 installation of a small, wheelchair accessible elevator just off the foyer and the 1997 redesign of the outside front entrance to incorporate a permanent ramp.

Although some discussion had occurred earlier, the Board of Governors seriously began planning barrier-free access in 1992, working with Dave Evans, the University architect.[63] In April 1993, the Governors authorized Quinn Evans, a historic preservation architecture firm, to proceed with construction drawings.[64] That fall, the Bureau of Michigan History, Michigan Department of State, approached the Governors and suggested they apply for state-administered federal historic preservation funds that could cover up to 60% of the costs of making the entrance and first floor barrier-

---

* See Chapter 8, Fundraising: Ensuring the Future.

free.[65] Unfortunately, the grant request was denied by the State Historic Preservation Office.[66]

In 1995, a lift was installed in a portion of the former coat room to carry a person from the foyer level to the main hallway, bypassing two sets of five steps that are the primary means of access to the public parts of the main floor.

Building Director Gloria Picasso reported to the alumnae:

> Great pains were taken to make it blend into the existing architecture. Old doors were refitted, recut and stained so that one can hardly tell they weren't always there. Old door latches were unearthed and are the same kind as used in that area of the building. The tiles were carefully chosen to match the marble sills originally installed in the building. It is a very handsome addition to the building and one which will actually enhance the appearance of the entry area. This effort will also allow many of our guests and devoted alumnae entry into the building where it might have been difficult or impossible before. We had a Dedication Tea on Friday, March 24 which included a ribbon-cutting ceremony.[67]

35. (kgm) Barrier-free access

Outside the front doors, a ramp was added in summer of 1997. Flanked by landscape plantings, it runs east from the central sidewalk, across the front of the Building. Extra outdoor safety lighting was added to the front entrance at the same time.[68] The barrier-free and lighting projects were made possible thanks to a gift from University President James Duderstadt who allocated $100,000 from his discretionary fund. Martha Cook paid the remaining $14,000.[69]

Still to be completed, to make the Building completely barrier-free, is the adaptation of bathrooms and some bedrooms to accommodate special needs. This redesign is scheduled to be part of the upcoming major renovation.

Safety and Security

The safety and security of the residents has always been paramount at MCB. The Building was constructed of poured concrete, a method which in 1915 was thought to be fireproof and would therefore protect the residents. While this is now known to be untrue, the concrete base of the Building is a first line defense for the Building's structure. To protect the inhabitants takes a little more effort and equipment.

It is not clear if a fire alarm system was in place from the beginning or if it was added at a later date. The first mention of a fire alarm in extant Martha Cook records was in October 1950, when Diekema informed the Governors that the existing system was inadequate and would be replaced at state expense.[70] In 1951, she told the Governors that two fire drills "must be held each semester—one which is announced and one which is unannounced."[71] In August of 1973, Olive Chernow, who had begun her tenure as Building Director just the month before, requested a fire and safety inspection from the University's fire marshal. The inspection found many violations including an inoperable fire box on the fourth floor and no fire extinguisher in the hood of the kitchen stove. The fire marshal required that all six hotplates in the kitchenettes be replaced and that storerooms be cleared of paper and boxes. He also suggested that combustion detectors be placed throughout the Building, especially in the sleeping areas. At her first meeting with the Board of

Governors in September, they accepted Chernow's recommendation to install a new fire alarm and combustion detectors in every room except the Gold and Red Rooms. For these two rooms, they felt the purchase of detectors that would blend with the décor was too costly. The project was completed in 1976 with the installation of a Larse Transmitter so that the fire alarm system would ring automatically in the Campus Security Office, eliminating the need for an emergency phone call in the case of a fire.[72] As part of the project to increase fire safety, the dining room doors were rehung in 1974 to swing outward into the hall rather than into the dining room.[73]

By the late 1990s, the alarm system no longer met code and the fire marshal required MCB to install a new system that would include both an alarm system and a fire suppression system, with the alarm to be completed first. In 1998, MCB was ordered to install battery-operated fire detectors in all resident bedrooms[74] and, in 2000, to hire a nighttime fire watch security officer[75] to remain on duty until the installation of the fire alarm, with hard-wired smoke detectors and flashing lights as well as a louder sound, was completed. The new alarm was installed during summer of 2001 at a cost of $535,000. MCB was able to pay all but $100,000 from reserve funds and borrowed the remainder from U-M; the loan was paid over five years. Summer of 2013 saw the installation of a fire suppression system which, since it had to be connected to a water pump in Lorch Hall (behind MCB), required digging up part of the Garden for the installation of pipes.[76] The water spigots in the Gold and Red Rooms were designed to blend with the decorative plasterwork ceilings. As part of the installation, a mass-notification loudspeaker system was installed to notify residents in case of a building or campus emergency. The cost of this project was approximately $2 million, with the down payment paid by Building reserves and the outstanding debt to be covered by the annual income from the Building's gift funds.

The inner front doors were first locked in the daytime and a buzzer system installed in September 1973.[77] In July 2007, the outer front door locks were changed to a keycard scan system and the buzzer system was eliminated.[78] Residents now have their M-cards coded to act as keys to MCB and visitors must call the front desk from the telephone kiosk on the front porch. The kiosk was added as a security measure at the same time the front entrance was made barrier-free in 1997, and replaced a temporary security phone installed outside the Building in early 1995[79].

Other security measures included the installation of main floor window locks and security cameras at the four exterior doors in 2008,[80] new lights with battery backup in the bedroom floor hallways in 2005[81] and on the first floor and in the stairwells in 2009,[82] and a cashless front desk in 2011.[83]

Roof

The original slate roof was replaced in summer of 2008* at a cost of $2.2 million.[84] A down payment of $1 million was paid from a combination of donations from alumnae, friends, and the Building's reserves fund. The remaining $1.2 million was funded by a multi-year loan from university to be repaid from donations and accumulating reserves. Slate for the new roof came from Vermont. Eight to ten tinsmiths at one time were required to install the copper flashings.

The installation of the new roof uncovered several deficiencies, all of which were repaired—rusting beams, bowed walls, deteriorated deck, paper-thin keystones.[85] Also revealed was an indication that MCB's original builders were running out of slate as

---

* Some of the slate was donated to U-M's Matthaei Botanical Gardens. It can be seen in the North Garden where the slates are arranged upright amongst low-growing groundcovers. There are also MCB slates in the Children's Garden for children to write and draw upon.

they neared the top of the roof because, as U-M Architect Trudy Zedeker-Witte told the Governors, "there are small pieces which may be leaking points. There is a running line across the roof at the point where this starts to be apparent."[86]

To celebrate the roof's completion, MCB held a party for its residents, their parents, and alumnae on Sunday, September 14, 2008.[87] The party was originally planned as a garden party but due to heavy rain, the remnant of Hurricane Ike, the party was moved indoors. Decorations for the event reflected a construction theme and included centerpieces made from toy trucks and construction equipment. Labels identifying the food were written on small pieces of the old slate. The meal for the event was a progressive affair with crudités available on the first floor, hot hors d'oeuvres served in the second floor library, and desserts offered in the third floor library.

Plumbing

From the Building's beginnings, Cookies were plagued by an imbalance of cold and hot water in the bathrooms. In 1997, the discrepancy was explained by MCB's Facilities Manager: "The cold water from the city enters the Building at 45 psi while the power plant hot water is entering at 75 psi. We do not want to decrease hot water pressure as it then would not be sufficient to reach the [fourth] floor."[88] All was well for women taking showers as long as no one flushed a toilet in the same restroom. Over the years, various attempts to control the shower temperature were made but none, including the 1996 replacement of shower heads with thermostatic control devices, were successful until the installation of a cold water booster pump in 1998.

The plumbing has been upgraded several times. In 1937, the entire plumbing system was renovated. "Care was taken to see that the bathrooms, with their white tile, marble walls, and original imported china fixtures were preserved."[89] Bathtubs and faucets were replaced in 1950.⁹⁰ In recent years, weakened pipes have burst and MCB's facilities staff has taken the opportunity while replacing the pipes to install additional shut-off valves throughout the Building. A complete replacement of the plumbing is planned as part of the upcoming Building renovation.

Heating, Cooling, and Electrical

In his deed of gift, William Cook stipulated, "the University shall at all times hereafter furnish heat, light, and power for the building free of charge."⁹¹ The University has faithfully paid the heating and electrical bills but gas for the kitchen stoves has always been paid by the Building.

36. (bh6) This early photo shows that women of the past, like their modern counterparts, opened windows on cold days to offset the Building's excess heat.

The Building does not have all-house air-conditioning or mechanical ventilation systems so the Building is cooled and vented primarily by its windows. From the beginning, the degree of heat supplied to the Martha Cook Building via U-M's steam plant has kept the Building warmer than most residents enjoy. Their way of coping has been to open windows, even on the coldest days.

Window screens

were not part of the original plan, but they were an early upgrade.[92] The first floor was screened in the fall of 1915, and, in 1918, after residents complained of troublesome flies and mosquitos,[93] the studies on the second and third floors were screened. All rooms have been screened since 1934. For many years, window air conditioners supplied cooled air to the computer room, front office, director's office, director's bedroom and living room, and the guest room. These are all rooms on the front end of the Building. In 2008, these units were determined to be security risks as they required windows to be left open; they were replaced with a central system. An all-house installation of air conditioning and ventilation systems, as well as an overhaul of the heating system, will likely be part of the Building's major renovation.

The Building's designers showed great forethought in determining the amount of electrical service that should be supplied to MCB for there has been an adequate supply for all of its 100 years. But code requirements both for wattage and type of wire will require the system, including a new switching station in the basement, to be completely redone as part of the renovation. Through the years, minor upgrades have been made to parts of the system. For instance the chandeliers in the Gold and Red Room were rewired in both 1974[94] and 1998.[95]

Over the last 100 years, increased enrollment of women at U-M, economic factors, two World Wars, changing safety standards, mechanical improvements, and social and technological changes have caused MCB to adapt its physical plant to new needs. While no one knows what the next 100 years may bring, it is certain that MCB will make the necessary changes to remain a viable, modern home within its traditional ambience.

CHAPTER SEVEN

Financial Well-Being: Income, Expenses, and Stewardship

The books and accounts appear to have been carefully and accurately kept in the period under review.
                                    Price Waterhouse & Co., 1927[1]

The economic well-being of the Martha Cook Building is dependent not only on its revenues—room and board from its residents and donations from its alumnae and friends—but also on the financial management provided by the Building's Board of Governors and Directors. It is through their excellent stewardship over the years, particularly their ability to find solutions in tough times, that the Building remains in good shape, both physically and financially.

For many years the Building's expenses were paid from accounts managed by the Treasurer or House Director, who also prepared the monthly and yearly financial reports. In the earliest years, these reports were monitored by William Cook's brother Chauncey, president of the Hillsdale Savings Bank. Copies of the reports were also sent to William and the proof that he personally reviewed them was revealed by a note, perhaps to his secretary, written by him on the report for the year 1924–1925: "Return this and send me the corresponding statement about a year ago so that I may compare the two. WWC."[2]

William Cook believed that the University's dormitories could and should be profit centers, but this has never proved to be a viable goal. The economic pressures of the Great Depression as well as later recessions and especially the modern belief that a college education is a universal goal have forced universities and colleges everywhere to keep costs as low as possible for students. Indeed, Cook himself was not consistent in his views on profits. In 1918 he wrote his brother, "I think the Governors should be very liberal in making any improvements in the furniture, equipment, etc., because there really is no need of building a surplus"[3] and in 1922, he wrote to Frances Mack, the Building's Treasurer, "Your finances have been well managed."[4] But in 1925, when MCB's cash assets of $16,524.94 (he specified the amount down to the penny) were about $1000 less than the previous year, he wrote:

37. (a17) Frances C. Mack

> There must have been extravagance and waste somewhere .... With 118 regular roomers and 118 registered boarders and no taxes or rent or interest or charge for heat, light, and power there should have been a substantial profit, even if the improvements in the past year cost about $1000 more than in 1924.[5]

The Martha Cook Building has experienced periods of financial angst but has always emerged in a better financial position. The financial situation in the first year seemed bleak, as revealed in extant letters from Mack. For example, she wrote to Regent Sawyer in November:

> The situation here is an impossible one and will continue to be so until the building is endowed.* The necessity of crowding in too many girls; the lack of funds to hire sufficient service or of room to house them, the inadequacy and inconvenience of dining room and serving room; the many inconveniences of a house planned by architects who did not understand the needs for which they built, are all some of the factors which make life too hard for those in charge .... The nervous strain of attempting to live up to the beauty and promise of the building and still make ends meet on an insufficient income is tremendous.[6]

Despite her fears, she managed to carry on for the next twelve years, and did indeed show a profit in that first year. Her end-of-year report showed a total profit for house and table (now called room and board) of $2,848.35 after wages, food costs, "expenses and replacement," and the purchase of almost $3000 in additional equipment.[7]

MCB experienced challenges during the Great Depression but weathered them. The banking crisis and ensuing bank holiday caused checks to bounce, both those coming in as room and board and those going out to pay bills. Payments made by MCB were reissued once the banks reopened but a folder of letters held by Sara Rowe, the House Director, indicate that many women ended up paying in cash, often in installments.[8] Although, as noted in the chapter on

---

* As noted in Chapter 1, William Cook did not endow the Building either during his lifetime or via his will. Today, Martha Cook's only endowed funds are the Anne E. Shipman Stevens Scholarship Fund, created in 1936 solely for the purpose of providing financial assistance to residents, and the Historic Preservation Fund, established in 1993 to provide future funds for the Building's long term maintenance. The creation of this fund recognized Mack's hopes but, as related in Chapter 8, does not yet provide income in the amounts needed for the renovation of the Building's infrastructure. The Martha Cook Annual Fund, a donor-sourced fund from which the capital as well as the income may be spent, will be a significant source of funds for the Building's renovation.

Scholarships, the Building was able to offer loans to several residents, cuts were made in other areas. The Alumnae Weekend of 1933 was cancelled. In March of that year, the Governors requested that both Rowe and Social Director Margaret Smith return for the academic year 1933-34 although their salaries were not guaranteed but would depend on the Building's revenues.[9] Then, in April, Dean of Women Alice Lloyd requested that Martha Cook reduce by ninety dollars its room and board for the following year and issue leases on a semester, rather than yearly basis. She also suggested a review of wage and salary schedules for all of the Building's staff but the Governors decided they would maintain the existing levels unless later directed by the University to alter them.[10]

38. (a33) Sara Rowe

Following World War II, MCB experienced some financial difficulties that called for cost reductions which in turn caused changes in the way business was carried out. Post-war inflation increased wages and other costs. At the same time, U-M chose to establish a retirement fund for its non-academic employees, requiring the various units to provide not only future monies but also to provide funds for back work credit to 1935. Martha Cook sent a good faith check of $2,500 and asked for a waiver on the back credit, since they had paid their employees at a higher wage rate than the rest of the University with the expectation that the employees would use the extra earnings to build their own nest eggs. The waiver was not granted. To the Governors' request to pay the back credit over a number of years, Herbert G. Watkins, Secretary of the University of Michigan somewhat condescendingly replied that "the Regents would not wish to impose a burden which would be embarrassing" so would consider allowing MCB ten years to make full payment. He continued, "It is ... to your advantage to liquidate this obligation in the shortest possible time ... nearly all of the similar units of the University have or are in the process of liquidating the past service credit liability."[11] The Board of Governors' response was to ask Rowe to sell securities held by MCB to cover the costs.[12] By November 1946, MCB had paid in full the $27,950 due to the pension fund for past service liability,[13] with $21,165 paid from the sale of US Treasury notes and $5,785 from the Building's cash reserves. Imagine the discouragement the Governors must have felt when in October 1948, following the yearly audit, U-M Vice President R. P. Briggs wrote to them, "It is a matter of considerable concern that the reserves for the equipment and building improvements total only $26,000."[14]

The Governors were also cognizant that operating expenses had been greater than revenues in 1947 and 1948 and had already begun cost-cutting efforts. They elected, for 1947–48, to forego the presentation of six partial room and board scholarships they had been awarding from the Building's operating funds. The Anne E. Shipman Stevens scholarship was still awarded.[15] Other cost-saving mechanisms included the 1947 transfer of supervision of the switchboard and housekeeping staff from the House Director to the Social Director,[16] and in 1949, bookkeeping was transferred to the University, the House Director position was replaced by a live-in dietitian and the secretary's position was eliminated.[17] In both 1950 and 1956, MCB increased admission allotments to raise revenues.

From the beginning, Martha Cook's financial health has been dependent on maintaining a full house of residents. The size of the house and the minimum level of staff required to operate on a seven-day schedule means that a vacancy of more than one or two occupant spots can cause havoc with the budget. For most of MCB's existence, freshman and to a lesser extent sophomore admittance to the Building was an on-and-off occurrence that coincided with a decline or increase in the number of upper-class applications for residency. In the early to mid-1990s, the Building experienced a severe drop in the number of admissions, causing the Governors to eliminate linen service and the poorly attended Sunday breakfast[18] and to also restructure room rates.[19] Until 1993, the cost of living at Martha Cook was the same regardless of type of room and fell halfway between the cost of a double and single room in the other University residence halls. In 1993, the scale was changed to different prices for doubles and singles and for deluxe or regular rooms, based on size, within each of the double/single classifications. Although prices tend to be slightly higher than those charged by University Housing, Martha Cook's price includes eighteen meals while Housing's only includes thirteen. Since 1997, the house has enjoyed full occupancy in most semesters, a waiting list is once again maintained by the Building Director, and the Building operates well within its budget.

In 1994, as another means of controlling costs, the Martha Cook Building contracted with University Housing to provide certain services to MCB and this agreement continues today. While there is a fee for the services, the total cost is lower than it would be if MCB were to handle these functions. The agreement designates Housing to operate as MCB's accountants and representatives to the Board of Regents and to provide human resource support, marketing of Martha Cook in Housing publications and on its website, resident life education programs, training of student counselor staff, and advice on capital improvements and service and maintenance arrangements.[20] The agreement further stipulates that MCB will maintain all its traditions. The staff are considered employees of University

Housing although their salaries and wages are paid by MCB. As was true prior to the agreement, Martha Cook staff positions nest into the same job classifications as employees in other residence halls and all Martha Cook staff members are ultimately employees of the University of Michigan and are eligible for the same wages and benefits as others in the same classification.

At different times, the Governors have looked into ways the Building might be used to bring in additional income, although the Building's founder was opposed to this. In July 1923, he wrote to U-M President Marion Burton, "I would ... like to have it settled that that building is never to be used for summer students. There should be a few choice things at the University beyond the reach of the flood. That building was not built for a boarding house."[21] The following April, he went even further in a note to Mack, "That building was not built for a hotel or boarding house or convention accessory or employment bureau. It was built for the cultivation of the graces and not for utilitarian purposes."[22] He formalized his feelings as a requirement of his deed of gift of the Legal Research Building (aka Law Library):

> ... the Martha Cook Building and the Lawyers' Club Building should not be (as they heretofore have not been) used for accommodation of summer students or schools; nor of organizations, conventions or associations; nor of meetings of any sort (except of the occupants thereof). Lest this rule be disregarded at some time in the future, I make it a further condition of the above offer that the rule shall be observed in perpetuity.[23]

But, just as Cook misunderstood the viability of running a dormitory for profit, he misunderstood the economic and political realities of running the house in isolation from outside forces. In the face of tough economic times and in the desire to achieve collaboration with units across the University and even with its own alumnae, there are times when the Building must be open to others.

The current bylaws of the MCB Board of Governors allow the following uses of the Building:

   a. The Building's main purpose as a residence hall is to provide a home for women students at the University of Michigan.
   b. Meetings of MCB alumnae bodies may be held at the Building if pre-arranged with the Building Director.
   c. Receptions, conventions, and similar gatherings may be held at the Building if authorized by the Board. The Board will review each request individually and will only authorize events which, in the best judgment of the Board, produce significant income or enhance the reputation of the Building within the University community.[24]

The first time the Governors broke Cook's summer school rule was in summer of 1944, although not for economic reasons but to help with U-M's housing shortage and they sought and received the Regents' approval to keep the house open.[25] The Regents ruled, "the provision of the donor of the building against the opening of the building during the summer session is not operative and binding for the war period." One hundred women lived in the Building that summer. In later years, summer sessions were held at infrequent intervals in an attempt to raise revenues, but were not the money-makers anticipated, particularly after U-M allowed women to live in apartments and MCB had to compete with summer sublet prices. Since 1964 when U-M adopted the trimester system with the third trimester split into two half terms, MCB has only been open for spring half-terms, preferring to keep the summer for maintenance and readying the house for fall occupancy. Whether the house was kept open in a given year depended on whether enough women signed leases to cover the cost of operation. In 1979, for instance, only nineteen women agreed to sign summer leases. Board fees for so few would not cover costs, so the spring lease was for room only.[26] The Building was required to be closed for spring and summer sessions during the installation of the fire alarm system in

2001, and since then there has not been enough interest from residents to warrant keeping the Building open when the winter term ends.

To keep costs as low as possible, MCB has always closely matched revenues to expenses, with a small residual allotted to reserves for future maintenance. MCB's main revenue source today is room and board, just as it was in 1915–16. Room and board revenues provide the funds for daily operation and the ongoing maintenance required to keep the Building functional on a daily basis. The first year revenues of MCB were just under $28,000,[27] an amount equivalent to $623,000 in 2014,[28] and are roughly equivalent to forty percent of the $1.6 million acquired in room and board revenues in 2013–14.[29] The significant increase in revenues is a reflection of increased wages across society in the last 100 years as well as an increase in the kind of expenses MCB and other University units face today. In his deed of gift, William Cook stipulated that the University would pay the Building's heat, light, and power (i.e., electricity) in perpetuity and the University continues to honor this commitment. But, changing technologies, cultural and social changes, and the University's cost-centered accounting system have added infrastructure fees to pay for services such as telephone and computer access, insurance, and security. In return for these expenses, MCB enjoys the benefits associated with the services provided and the mass purchasing power of the University.

Over the years, the Building's Directors and Governors carefully husbanded the "net remaining after expenses" and accrued a reserve account for future major projects. From the first year's "unexpended profit" of $2,848.35, MCB's reserves grew to almost $1.5 million by June 30, 2012, before being reduced by two-thirds in fiscal year 2013 to pay the down payment on fire suppression and mass notification systems. Since fiscal 2001, MCB has designated five percent of its total operating revenues for reserves to cover long-term maintenance needs.³⁰ In addition, beginning in fiscal 2004 and continuing through today,³¹ the Regents of the University have stipulated certain portions of room and board increases at all residence halls be dedicated to long- term resident life initiatives (RLI) such as renovations or for programs and projects that will benefit the quality of life in the residence hall and go beyond the scope of operating expenses. These monies have been added to MCB's reserve account.

Martha Cook's alumnae, determined to maintain the Martha Cook community, have been generous. The Building's donor gift funds have accrued, especially since 1998, so that they totaled $4 million at the end of June 2014.³² (Just under three-quarters of this amount belongs to endowed funds from which only the income can be spent.) The Martha Cook Alumnae Association's Memorial Fund, which benefits the Building and its residents, holds another $77,000.

Over the years, the Building's reserves have paid for many repair and replacement projects, including a new elevator in 1958* and the redecoration in 1965 that turned the Blue Room into the Gold Room. In recent years, the reserves and gift funds together have paid for a state-of-the-art fire alarm system, safety lighting throughout the Building, security cameras, wireless computer access to all rooms, the down payments

39. (kgm) Resident using wi-fi to study in the Sparking Room.

---

* The 1998 replacement of this elevator was a gift to Martha Cook from the University as was the 1997 installation of the barrier-free front entry.

and yearly debt payments for the roof and fire suppression systems, restoration of the Gold Room's art-carved piano, and scholarships and grants in an amount approaching $60,000 per year. The reserves and gift funds will provide the footing for a campaign to raise the approximately $30 million needed for a "deep renovation" of the Building's infrastructure, currently scheduled to begin in 2018. As past experience has shown, the Martha Cook community depends not only on excellent financial management by the Building's Governors and Directors but also on the goodwill and stewardship of the staff, residents, alumnae, and friends. With their help, the community will maintain a strong financial position through and beyond the twenty-first century.

CHAPTER EIGHT

Fundraising: Ensuring the Future

I trust that this gift of my residuary estate may cause others to realize that ... they should be generous in their financial support.
William W. Cook[1]

Because William Cook did not create an endowment fund for the Building, MCB has counted on its alumnae, friends, and Directors to step forward whenever Martha Cook has needed funds beyond those provided by room and board. Not only have these groups donated generously but they have also carried out the various tasks associated with seeking donations.

The first such need concerned scholarship dollars. William Cook expected the Martha Cook Building to turn a profit and his deed of gift stipulated that any excess income remaining after the purchase of "furniture, furnishings, works of art and improvements" should be "used in the following year to give lower or free rates" to needy residents. Profits did not roll in as Cook expected, and there was soon a need to find additional funds to provide the financial aid Cook desired. MCB's alumnae created an additional loan fund in 1924 and in 1936 Governor Anne Shipman Stevens became the first donor to the scholarship fund that would bear her name.[*]

Except for a letter campaign in 1939, solicitations for the fund remained low key until 1949 when Building Director Leona Diekema spearheaded a campaign to raise donations to the Anne E. Shipman Stevens Fund from the Building's alumnae. She sent her annual holiday letter to 220 alumnae and in it she appealed for donations of $10.[2] She also called upon the Martha Cook Alumnae Association (then called the Martha Cook Alumnae Association of Detroit) to help her raise additional monies so that the total added to the AESS fund would be $4,000 to $6,000. On November 3, 1951, the MCAAD held the first of several yearly bridge parties to raise funds for scholarships. The party was held at the Detroit Edison headquarters. About eighty women enjoyed an afternoon playing bridge at the first party, which netted about $100 for the scholarship fund. Detroit Edison provided the space, tables, chairs, coffee, and dessert. Detroit retailers and the MCAAD provided table and door prizes.[3] Around the same time, the MCAAD mailed 2000 letters to alumnae soliciting scholarship funds; the letter campaign yielded $1,566.70.

Later, the MCAAD (and its successor, the MCAA) discontinued the bridge parties and instead devoted one of their luncheon events each year as a fundraiser for the scholarship fund. In 1971, the MCAAD established the Martha Cook Alumnae Memorial Fund, first designated an emergency loan fund and later converted to a discretionary fund. By 1977, this fund replaced the scholarship fund as the focus of the MCAAD's luncheon fundraising efforts.[4] The Memorial Fund is set up as an expendable account but is managed like an endowment. The gifts from this fund have provided both equipment and scholarships over the years and have funded $7,000

---

[*] See Chapter 15, Scholarships: Room, Board and Encouragement.

in matching gifts for the renovation of the Steinway art-carved piano in the Gold Room.

Requests for gifts to both the AESS Scholarship and Memorial Funds continued in a low key manner. They were the only types of fundraising done until 1993 when the Governors began to realize that the Building, at seventy-seven years old, was going to soon need major restoration, repairs, and renovations of its infrastructure. The most immediate need at that time was the installation of the barrier-free front entrance and elevator, but the Governors also envisioned other needs arising very quickly. They established a new fund as an endowment, The Historic Preservation Fund, in which only the investment income could be spent, the principal "meant to grow and safeguard the building from inappropriate change in the future."[5] They first introduced this fund to the Building's alumnae via the *Martha Cook Alumnae Association International Newsletter* in spring 1994[6] and referred to the need for "big ticket items" for the first time in the fall 1994 issue of the Newsletter.[7]

The Board of Directors of the MCAA desired to help and five members of the group met with Building Director Gloria Picasso, Governor Connie Butler Amick '57, Former Governor Nancy Howe Bielby Sudia '56, House Board President Christa Alessandri '90, MBA'95, and resident Marisa Szabo '89, JD'95, who had earlier presented a fundraising marketing proposal to the MCAA.[8] Maria's proposal, which included selling merchandise and tickets to some of MCB's traditional events, was deemed to have merit but would take a lot of time and effort for a return too small to meet MCB's needs. Instead, the group suggested a committee be formed to work on an annual drive soliciting outright cash gifts.

In the meantime, the Building received a bequest from Louise Pressler '27, who died in 1992. She left $25,000 and her will stipulated the gift was "to be used as part of a scholarship fund or other memorial in memory of the class of 1927, at the direction of the Board of Governors of the Martha Cook Building."[9] Recognizing the significant need for preservation funds, the Governors asked U-M if the interest could be deposited in the Historic Preservation Fund. Upon learning that it could be, the Governors designated the Pressler Fund for historic preservation but elected to keep the money in its own fund rather than merging with the Historic Preservation Fund.[10] To date, the Pressler Fund has provided new exit lights, lighting with emergency backup in the hallways of the bedroom floors,[11] and ground fault circuit interrupters, mirrors, and shelves next to each sink. The remainder of the fund continues to earn income for future safety and preservation needs.

Donations for the Historic Preservation Fund continued to trickle in small numbers and small amounts and $5200 was accrued by November 1996.[12] In spring 1997, the Governors recognized an urgent need to more quickly build a fund to handle existing critical needs. They asked the MCAA to form a committee to work with the

40. (cjd) Mailing party in the Red Room, 2003

Governors and former Governors to undertake a more intensive fundraising campaign. The first meeting of the new group, the Martha Cock Building Fundraising Committee, was held a year later on April 14, 1998.[13] By June,[14] the committee had elected Debra Ball McMillan (now Johnson) '80, MArch'82 and Barbara Osborne Osborn '46, MA'71 as the group's first chairpersons and planned an introductory solicitation letter to be sent to almost 2000 alumnae

Over the next eight years, the MCB Fundraising Committee added members and met monthly in what would prove to be a long-term learning experience, requiring flexibility to adjust to changing needs and constraints. Representatives of the Board of Governors, former Governors, the MCAA Board, and alumnae members-at-large were active committee members as, for the first four years, were the House Board presidents. Advice was provided to the group first by Janet Kreger '72, a historic preservationist with major gift experience at both U-M and Michigan State University, and, after 1999, from representatives of U-M's Office of University Development.

In 2000, the FC elected to hold a Coming Home Spring Tea for alumnae and friends, with proceeds to benefit the Historic Preservation Fund. This event has become an annual rite of spring, although the proceeds now benefit the later-created Annual Fund (see below). The MCAA, the Ann Arbor Alumnae, House Board, and Building staff assisted with the tea until the dissolution of the Fundraising Committee in 2006. At that time, the MCAA and the Building staff took over full responsibility for the presentation of the tea.

Initially, the goal of the FC was to raise $1 million dollars, in the form of 1000 gifts of $1,000, within three years.[15] This was quickly retracted because they learned that projects needed to be completed soon—fire alarm, fire suppression system, new roof—would cost more than $4 million. The committee recommended a goal of $5 million in five years for MCB's Capital Campaign, a goal which proved to be too large for a fledgling campaign.[16,17] The first major "ask" for donations was mailed in November 1999[18] and by the end of the fiscal year in June 2000, the Capital Campaign had received $90,000.[19]

The first major gift of the campaign was a gift of $50,000 from the estate of Mary Ann Tinker '60, MD'64 realized in spring 2000. With the permission of Mary Ann's brother, the gift was publicly recognized in that spring's issue of the *Martha Cook Alumnae Newsletter*.[20] At the Ninetieth Anniversary of MCB in October 2005, the Mary Ann Tinker Society was announced as MCB's way to recognize gifts of $50,000 or more. A plaque to record members of the Tinker Society was hung in the Building's foyer.[21]

One issue of concern to the FC was the potential effect on MCB's ability to keep up with scholarship needs as donors' priorities shifted to the building's preservation. Would the AESS Fund continue to provide enough income to cover need as board and room rates increased? The problem was solved by a bequest from Elizabeth Thompson '30 who passed away in April 2000.[22] When completely distributed, her estate awarded $822,152[23] to the AESS Scholarship Fund, making it possible for MCB to increase both the number and size of scholarships awarded to residents. The addition to the scholarship fund ensured an income great enough to meet the needs expressed by scholarship applicants so MCB's fundraising could be focused on preservation needs for the next decade and a half.

Following a fatal fire in 2000 in a residence hall at Seton Hall University in New Jersey, U-M Regents mandated replacements of the fire alarm systems in all residence halls, and MCB complied by installing a state-of-the-art system in summer 2001. Donations to the endowed Historic Preservation Fund had not been sufficient to provide the income necessary to pay the $535,000 cost. To cover this price, MCB turned to the University for a loan. The Building was required to pool its gift income with its Building reserves to cover the first $435,000, temporarily depleting the bulk of MCB's funds. U-M then extended a loan over five years for the remaining $100,000.

During the loan negotiations in fall 2000, Norman Herbert, U-M's treasurer, encouraged MCB to establish a second fund, the Martha Cook Building Capital Fund, as an expendable fund to meet immediate capital needs. He recommended that the Preservation Fund be retained as it would be important to MCB's future but that it be given less prominence and the Capital Fund become the primary focus for fundraising for the immediate future. In 2007, MCB's financial consultants at University Housing suggested that in order to cover all needs, including those not specifically considered capital in accounting terms (e.g., furnishings), the Building should instead raise funds for a discretionary fund. The Martha Cook Annual Fund was created and became MCB's primary fundraising focus and funds were no longer actively solicited for the Capital Fund.[24] The Annual Fund continues as MCB's top fundraising priority and will probably be the primary source of funds for MCB's renovation although the remains of the Capital Fund will also be used for this.

After the creation of the Capital Fund, and with the advice of the University's Office of Development, the FC established a door plaque program to begin fall 2001 to encourage larger gifts. First suggested by Carol Giacoletto '72, who was one of the first plaque donors,[25] the program allowed women who donated $10,000 in unrestricted gifts to the Capital Fund

41. (bgm) Room plaque

to place their name in the door frame of their student bedroom. The brass plaque is of similar size and design as the paper name cards that adorned the door when the Cookie was a resident. Only one name can appear on each plaque but up to ten names can be placed by each door. The program was modified to also recognize donors to the Annual Fund as well when that fund was established. As of January 2015, to comply with University naming requirements, the gift size for name plaque eligibility was raised to $25,000.[26]

In 2003, an intriguing gift was pledged to MCB. Learning of the Building's needs, International artist Edwina Jaques BFA '70, MFA '75 decided to use her talents for the benefit of Martha Cook. She designed a statue* to which individual donors can add inscribed polymer hearts representing gifts to the Annual Fund in six specific sizes from $200 to $1000.[27] A special glass case to hold the statue was contributed by U-M Vice President of Student Affairs (now Student Life) E. Royster Harper.[28] The statue was dedicated at the Building's Ninetieth Anniversary Gala.[29] To date, the hearts have accounted for more than $30,000 in gifts.

42. (wjd) Edwina Jaques with *Edwina* at the 2005 dedication.

In 2004, the Martha Cook Building joined U-M's Michigan Difference campaign.[30] The goal for this campaign was set at

---

* See Chapter 4, The Art of Martha Cook: Ornaments of Gracious Living.

$3 million, the expected costs at that time to replace the roof and install a fire suppression system. When the campaign ended in December 2008, the amount of donated funds at $2.5 million fell just short of the goal and the roof, at an actual cost of $2 million, had been replaced by combining donated funds with Building reserves and a loan from U-M.[31] Plans were being made to install a fire suppression system. This system, combined with an emergency mass announcement system, was installed in 2013 and cost approximately $2 million and was again paid by a combination of Building and donor funds and a loan from U-M.[32]

In the final year of the Michigan Difference campaign, it became apparent that the Building's dining room chairs had reached the end of their life span, so a campaign within the campaign began.[33] The Building loaned itself the funds to buy the chairs and paid the monies back through specified gifts of $1000, the gift recognized by the donor's name placed on a plaque on the back of the chair. The MCAA donated ten chairs, in honor of Cookies in each decade from 1915-2009.

Fundraising at Martha Cook continued after the closure of the Michigan Difference campaign, although in a less intensive manner. MCB informed its alumnae in 2010 that the Building would soon face the deep renovation predicted by the Governors when they first established the Historic Preservation Fund in 1994. The Governors announced that due to economic changes and a better understanding of what the deep renovation would entail, costs, as estimated by MCB's financial consultants at University Housing, were now expected to be near $30 million.[34] MCB paid for a study done in 2012 by the architecture firm Lord Aeck Sargent. This firm, working with U-M's Department of Architecture, Engineering and Construction, provided a similar estimate, with the proviso that the estimate was only good through 2018 and was subject to change depending on economic conditions.[35] It should be noted that actual costs will not be known until final architectural plans are drawn and the U-M Board of Regents approves the renovation.

The Victors for Michigan campaign, announced by U-M in 2013, was the stimulus to once again seek donations in a more aggressive manner. The Building held its own kick-off tea in conjunction with other University events on November 9. The Board of Governors announced that each member had made a "stretch gift" and encouraged MCB's alumnae and friends to also make gifts that stretched their limits.[36] In August 2014, the Board of Governors announced a goal of $5 million to be raised during the Victors for Martha Cook, Victors for Michigan campaign, scheduled to end in December 2018.[37] They encouraged alumnae and friends to donate to either the Annual Fund or the AESS Scholarship Fund. The Governors stressed these campaign aims were intended to lay the foundation for the greater goal of raising $30 million for the renovation and to prepare for future scholarship needs.

It is safe to say that Martha Cook's needs will not disappear when the campaign ends. Fundraising has become a way of life for MCB. New donor campaigns will seek additional funds, and, if the past is any indication of the future, the Building's alumnae and friends will continue to be the benefactors of the unique community of women housed at the Martha Cook Building.

CHAPTER NINE

A Board of Women

When the Martha Cook Building was built I thought the occupants should be self-governing, like a sorosis.* *President Hutchins and my brother Chauncey persuaded me to add a board of governors. That was wise.*

William Cook[1]

MCB's Board of Governors plays a vital role in the stewardship of the Building. Its members are appointed today by the U-M President and all serve without financial compensation. The role they carry out is described in their bylaws[2]:

> The function of the Board of Governors, with the approval of the President of the University of Michigan, and within the University structure, is to set policy for the management of the Martha Cook Building (MCB), to maintain and foster an environment of congenial living and growth, to maintain the traditions of MCB, to approve the budget and expenses of the Building, to maintain the historic Building itself, and to oversee the Building's staff. The Board will also foster good working relationships with other departments of the University.

Organization of the Board

Cook's decision to have a Regent-appointed board of women to oversee his new dormitory was made public in the 1914 deed of gift.

---

* Sorosis was the first professional women's club in the US, organized in New York City in March 1868 for the purpose of furthering women's educational and social activities.

At the February 1915 Regents' meeting a year later, when construction was well underway, the first Board was appointed and guidelines were formally established. The Regents' Proceedings state that the Martha Cook Building was to be "placed under the management and control of a board of three women." Terms were to be three years, but staggered, so that future turnover would be smooth. Finances were to be handled according to University procedures, and the women "shall have no authority to enter into any obligations which will involve a liability without having first obtained the authority to do so from the Board of Regents, or its authorized agents." Louise Stock Cook of Hillsdale, Grace Grieve Millard of Detroit, and Anne E. Shipman Stevens of Detroit were then appointed to terms ending in 1918, 1917, and 1916 respectively.

The Governors' terms are still three years. The Regents resolved at both their June 16, 1933, and April 27, 1934, meetings that the boards of the women's dorms were only to be appointed for two consecutive terms. In addition, it was resolved that "governing boards of dormitories in making nominations to the President shall submit at least two names for each vacancy to be filled."[*] The MCB Governors remain limited to two consecutive terms with a minimum of one year off before being reappointed. Submitting two names for each open position, documented several times in the 1950s Governors' Minutes and again in the early 1990s, has since been simplified to one. By the mid-1990s the Regents delegated responsibility for approval to the University President.[3] Today, the Chairwoman of the Board of Governors writes a letter citing the candidate's qualifications and the U-M President makes the official appointment.

During MCB's first fifteen years, the Governors lost track of when their terms ended. The April 1931 *Regents Proceedings* have

---

[*] Letters with this information were filed in the Director's Notebook under U-M Correspondence, illustrating that the MCB staff assisted the Governors with following University procedures, just as is done today.

the startling entry: "The Board received the resignation of each of the three members of the Martha Cook Board of Governors." However, there was no drama after all, as all three women were immediately reinstated, each in turn with terms ending in December 1931, 1932, and 1933.[4] In 1946 the term-endings changed from December 31 to June 30 to coincide with the conclusion of the University's fiscal year.[5]

The Helen Newberry and Betsy Barbour residence halls, which opened in 1915 and 1920 respectively, also had Regent-appointed female boards. They were sometimes referred to as Governors but often as Patronesses, a term the MCB Governors disliked being applied to themselves. Florentine Cook Heath '17 wrote testily to U-M President Ruthven in 1945, "... will you see that the proper authorities make note of the fact that we serve as a Board of Governors appointed by the Regents and not as a Board of Patronesses as now the University records?"[6] Presumably, the term "governor" implied greater authority and responsibility than "patroness."

Choosing Governors

The first three Governors had strong connections to Cook or Hillsdale, so the reasons they were chosen can be surmised. Grace Grieve Millard was an 1897 U-M graduate, former Dean of Women at Hillsdale College (1906–10), and was teaching in the Latin department of Detroit Central High School at the time of her appointment. Hillsdale is a small town and it is highly likely the

43. (a19) Grace Grieve Millard

Cook family and Dr. Sawyer were acquainted with her. It is noteworthy that a woman with a college degree and career was chosen to be one of the original governors.

Louise Stock Cook, wife of William's brother Chauncey and living in nearby Hillsdale, was intensely involved in the residence hall project from the outset. Her selection is the only one where a fragment of the reasoning was recorded, although several years after the fact. Cook referred to her appointment in a June 30, 1920, letter to U-M Regent Dr. Walter Sawyer:

> You will recollect that I acquiesced in her appointment originally by reason of your recommendation. I did so largely because I thought it would interest my brother intensely, and that it would do him much good, as it did. On the other hand, you know my idea has always been that my family should not interfere with the management of the building, and now that my brother is gone, it seems to me that it would be well to carry out that policy, especially as I carefully refrain myself from making requests, except on very important matters, and in fact, keep away from the building entirely.[7]

44. (a19) Louise Stock Cook

Sawyer responded favorably regarding Louise's appointment: "I must say she has been so efficient and faithful to the task that I had hoped her service might be extended. I know she very much enjoys the work and relationships."[8] Cook wrote back: "I have carefully considered all that you say, but still think that my family should be disconnected from the day by day management of the Martha Cook Building. Moreover, Louise is not in sympathy with the Senior Class policy* of the building ...."⁹ A month later Sawyer commented, "Your wishes, of course, will be complied with; however her term of office does not expire for a number of months so I had not thought best to discuss the matter with her until some time a little later ...."¹⁰ Louise Cook remained on the Board until the end of her term and formally resigned via a letter presented by Sawyer at the January 7, 1921, Regents meeting. In it, she "stated that she expected to travel for a considerable period and would be unable to attend to the duties of membership in the Board."¹¹

Anne E. Shipman Stevens was Cook's personal friend and well acquainted with Dr. Sawyer, too.¹² She was a community leader with a wide range of philanthropic and volunteer activities in the Detroit area.† Her personal relationships and experience made her a natural choice, and indeed, she devoted a great deal of time and energy to the Martha Cook Building until her death in 1939. Stevens is MCB's longest-serving governor, remaining in office from 1915 to 1934. She stands tall as a role model for Cookies and all governors who have come after her. One hundred years after she began her first term, she still merits

45. (a19) Anne E. Shipman Stevens

---

* Cook increasingly wanted to exclude younger women from MCB, first saying that only juniors and seniors should be accepted and then, only seniors with a very small number of exceptional juniors. The Building never completely complied. See Chapter 13.

† A noteworthy sidelight to Stevens' philanthropy, unrelated to MCB, is that multiple purchases by the Detroit Institute of Art's Founders Society were made with the Anne E. Shipman Stevens Bequest Fund.

individual mention for her enthusiasm, interest in the residents, participation, and creativity in helping mold Martha Cook Building culture.

The chairwoman for the 1938 Christmas breakfast called her "the foster-mother of the dorm."[13] Often referred to as Martha Cook's fairy godmother, Stevens provided Christmas carol leaflets, music scores, the guest book, volumes for the library, and two enormous scrapbooks which residents filled with newspaper clippings relating to MCB, current events, University events, William W. Cook, and alumnae. She was also committed to assisting residents financially, personally donating to the scholarship fund that eventually came to bear her name. That her efforts were appreciated in her lifetime by the women she influenced is borne out by a memorial tribute in the 1939 *Annual:*

> Through her own sincerity, devotion and service, she has caused the beauty and strength of the Building itself to be impressed upon the character and personality of every girl who has lived here. Her deep and continued interest in every Martha Cook girl ... will ever be a cherished memory for everyone whose good fortune it was to know her.

The following autumn, in the *Jubilee Bells* alumnae newsletter published to commemorate MCB's Twenty-fifth Anniversary, Thelma James '20, who as a student and as an alumnae volunteer knew Stevens well, wrote a lengthy tribute which concluded, "No one will ever know how many girls she helped financially and with wise counsel, but all of us have shared in her gifts of the spirit and are thereby the richer."[14]

Because discussions regarding potential new appointments have been conducted privately and are not included in any of the Governors' archived minutes or letters, it cannot be determined whether the Regents, Dean of Women, or other University personnel contributed to choosing early nominees. Sawyer referred briefly to the process in a 1924 letter to Cook, implying that the Board was at least largely responsible for choosing members:

> The Board of Management has been largely self-perpetuating. The Regents have felt that those in control were best fitted to make choice of successors and we have approval of the recommendations made by them. In general I think this is wise and I had thought that the end was accomplished with this governing body. President Burton, I think has felt at times that there should be more direct control by the Regents. With this I have not been in accord as I have felt that your original plan was the wise one and should not be changed. In fact, you have more carefully thought out this problem than anyone else has and I rely absolutely upon your judgment and conception.[15]

Cook confused the issue in a 1920 letter to Sawyer:

> When your Board of Regents selects another Governor I hope they do not select anyone living in Ann Arbor, for various reasons, one of which is that the resident Governor would be liable to interfere with the day by day management of the building and there would be friction all the time.[16]

Amusingly, Governor Florentine Cook Heath '17, Cook's favorite niece, wrote in 1938, "Since [Cook's] time we have had an Ann Arbor member – a very happy choice for the building."[17]

Cook weighed in again on the composition of the Board when writing to President Burton in July 1923: "Further, I think the Governors should not include the Dean of Women. A little friendly rivalry in management and ideas is desirable. Moreover, it is not well to reduce all things to a dead common level."[18] The Dean did sit on the Boards of Betsey Barbour and Helen Newberry.

Although Cook said he wanted his family to distance itself from MCB management, female members sat regularly on the Board into the 1990s. Cookies have viewed this very favorably, appreciating the tradition and connection to their benefactor. Florentine Cook Heath was the second family member as well as the second MCB alumna on the Board. She was the daughter of Chauncey and Louise Cook, and served three separate times (1933–38, 1945–51, 1955–61). Jane Whitney Cook, Louise Cook's daughter-in-law, was the third relative

(1939–45). Ann Bradford Cook '45, daughter of Jane and Chauncey Jr. and hence Cook's great-niece, served two terms (1961–69 and 1975–81), and her sister, Martha Cook Nash '40, was a Governor from 1969–75 and 1981–84. Martha's daughter-in-law, Sharon Warnock Nash, MD, volunteered her time from 1984–1996. Martha's daughter, Martha Cook Nash Campos '72, AMLS '74, was the Building's Assistant Resident Director in 1973-74.

MCB alumnae have been traditional choices for governors and Cook himself was very much in favor of it. He wrote to Sawyer in 1925, two years after Emilie Sargent '16, the first House Board President, joined the Board:

> ... ten years from that building and one of them is now one of the three governors of the building, and I think the time has come to select future governors from non-resident graduates from the building itself. The reason is that those who have lived in the building know better what it needs and are more interested in it than an outsider.[19]

The next alumna to serve as Governor was Florentine Cook Heath in 1933. She was followed in 1937 by Marguerite (Marnie) Chapin Maire '20 who served on three different occasions. Alumnae have typically been chosen from the pool of women either actively engaged with the Martha Cook Building as volunteers or who were employed as U-M staff members.

However, despite Cook's express blessing regarding alumnae overseeing Martha Cook Building management, the Board continued to include many non-Cookies until 1961. These women were wives of University officials or U-M alumnae. The latter must have been active in alumni activities or otherwise known to sitting Governors, the Director, or Dean of Women. Dora Van Den Berg Perrett '30 (in June 1961 the only Governor to die in office) was the last Governor who was neither an alumna nor a Cook until Margaret Leary was appointed in 2013. As the retired Director of the U-M Law Library and author of the William W. Cook biography *Giving It All Away*, Leary came with unique ties to the Cook legacy.

The Governors have been a mix of professional women and homemakers, all dedicated volunteers with a wide variety of skills and knowledge. They have resided in Ann Arbor, greater Detroit, or the Lansing to Grand Rapids corridor, thus able to attend meetings.

Meetings and Minutes

The first meeting was described in the 1921 *Annual:*

> And looking into the past again, by the light of a candle, flickering over piles of debris in the Director's office and casting weird shadows about, we see Miss Millard seated on a packing box, jotting down the minutes of the first Board meeting.

Unfortunately, those minutes are lost. The first available minutes begin in 1933, so it is unknown how frequently meetings originally were or where they were held. Ann Arbor is a midway point between Detroit and Hillsdale, however, and it is probable that most were held at Martha Cook, albeit in more comfortable conditions than the one described! Later minutes place the majority of meetings at MCB with a few taking place in the Detroit area at clubs, the governors' homes, or other locations in Ann Arbor. They gathered in the Social Director's apartment or office, the Dining Room, and at least once in the House Director Sara Rowe's new suite when that had been a major summer project. Under Director Marion Scher Law in the later 1990s and 2000s, the Red Room with folding tables covered by white tablecloths was the typical venue, affording plenty of space for guests, but occasionally the Governors met offsite on campus. In 2011 the Guest Room was repurposed as a conference room, providing greater privacy and leaving the public rooms free for residents.

The minutes indicate that the Director has been on hand for most meetings. In the days of a Social and a House Director, both attended regularly. University officials, particularly those in the financial offices, have been invited to meetings as needed to discuss special topics as have MCB employees, residents, and alumnae. U-M President Ruthven is the only University president documented as having come to a Governors' meeting.[20] Dean of Women Alice Lloyd was frequently present for at least a portion of most meetings during her tenure. She kept in close contact with MCB administration and her approval was required for many decisions affecting residents. The extant letters between Dean Lloyd and the Governors are very cordial and cooperative, and there are no negative references to her. She was invited to dinners, dances, Christmas Breakfast, and other social events. Subsequent Deans of Women confined the majority of their MCB interactions to the Director.

Communication between the Governors has been in person, by telephone, and by mail, often with the chairwoman or Director as go-between, and some situations have by necessity been dealt with that way. The advent of personal computers and email in the late twentieth century facilitated conducting group business between meetings. It is also now possible for members to contribute to meetings virtually when necessary, via telephone or internet.

21st Century Changes

Although there was a brief trial period with four Governors in 1997-98, the Board began the process of increasing their number from the original three to a maximum of five in 2000.[*] The June 28, 2000, minutes assert:

> The number and kinds of decisions being made, and the difficulty in arranging convenient meeting times for all governors, justify the need for an enlarged board. The larger board would ensure that enough governors would be in attendance at any given meeting for a meaningful discussion. The change in the number of governors will require a change to the [governors'] bylaws.

---

[*] The 1935 and 1936 *Annuals* list four Governors (Heath, Baits, Bruce, and Stevens), although Stevens resigned from the Board in December of 1932. Perhaps Stevens was simply considered an honorary Governor.

The adjustment was accomplished by sending an explanatory letter to President Lee Bollinger through VP for Student Affairs, E. Royster Harper, and VP and Secretary of U-M, Lisa Tedesco, who discussed it with Bollinger."[21] Official University approval was granted in time for the Governors' February 7, 2001, meeting. The board officially grew to four in 2004 and five by 2006, and it has remained at that number to the present.

As the internet became increasingly central to people's lives in the 1990s, the Governors first brought up the subject of their own website at their April 1997 meeting.[22] While email communication with alumnae grew with the help of the MCAA and the University Development office's email lists, it was not until April 2015 that the Governors finally launched a Martha Cook Building website. This was spurred by the Victors for Michigan fundraising campaign and Martha Cook's 100th Anniversary, and accomplished with the expertise of Governor Marie Fox Skrobola '95, the longtime MCAA webmaster, and assistance from the Fundraising Committee and MCAA Board. Official MCB Facebook and Twitter accounts preceded this by a few months.

Relationship with Residents

Maintaining a good relationship with residents is a continuing effort. Lunches and teas with House Board and residents in general have traditionally taken place throughout MCB history. Day-long retreats were held a few times beginning the 1999-2000 academic year. In 1962 House Board even proposed a student liaison position, to possibly be shared between House Board members.[23] This never came about, but twenty years later the Governors organized their agenda to accommodate individual reports from staff and a time "when residents may meet in private with the Governors. Goal: to improve communication with the students and with building personnel."[24] While done on occasions, this has not been the norm and today residents attend the meetings on an as-needed basis.

The Resident Satisfaction Survey was first executed in spring 1996 to gain insight into residents' feelings about a multitude of areas including food, courtesy of staff, front desk operations, aspects of the MCB experience, male visitation hours, computers, House Board's effectiveness, cleanliness of bathrooms, and more.[25] The survey proved useful and has been done ever since, changing from a hand-tabulated project to an online survey as technology advanced.

The Challenges of Stewardship

The introduction to the Martha Cook Building By-Laws, last revised in 2004 and reviewed in 2008, reads:

> Today's Governors and Building Director face challenges not anticipated by Mr. Cook or the Board of Regents when the Martha Cook Building was deeded to the University of Michigan. Changing societal and governmental rules, the need to seek funds beyond those available from board and room revenues, the perpetual determination of the Governors since 1915 to maintain Martha Cook as an independent residence hall, and the moral imperatives to maintain a diverse resident body and foster human understanding are the foundations for all decisions made by the Board of Governors of the Martha Cook Building.[26]

The Governors, with the Director and staff, have striven to uphold MCB's ideals, preserve the structure and see that it continues to provide a college home for its residents. They have been good stewards. Most have probably hoped at one time or another that Cook would be pleased with the choices they have made over the decades. That he was satisfied with them in 1927 is clear. He wrote to Professor Grismore, Secretary of the Lawyers Club, to express concerns about the Club's management and compared it to MCB:

> They keep up their building and park in splendid shape and pay for that too .... The Martha Cook organization settles its own troubles and problems and never thinks of running to the Regents about them. How would it do to swop managements?[27]

CHAPTER TEN

The Staff: Providing the Comforts of Home

Their jobs well done have enriched the lives of us all. We salute them now, with profound appreciation and respect.
MCB's Seventy-fifth Anniversary booklet[1]

Certainly, the Board of Governors can be credited with wise oversight and the residents with the ideas and activities that lead to a community, but it is the staff who are responsible for making all the ideas fit and work on a daily basis. Often the results of their work are unremarked but if it were not for their skills in managing the Building, preparing and serving meals, and keeping and maintaining the house, life for the residents would not be gracious nor harmonious. At Martha Cook, perhaps because of the relatively small sizes of both populations, staff and residents develop a familiarity which allows them to know each other by name and to learn and respect the abilities of each individual. In this way, the staff is truly part of the community to a degree that is seldom found in other living experiences.

For MCB's first twelve years, day-to-day management was carried out by three women, all of whom lived in the Building: the Social Director, the House Director, and the House Treasurer and

Accountant (called the Business Manager until 1921). Although there are no extant organizational charts from the early years, it seems apparent that the Social Director was the senior manager. William Cook described the Social Director as the one "who will be held responsible for results, financially, socially and as to the welfare and proper care of the young women in the building."[2]

In 1994, MCB contracted with University Housing for facilities management services.* As part of that contract, which has been renewed several times and is in force today, all non-student employees are considered employees of University Housing, under the overall managerial supervision of the Director, and all salaries and wages are charged against MCB board and room revenues.

Social Director/Director

The title of the primary manager of MCB was Social Director until 1956 when it became Director of the Martha Cook Building.† That has remained the official title although the woman in this position has sometimes since been referred to as Building Director or Resident Coordinator. In the 100 years of the Martha Cook Building's existence, eighteen women have held this position.‡ From the

46. (a17) Gertrude Beggs, first Social Director

---

* See Chapter 7, Financial Well-Being: Income, Expenses and Stewardship.
† Their Minutes of April 2, 1956, state that the Governors had met with candidates for the position of Social Director but May 14 minutes refer to Margaret Blake, "who has accepted the position of Director of the Martha Cook Building."
‡ See Appendix C for biographies.

beginning, the Director was responsible for acting as hostess to the Building, selecting the women who would live there and regulating all matters pertaining to the students.³ When House Director Sarah Rowe resigned in 1949, much of the business management was transferred to the Social Director.⁴ The task of fundraising for scholarships was also added to the Director's role that year.⁵ When the Governors confronted the need to acquire funds for the historic preservation of the Building in the late 1990s, it became apparent that the Building Director, primarily through her good will and engagement of residents and alumnae, would again play a significant role in the raising of funds for the Building's repair and renovation. Tasks associated with this were added to her job description in January 2004.⁶ Over the years, the Social or Building Director has been tasked with maintaining the records of the Building. The Director acts as liaison to University officials, has served on University committees, has been active in community events, is the primary contact between MCB and its alumnae, and, of course, remains the overseeing manager of all staff.

In the selection of residents, the Director has had almost complete authority, although the Dean of Women (when such a position existed) often suggested women for consideration and was even known to offer a Martha Cook scholarship to a non-Cookie to encourage her to move to the Building or transfer to U-M.*

The greatest influence of the Director has been on the Martha Cook residents. Most directors used their role as official hostess of the Building to be a guiding example to the women, instructing chairwomen and committees to arrange appropriate events and greet guests. The Directors have been available as counselors to the women in personal matters and, in the earlier years, served as academic counselors for those women in danger of or on academic

---

* Details on the selection and scholarship processes are explained in Chapters 13 and 15.

probation at the University.[7] Each has added social instruction in her own way, always through example and sometimes via specific instruction. For example, Leona Diekema led weekly sessions on

47. (a41) Leona Diekema, 1941

current events[8] and Cookies of the 1960s will remember Isabel Quail's "ice cream speech." The latter was a lecture on dining etiquette, delivered at dinner one evening early in each semester. The eponymous title of the speech comes from the instruction as to the proper way to eat ice cream, placing on the spoon only an amount that can be slid into the mouth at one time, i.e., licking or biting pieces from the spoon would not be permitted.

In her role as conservator of MCB's records, Olive Chernow toured the new Bentley Historical Library in 1974[9] and determined that it, with its archival safeguards and unlimited availability to the public, was a better place than the Building to store the records. In 1976, with the approval of the Board of Governors, she arranged to house the bulk of MCB's records through 1973 at the Library.[10] Rosalie Moore later added some records through 1979. Records of the years since then have remained at the Building but plans are being made to move additional material to the Bentley.

For many years, Leona Diekema held the record for longest term served at seventeen years, but was surpassed in spring 2015 by Marion Law who completed her eighteenth year as Director. Other long-term directors were Rosalie Moore with eleven years and Isabel Quail with ten.

48. (a05) Olive Chernow, Marion Law, and Rosalie Moore, Messiah Dinner 2005

The Board of Governors were and are responsible for hiring the Building's primary director, but William Cook certainly informed them of his desires as to the characteristics of the woman involved. In a long letter of July 8, 1925 to Governor Anne E. Shipman Stevens, Cook laid out his thoughts:

> The social director is there to teach the social graces to the young women. She should be competent to give them what the "finishing schools" in New York and elsewhere give. They will learn even more by example than by suggestions. How to act is as important to a woman as how to think.

The social director should make that building the social center of the University as it was formerly. Distinguished visitors to the University should be entertained there. Receptions and occasional parties should be given. The Lawyers Club should be civilized. The social life of the University should be dominated, led, moulded [sic] and perfected by the charm of the Martha Cook Building.[11]

Other Management

For the first twelve years, the housekeeping and dining room were managed by the House Director and the business affairs were handled by the Business Manager, whose title changed to House Treasurer and Accountant in 1921.[12] During these twelve years, four different women served as House Director but only one, Frances Mack, held the business position. When Mack retired in 1927, the House Director and Treasurer positions were rolled into one under the title of House Director. In 1949, when responsibility for the Building's bookkeeping was transferred to the University and the Social Director assumed more responsibility for the business end of MCB's management, the administration of kitchen and dining room remained the purview of the second in command, a position retitled as Dietitian. In 1964, the dietitian's title became Associate Director.[13] The latter title was scrapped in July 1973, following the retirement of Ellen Scott, when it was decided that the Dietitian, now officially titled Food Supervisor although sometimes still referred to as Dietitian, did not need to live in the Building. The Governors instead appointed a graduate student as Assistant Resident Director to assist the Director and administer the Building in her absence. The Dietitian/Food Supervisor was responsible for seven-day oversight of all meals until fall 1975 when a Cook III/Supervisor was hired to oversee the weekends.[14] In, 2000, a chef was hired.[15] Today, the Dining Services management team consists of a Manager, Supervisor, and Chef.

Housekeeping (today called Facilities Services) was established as a separate organizational department in 1973 when Director Olive Chernow appointed Vivian Jones as Housekeeping Supervisor. Hired in 1950, Vivian was the first African-American to be employed at MCB. A retirement tea celebrating her 47 years at the Building—the longest tenure of any MCB employee—was held in the Gold Room in April 1997.

49. (a76) Vivian Jones, 1976

For the years 1997–2001, Martha Cook shared a Facilities Manager with the Lawyers Club[16] but since then with the exception of 2012–13 when the position was again shared with the Lawyers Club, MCB has had its own Facilities Manager. In fall 2001, supervisory responsibility for the front office transferred from the Social Director to the Facilities Manager.[17]

Support Staff

The types and numbers of support staff have varied over the century. Early on, the staff included a seamstress, elevator operator, switchboard operator, and maids as well as cooks, pantry workers, and maintenance personnel. In 1949, F. C. Shiel, U-M's Business Manager and Director of Residence Halls, reported to the University's Vice President for Business and Finance that Martha Cook's staff included a secretary, four maids, a seamstress, and two janitors, one of whom was a part-time employee.[18] By fall 1973, two full-time and one part-time maid fulfilled the housekeeping functions.[19]

50. (a34) MCB Staff, 1934

Maid service was provided weekly to residents (dusting, mopping, and vacuuming only—residents were responsible for making their own beds and keeping their rooms tidy) through winter term 1977, then was eliminated as a cost-saving measure.[20]

The current support staff at MCB consists of three cooks, two food service workers, one kitchen cleaner, two and one-half custodians, and one maintenance mechanic.

Some Martha Cook annuals describe the affinity and fondness between staff and students. The 1940 *Annual* recorded that Miss Bentley, the secretary, "takes money for room and board bills," Ellen, who was responsible for the switchboard and mail, "remembers the names of all our boyfriends," Southey in the kitchen "remembers whether you take coffee or milk and how much cream you like in your coffee," and Mrs. Richeson who ran the elevator "knows where each of us live and is always willing to hem a dress or take in a seam on five minute's notice."[21] "Whistley Mr. Nissle," the longtime handyman who endeared himself to residents by fixing their radios and whistled while he worked, was the subject of poem which says in part:

Who is it chases ants galore,
Once saved us from the danger sore
Of a bat that terrorized third floor? Mr. Nissle.
When cleaning day comes round each week,
Who is it makes our rugs look sleek,
Braving the snakelike vacuum's shriek? Mr. Nissle.
Ah, when our husbands fail to do
The little things we ask them to,
How we'll tell them tales of you, Mr. Nissle![22]

51. (a41) Mr. Nissle

Residents of the Martha Cook Building have always been fortunate that both management and support staff are willing to support the student activities in addition to carrying out the day-to-day tasks of their positions. For example, Dining Services management has routinely provided consulting services to the student chairpersons of special dinners, Chef Gary Marquardt designed a flying Harry Potter for a Hogwarts dinner, and the dining staff has willingly created everything from the multi-course Messiah Dinner to ethnic delicacies for the International Tea. Similarly, the Facilities staff have always put up the trees for the annual Holiday Decorating Party and helped with constructions of props for dances and parties.

Student Staff

Unlike permanent support staff who hold their positions across years, student staff are interviewed and hired on an annual basis.

When Ellen Scott retired as Dietitian at the end of the 1972–73 school year, the Board of Governors hired Marilyn Hoag, a married woman with children, to be the new Dietitian. Not surprisingly, she preferred to live in her own home rather than at MCB. Upon the recommendation of Building Director Thelma Duffell, who was also retiring, the Governors decided to hire a graduate student for the following school year to serve as an Assistant Resident Director. She would live in the apartment previously used by the Dietitian and assist the Director and administer the Building during the Director's absence.[23] The ARD would also be available for counseling residents when needed and, by fall 1975, the ARD was also the supervisor of the residents who worked as office assistants at the front desk.[24] The first woman to fill the ARD position was Martha Cook Nash '72, AMLS'74, a graduate student in library science who was William Cook's great-great niece. Martha had previously lived at MCB during her junior year. In addition to assisting Director Olive Chernow, Martha undertook the task of cataloging MCB's libraries. In fall 1977, the position of ARD was filled by an undergraduate, Deborah Ahern Larson '78, for the first time.[25]

The ARD position was eliminated for one year, 1978–79, when the Governors once again required the Dietitian to live in but they retained a student, Patricia Duch '80, as a Student Services Assistant II to supervise the front desk.[26] However, the Dietitian, Margaret Bergren, requested to live out of the Building the following year and Patti recommended to the Governors that the Student Services Assistant position be replaced by restoration of the ARD position for the school year 1979-80. The position remains in place today as a twenty-hour per week commitment. In 2013-14, upon the recommendation of University Housing, a ten-hour Assistant Resident Advisor/Peer Academic Student Specialist position was added to better provide the availability of student counseling required by the University. Compensation for the ARD includes room and board plus a small stipend. The Assistant RA receives room and board. The women are selected in late fall for the following fall's positions and, along with the Multi-Cultural Peer Advisor, must take a one-term, one-credit class offered by the University.

Another type of counseling service was provided to the residents when the Multi-Cultural Peer Advisor position was created in 1995[27] following a period of racial tension on campus and a harassment incident at Martha Cook in 1994.* The role of this job includes counseling and educating both individuals and the Building's student body as a group[28] and is now titled Assistant RA/MCPA. The position is different from the House Board elected role of Ethnic Chair in that the latter is primarily focused on social events, but the women in the two posts work closely together. Martha Cook's MCPA receives her room and board as compensation.

52. (bgm) Office assistant, 2014

Currently, these three positions are considered to be part of the MCB management team, but they are not the first nor only types of student employment at Martha Cook. Cookies can earn wages at MCB by working as office assistants at the front desk, waitresses in the dining room and pantry, and as pot and dish washers in the dish room. The latter is an adaptation of the previous post of busman, which lasted from the first day through 1998, in which young men earned meals by carrying out the heavy work of dining services. The increase in off campus eateries and the advent of microwave ovens

---

* See Chapter 13, The Quest for Diversity.

and ramen noodles decreased the interest in working for meals and the ideal of equal work for both sexes made it possible to offer the heavier-duty positions to women within the Building before seeking outside assistance. Today's student employees at the University of Michigan earn roughly $10 per hour for tasks within the residence halls. This contrasts with student wages for 1934–35[29] when waitresses and those working the switchboard or doing clerical work received thirty-five cents per meal and elevator operators received twenty-five cents per hour.

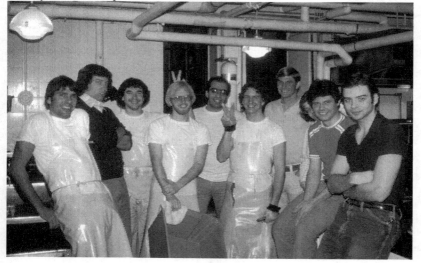

53. (mbs) MCB busmen, 1979

Other student positions which no longer exist include the Nurse and Night Chaperone. The Nurse, sometimes called the Health Chairman, was a registered nurse enrolled at the University as a graduate student in either nursing or public health.[30] She was responsible for checking each girl who was ill, determining whether the resident needed to see a doctor, and writing the notes needed for excused absences from class as well as providing daily reports to the Building's Director and a monthly report to University Health Service. In 1935, there were nurses in five campus dormitories, but the program began at Martha Cook in 1924–25 when resident Genevieve Hoilen, a junior in public health nursing, volunteered her services at the suggestion of Professor Barbara Bartlett. Professor Bartlett arranged the next year for MCB's nurse to be compensated by receiving free room and board, and this compensation, along with fourth priority in room draw,[31] continued until the elimination of the position in 1961.[32]

The Night Chaperone's responsibilities included locking the Building's doors and windows, admitting students out after hours, filing lists with the Dean of Women of those women coming in late, manning the front desk in the evenings and taking all phone calls after the closure of the front desk.[33] The Night Chaperone received room and board[34] and originally was given fifth priority in room draw[35] but later, the after-hours phone line was permanently directed to room 104 on the North Mezzanine and this became the automatic room of the Night Chaperone. With the permission for women to permanently hold keys to the Building—obtained in the mid-1960s—and the installation of in-room phones in 1975, the position became obsolete. The Building's Director and ARD assumed responsibilities for night lockup, or delegated it to an office assistant. Today, the ARD and the two Assistant RAs share the responsibility for ensuring the Building is locked at night.

Together, the Building's management, support, and student staffs provide a constant foundation for the students. It is thanks to the staff members that MCB runs efficiently and effectively. The homelike, family atmosphere that makes Martha Cook so different from other dorms is due in a large part to their presence.

CHAPTER ELEVEN

The Residents: Choicest Spirits of the University

The phenomenon of more than one hundred girls living in a community situation can be a very powerful, spirited kind of experience for everyone involved.
Joan Woodward, House Board President, 1971-72[1]

In 1923, William Cook wrote to the residents of the Martha Cook Building, "Your building was built to gather together the choicest spirits of the University, for their influence on each other and on the University itself …. it is for you to take the torch and carry its flame."[2] And, indeed, the women of Martha Cook have done just that. They determined a code of honor, developed a student government, created events that have become traditions spanning generations, served their University, established an active alumnae association, and found friendships that last a lifetime. While living in the Building and long beyond graduation, the women who call themselves Cookies experience a sense of unity that is the result of a shared culture.

There are no secret handshakes or rituals held in secret rooms, but there are a variety of activities unique to the Building. Three symbolic events*—Dinner for New Women, Turnover Dinner which recognizes the continuation of a strong student government, and Dinner for Graduating Women—are traditions with underpinnings dating to MCB's first year and were designed by the women specifically to ensure the continuance of the community. Opportunities to share academic interests or to learn of others' ethnic backgrounds and occasions to relax and forget school for a while, whether it be at afternoon tea or the Halloween party, add to the camaraderie of the residents. As in all relationships, the smaller things—singing the grace, gathering in a kitchenette for coffee and sweet rolls on Sunday or sharing Michigan pride on a football Saturday—also play a part in creating closeness among Cookies.

54. (avr) Maize and blue Cookies, 2013

---

* See Chapter 19, Tradition: Parties and More.

Student Government

As indicated in his deed of gift, Cook's original intent was to include the women of the Building, under the guidance of a Board of Governors, in the decisions relating to the Building's daily operations and oversight. But, he was convinced by his brother Chauncey and U-M President Hutchins that the Building would be better served if the Governors were the controlling body[3] and

55. (a17) House Board, 1917

this was made the rule by an act of the Regents.[4] Nevertheless, the residents developed their own student government and created a community run by their own leadership. From the beginning, they, acting as the Martha Cook Student Organization, elected officers to serve as a House Board. The earliest boards consisted of a president, vice president, secretary, treasurer, and one representative for each class (e.g., junior-class representative), all elected in the fall. By 1931,[5] the president and vice president were elected in the spring for the following school year so that they could make plans over the summer for Building activities to coincide with the University's orientation week. Upon her election, the president appointed a temporary secretary and treasurer to serve until permanent officers were elected in the fall. In 1938, the elections of secretary and treasurer were moved to the spring[6] preceding the term of office and in 1948, the residents' constitution was revised to include the election of junior and senior representatives at the same time as the rest of House Board, beginning that spring.[7] In 2014, elections of next year's officers were moved to the end of January with turnover of office taking place before spring break. This was done so that MCB's room draw for returning residents, when officers get first choice of rooms, could be held in early February, to coincide with the rest of the University's residence halls.

For many years, the Martha Cook Student Organization ran on a democratic basis, with decisions made at all-house meetings. The primary purposes of the House Board were to plan the agenda for and run the all-house meeting and to coordinate punishments of

56. (a37) House Board on the terrace, 1937

women who stayed out at night beyond closing time or who did not meet the standards of the Room Inspection Committee. Standing committees—running the gamut from a Flower Committee, which organized the ordering of flowers for special events, to the Magazine Committee, which chose and ordered the Building's magazine subscriptions, to the Activities Committee, which kept the residents informed of campus events—provided leadership opportunities for women not on the Board. As the years progressed, the number of standing committees decreased as interest in the various activities waned or as the positions became large enough to warrant an elected position on House Board. For instance, the Service Committee was originally established to draw up the schedule by which Cookies would perform their house service of setting up or cleaning up Friday tea, serving salad at Sunday Tea (sometimes called Sunday Supper), or delivering copies of the Sunday *Michigan Daily* directly to subscribers' rooms. Establishing the schedule required a few hours of committee time at the beginning of each semester. By the 2000s, however, Sunday Tea was replaced with a regular dinner and residents picked up their own copies of the *Daily,* now a free publication, in the Martha Cook foyer. The Service Chair of today, now a House Board position, is responsible for scheduling house services but also plans exam snacks and directs the residents' charitable activities throughout the year. At different times through MCB's history, the residents have voted to include non-elected student officials such as Head Waitress, Health Chair, Chorister, Assistant Resident Director, or Multicultural Peer Advisor to also sit on House Board.

As of the 2015–16 school year, there are thirteen positions on House Board.[8] Committees, fewer than in the past and mostly associated with social activities, still provide leadership roles for non-Board residents.

House Board minutes indicate that the Building's women have had very similar concerns regardless of when they lived at MCB. Except for those times when a controversial Building policy, usually associated with in loco parentis issues, upset the residents, all-house and House Board meetings concerned themselves with plans for the social calendar, the choice of house charitable projects, and the compromises required to maintain a comfortable group environment. Over and over again, meeting minutes were filled with reminders that the Gold Room piano is not a practice piano and cautions to lock bedroom doors when leaving the floor, yell "shower" when flushing the toilet, fulfill house duties, avoid effusive, embarrassing public displays of affection, not remove food from the dining room, not place coats and books on the benches in the hall, and not sit on one's feet on the cane seats of the dining room chairs.

The residents have not always agreed with the rules and policies established by the Board of Governors. Sometimes they were able to effect change to policies, although it often took several attempts, and sometimes they rebelled against authority and were reminded, as in 1937, of "the method by which problems are treated—first through the Student Board to the Directors and through them to the Board of Governors"[9] or as in 1971, "the Board of Governors must always approve a change of policy."[10]

All-house meetings were held twice-monthly for many years and, for the most part, were compulsory. By 1960–61, all-house meetings were held on "an average of once a month lasting approximately one hour."[11] The meetings were held at night, after the house closed. Residents could wear pajamas and curlers although, at least in 1953-54, "Combing hair or putting up hair is prohibited."[12]

57. (a20) A sketch by Juliet Peddle '22 reveals the solution to overly-long meetings.

Many residents were unhappy with the amount of time spent in all-house meetings and efforts were made to shorten their duration. In her end-of-year report for 1942–43, House Board President Virginia Capron Livingston '43, MS'45, reported,

> Meetings were kept as brief as possible. When controversial matters were to be taken up in house meeting, a few girls were selected to discuss the issue thoroughly before house meeting and then present their conclusions to all the girls at the meeting.[13]

In December 1943, Diekema, reported to the Governors, "To save time for the girls, as much business as possible has been handled in the dining room,"[14] presumably as dinner-time announcements. In spring 1955, a motion was made, tabled, then defeated to hold shorter corridor meetings in place of some all-house meetings.[15] Fines were often imposed to ensure attendance. Proposals were made to make attendance at meetings honorary rather than monetary, but the dearth of attendees caused the Governors in 1961 to reinstitute mandatory meetings.[16] Finally, in 1969–70, the residents voted 136-1 to change their democratic form of government to a republican—or representative—one and the Governors approved the ballot proposal.[17] The new organization, still in effect today, calls for one mandatory all-house meeting each semester, primarily for introductions and discussion of the Building's rules. After that, House Board meets weekly to make all decisions related to the student organization except those dealing with policy changes. The latter are decided via a balloting process where each resident has a vote. All residents are encouraged to attend the House Board Meetings to share their opinions and the chairpersons of events must present their proposals and requests for funds to the Board. Minutes of all-house and Board minutes were posted publicly, either on bulletin boards next to the elevators on each floor, or on the back of bathroom stall doors. Currently, minutes are posted online as well as in bathroom stalls and on the resident information table in the main hallway.[18]

Community Building and Social Activities within MCB

All activities and events at Martha Cook have an aspect of camaraderie. Some, though, are aimed specifically at building a sense of community. Their aim is to initiate relationships, establish communication, encourage trust, create unity, and overcome differences within the MCB population. The most significant unifying activity from 1916 through the present day has been the singing of the *Martha Cook Grace*. More than anything this grace has united Cookies across the generations as it is not only sung at every sit-down dinner at the Building but is also the opening ritual of every alumnae brunch or dinner. The largest community building action of each year—and a tradition in its own right—has been the series of events that make up what is now called Welcome Week but for years was labeled as the University's Orientation Week. During the school year, House Board organizes and different residents serve as chairwomen of events, both those open to residents and their guests and those for MCB women only. Over the years, the latter have ranged from special tea dances to movie nights to Girls Night In, a first floor pajama party event.

58. (a06) Welcome Week, 2006

The college experience is not complete without a social life. Cook himself recognized this when he wrote to Anne E. Shipman Stevens in August 1925 that MCB should be "the social centre of the University .... Receptions and occasional parties should be given."[19] Cookies have taken this advice to heart and producing some of the grandest, most elegant, and most fun dances and parties imaginable has become tradition at Martha Cook.[*]

---

[*] See Chapter 19, Tradition: Parties and More.

Educational Experiences

When it came to educational activities within the Building, William Cook was very definite in his opinion, or almost definite. In that same 1925 letter, Cook wrote, "That Building is not an educational institution. The University attends to that."[20] Yet, he also stated, "Distinguished visitors to the University should be entertained there" and he must have realized that inquisitive young minds would learn much from meeting these notable guests. And he was not beyond wishing that the Martha Cook Building would stimulate academic thought, for he wrote in 1929 to his friend, author and actress Cornelia Otis Skinner, "... I think that the magnificent equipment of our universities enlarges the vision, gives an inspiration and stirs the imagination of the students. Otherwise I would not have built those buildings."[21]

Whatever Cook's thoughts, the women of the Building have always had minds of their own. To them, education within the residence hall has been as important as in the classroom. University presidents and faculty members have visited for dinners and informal conversations and fireside chats after dinner with famous guests to the Building were part of the Martha Cook way of life from the beginning. In 1921, the Building hosted a dinner party for Emmeline Pankhurst,[22] the leader of the women's suffrage movement in England. She had served jail time for her militant tactics, including hunger strikes and assaulting policemen, actions which must have been an anathema to Cook who placed ladylike grace above all else.

In October 1929, MCB not only hosted a dinner and fireside chat in honor of Cornelia Otis Skinner, but some of its women were in complete charge of Skinner's presentation at Mendelsohn Theater. "The Committee Chairman assumed all the responsibility for the performance and worked with the Director of the Theater."[23] Ms. Skinner visited again in 1936.[24]

Eleanor Roosevelt visited on October 26, 1939, and Diekema reported to the Governors,

> It was a momentous occasion at the corner of Tappan and South University, even raising the excitement of the Lawyer's Club to the point where its occupants took their binoculars to their positions on the windowsills of their cloister. Needless to say, it was one of our most popular teas.

Journalist Eve Curie, daughter of Nobel Prize winners Pierre and Marie, stayed overnight at MCB on February 15, 1940.[25] That same evening, she gave a presentation to the University community. The next day, after touring the campus and lunching at West Quad, she was the honored guest at MCB's tea, to which about 200 campus women were invited. She dined with the House Board officers, then toured the Building, and joined the house in the Blue Room until train time. MCB women held receptions for conductor Zubin Mehta and his wife Nancy Kovac Mehta '55, a Cookie, and the members of the Israeli Philharmonic Orchestra in 1972, 1976, and 1989.[26] The Mehtas and the Los Angeles Philharmonic Orchestra were guests at an MCB reception in 1975.

President Gerald R. Ford was a dinner guest on April 5, 1977.[27] Following dinner, several Cookies joined off-duty Secret Service members for libations at Dooley's, a local watering hole.[28] In 1984, movie director Robert Altman turned the Red Room into a replica of the study in former President Richard Nixon's New Jersey home and filmed *Secret Honor,* a fictional

59. (clr) President Gerald R. Ford in the Gold Room, 1977

one-man performance intending to give insight into President Nixon's beliefs and actions starring Philip Baker Hall.[29] A special private showing of the completed movie was held for the residents in the Gold Room on February 4, 1985.[30]

Over the years, the residents have entertained other famous guests, some for dinner, some for tea, some for honorary receptions, and some for simple tours of the Building. They have included[31] social worker Jane Addams in 1926; Ossip Gabrilowitsch, pianist, conductor, founding director of the Detroit Symphony Orchestra, and son-in-law of Mark Twain in 1931;[32] Korean nationalist and later president of South Korea Syngman Rhee and poet Edna St. Vincent Millay, both in 1933; journalist and radio broadcaster Dorothy Thompson in 1936; novelist Frances Parkinson Keyes, actor Conrad Nagel, and Senator and Mrs. Arthur Vandenburg, all in 1941; journalist Pierre van Paassen and actress and novelist Ilka Chase in 1942; Vijaya Lakshmi Nehru Pandit, the Indian nationalist who later became India's ambassador to the US and the first woman president of the UN General Assembly, in 1945; the Netherlands Ambassador to the US, Dr. J. H. and Madame van Roijen in 1953; Senator George McGovern in 1969; pianist Vladimir Horowitz in 1975.[33] During a visit to perform and teach at U-M, cast and crew of the Royal Shakespeare Company joined residents for tea on November 3, 2006.

Educational moments were not always brought into the Building for the residents, but sometimes originated in the Building and were led by the residents themselves. A 2013 celebration of Diwali, the Hindu festival of lights, planned by resident Aashka Soni for her fellow Cookies, earned MCB the U-M Residence Hall Association's award for best religious program.[34] Sometimes a Cookie inspired event was opened to the campus. In 2014, Service Chair Michelle Zaydlin '15 organized a community walk to bring awareness to eating disorders and to benefit the National Eating Disorder Association (NEDA). She and the MCB Service Committee created a day-long event that combined educational seminars with a walk around Palmer Field, raising $16,000 for NEDA and earning MCB the award for best educational program.[35] The annual International Tea is an example of an event that was originally a Martha Cook event but has transformed over the years into a premier campus event.

Campus Activities

From the Building's earliest days, MCB residents have been strongly encouraged to participate in a volunteer capacity that will benefit either the house or the campus. This is in addition to the one required "house service" described above. In earlier years, many a Cookie served as an officer of the Michigan League, the Assembly (the independent women's organization), or the Women's Athletic Association or participated in events of those organizations. It was not unusual for MCB to place among the top competitors in skit

60. (a30) Intramural hockey team, 1930

nights, Lantern Nights (singing contests), or intramural athletic events. In November 1941, Diekema reported that MCB ranked second in per capita participation in campus activities (Collegiate

Sorosis was first).[36] In addition, MCB women often prepared exhibits or floats for the Homecoming and Michigras parades. (Michigras was a fun-fair-like event held during winter term at the Intramural Building.) Today, residents still participate in intramural athletic contests and, as members of the Resident Hall Association, are represented by two House Board officers at the regular meetings of this group. Martha Cook has won several awards from RHA (e.g., Best Educational Program, Best Non-Advisor Resident Staff Member, and Best Dining Services in 2014[37]) and in spring 2006 was awarded RHA's highest honor, "Residence Hall of the Year."[38] Individual MCB women have been writers and editors for the *Michigan Daily*, *Michiganensian*, or *Gargoyle*. Others have sung in groups such the University Arts Chorale or U-M Gilbert and Sullivan Society or played in the Marching Band. Some have addressed global and domestic issues through Model UN and other policy organizations, enrolled in ROTC, joined club activities such as the U-M Ballroom Dance Team, participated in religion-affiliated groups, or were otherwise active in extra-curricular endeavors.

61. (jm) Intramural football, 1981

Activities to Benefit Others

Charitable activities are tradition at Martha Cook. As part of some Christmas Breakfast celebrations,* the residents collected small

---

* See Chapter 19, Tradition: Parties and More.

toys for children in the University hospital. Residents have actively participated in U-M campaigns to raise funds to build the Michigan League,[39] the Burton Memorial Tower,[40] the women's swimming pool,[41] and the Michigan Memorial Phoenix Project, an undertaking "launched in 1948 to engage in research and other activities that support the peaceful uses of atomic energy" and dedicated to the 579 members of the Michigan community who gave their lives in World War II.[42] In spring 2008, the residents assisted in the renovation of their own college home, holding a talent show, cleverly called "Raise the Roof," to raise funds specifically earmarked for the Building's roof replacement project that summer.[43] They sponsored orphans several times[44] and raised awareness for eating disorders,[45] world hunger[46], planet sustainability,[47] and other causes. In the springs of 2013, 2014 and 2015, a team of Cookies participated in the U-M Dance Marathon, with proceeds going to different children's funds.[48]

The two World Wars provided many opportunities for civilians to support the war efforts and Cookies were campus leaders in the endeavors. According to the 1918 *Annual,* every Cookie was a member of the Red Cross and fifty-two of the girls had purchased Liberty Bonds that year.

> The girls determined ... to buy bonds through their own efforts, either by foregoing pleasures or by earning the money. When the tasks in the Building were all taken – such as waiting table, toasting bread and relieving the elevator operator, schemes were devised whereby the bond payments could be met .... Shoe shining, sewing, mending, scalp massaging, errands and fortune telling were among those offered for sale.

World War II service activities were even more abundant and were completed with great gusto. At an all-house meeting on January 12, 1942, the women decided to establish a Red Cross knitting and sewing unit at the Building and twelve sweaters were knitted during February.[49] During that same time period, Cookies registered through the Michigan League's branch of the Office of Civilian Defense, for courses in home nursing, nurse's aide, nutrition, first aid, braille, typing, children's aid, motor mechanics, and radio communications. Different University departments also offered courses taken by many Cookies—military map making, cryptanalysis, stenography, special math and sciences, camouflage, radio wiring, and petroleum chemistry.[50] Many of the women helped in the hospital, sold stamps and war bonds, or prepared surgical dressings.[51] In each of 1943, 1944, and 1945, Martha Cook won the League War Council's plaque for the highest percentage of activities in war work participation.[52] Diekema reported in June 1944 that the average for the year was 28.21 hours per person, but that second semester participation averaged 42.07 hours per person.[53] In addition to their time, Martha Cook women gave their money to community war chest drives[54] and to the Bomber Scholarship Fund.[*] The latter was a campus-wide effort to raise $100,000 (the cost of a light bomber plane, hence lending the sobriquet to the fund), to purchase war bonds, the interest from which was used for scholarship aid to students, both men and women, whose University careers were interrupted by the war.[55]

Passing on a Legacy

Through the organizational structure and activities of Martha Cook, each Resident found her own niche at Martha Cook and in so doing not only discovered herself but also added meaning to the lives of her fellow Cookies, a legacy best described in Lynn Zimmerman

---

[*] "The Bomber Scholarship, supported by funds raised by students during the years of World War II, was ... intended, originally, to provide tuition for students who had had their education interrupted because of war service. When the United States Congress passed the G. I. Bill, the Bomber Scholarship, in the form of grants of $100 a semester, was set up to give supplementary assistance to deserving veterans. Several hundred students received assistance through this program between 1947 and 1952." Source: Wilfred B. Shaw (ed.), *The University of Michigan: An Encyclopedic Survey, Part 9* (Ann Arbor: U-M Libraries, 1958), p 1853, <googlebooks.com>, (June 27, 1015).

Bloom's '56, MA'57, PhD'63 essay in MCB's Seventy-fifth Anniversary booklet:

> We not only became part of each other's maturation process, we helped to humanize, civilize, and socialize one another. Through living in Martha Cook we enhanced each other's self-esteem, as well as our own. These influences last more than a lifetime, for we transmit the legacy of honor, intelligence, commitment, and grace to our children, daughters and sons alike. This legacy extends to our grandchildren as well, generations past, and passing, and to come. That is the overarching virtue, the ultimate value of residence in Martha Cook.[56]

CHAPTER TWELVE

Alumnae: Beyond Graduation

Oh guard our friendship circle ever,
see that naught its firm bands sever
                                        Martha Cook Grace

Most Martha Cook women make at least one lifelong friend during their stay in the Building. Most also find that being a Cookie becomes part of their identity, much as they feel enduring kinship with fellow U-M Wolverines, and they enjoy preserving their ties through the Martha Cook Alumnae Association. The Martha Cook Building has also reached out to alumnae since 1916, made them feel part of the community and facilitated their efforts to organize. The ways in which alumnae and the Building maintain their relationship have changed and modified over the years, but the spirit behind it is timeless. The words to the *Martha Cook Grace* could not have been more appropriate.

Organizing the Martha Cook Alumnae Association

Alumnae first formally organized in 1918, and this was commemorated in the *Annual*:

gradually throughout our lively student organization (it may at times have seemed hazardously so), there has permeated that oneness and integrity which could not fail to develop in a college home so thoroughly planned and so marvelously executed. It is this consciousness of our unity as an organization and the ties that have become established among the varied types of Martha Cook girls, that have made it seem necessary and fitting that the graduates who leave the Martha Cook Building organize an Alumnae Association.

The alumnae, largely from the Detroit and Ann Arbor area, gathered at MCB during commencement week in 1920. As noted in the residents' 1921 *Annual*,

Winona Beckley Matthews suggested that the money in the treasury of the association be used to publish a paper containing news of the alumnae so that the association would begin to more nearly fulfill its purpose, namely, to keep the girls in touch with each other.

They formed a committee with members from each class, notified alums and, "after a few meetings at the home of Mrs. [Delicia Gilbert] Deming the paper became a reality."[1] At least one issue of *The Wide, Wide World* was published but no known copies survive.

In addition to alumnae updates, *The Wide, Wide World* also featured the MCAA constitution of that time. The complicated sections on eligibility for MCAA membership were quoted in the 1921 *Annual*. Graduation from U-M and living at least the second semester of senior year in the Building, or a full year in MCB "without spending a continuous year of residence elsewhere on campus subsequent to her residence in Martha Cook, " were the rules, probably in an attempt to exclude anyone who left to join a sorority. There are not enough existing and dated constitutions to check for sure, but the current stipulation of a semester in residence has probably been closer to the norm. Also, the 1920 system where the House Board President automatically became the MCAA President did not last for long.

The women reorganized again on February 19, 1927, calling themselves the Detroit Alumnae Chapter for the Martha Cook

62. (a28) Alumnae meeting in the Blue Room, 1928

Building. At this time, the impetus was the idea of encouraging additional chapters around the country as well as raising money for scholarships. Approximately seventy were in attendance at the College Club of Detroit, including Governor Anne E. Shipman Stevens and Social Director Elva Forncrook as guests of honor. The women planned to make a yearly donation to the MCB scholarship fund and Stevens, always a staunch supporter, donor, and event attendee, gave $100 on the spot.[2]

Then, in 1935 the women renamed themselves the Martha Cook Alumnae Association of Detroit. Many alums still refer to "the Detroit Group." Fostering ties between alumnae and the Building as well as socializing and benefiting residents by raising money for scholarships continued to be at the organization's heart just as they are now. The Building's Director and Board of Governors (seldom alumnae themselves in the early years) regularly attended these social gatherings, as they do to the present day.

The MCAAD's constitution has been regularly updated, most recently in 2009, and the club has remained the core alumnae force, organizing teas, luncheons, bridge parties, and fundraisers, and working closely with the Building Director and Governors on special events. In 1992, the MCAA voted to delete "Detroit" from its name to better describe its role as the association for all Martha Cook alumnae, "now residents of the world."

The MCAA Board has typically held meetings monthly except for December, April, July, and August. After meeting in Detroit for decades, often in the Rackham Building, in 1976 the Board changed its meeting location to Dearborn's Fair Lane Mansion because it was more central to board members' residences.[3] For a while, the Board met in members' homes. By the early 1990s, Ann Arbor became more convenient, and the group met at a board member's apartment complex before finally convening at Martha Cook which has continued to be the board's usual venue. When MCB is closed for the summer, the group usually meets at a campus area restaurant.

The MCAA Board arranges two events per year, down from three when, in 1952, the constitution was unanimously amended to combine the annual meeting with the spring event.[4] In 1969, the Board discussed reducing the number of events again,[5] but chose to continue with two. The MCAA Board also manages the Memorial

Fund, donates the Outstanding Resident Award gift[*], assists with AESS Scholarship interviews, and coordinates or helps with special projects.

The Ann Arbor Alumnae Association

The Ann Arbor Alumnae Association was founded in 1962 by Connie Butler Amick '57[6] as a separate social organization for the women living in the Ann Arbor area. They first gathered in the Red Room, but after two meetings were asked to convene elsewhere, perhaps due to an overly literal understanding of the rule that the Building is only to be used for residents. They did not meet in MCB again until Olive Chernow became Building Director in 1974 and invited them back.

In the spring of 1964, Connie Amick wrote to the Governors informing them about the organization, and Elizabeth Black Ross '29 responded that the Governors were pleased, especially as there would be work to do for the upcoming Fiftieth Anniversary.[7] As an "on the spot" club, they were well placed to assist the MCAA and the Building, and organized local projects such as bed and breakfast accommodations for out-of-town Cookies attending the Fiftieth, Seventy-fifth and Ninetieth Anniversary Weekends. They joined the Governors, Fundraising Committee, MCAA, and residents in organizing the first Coming Home Spring Teas in the early 2000s. The group had its own interests, too. Some years, they sponsored needy families at Christmas through the Washtenaw County Social Services. They customarily gave practical gifts to the Building, and in 1993 they created their own scholarship fund for a Minority Merit Award.

The Ann Arbor alumnae traditionally held two meetings a year at MCB, a holiday evening in December while the decorations were

---

[*] See Appendix G, Outstanding Resident Award.

still up, and a spring salad pot luck luncheon after residents had moved out. They eventually worked with MCAA to develop chapter guidelines which were put to a vote in the fall 1997 MCAA newsletter. They became the first chapter in 1998 but disbanded in 2005 as a formal non-profit group. They met informally a couple times afterwards. Chaptering, which has been discussed and encouraged many times over the century, has never taken hold, although small groups of friends get together informally around the country. The Ann Arbor Chapter, however, had a terrific run of over forty years and set the bar.

Communication – Letters and Lists

Staying in touch is a hallmark of the Martha Cook Building and its alumnae, both individually and as a community. While far from unique among college alumni, it is nonetheless the foundation for MCB's post-graduation culture, and it hearkens back to the Building's earliest period as demonstrated with *The Wide, Wide World* and the yearbooks.

Were the MCB annuals mailed or sold to alumnae? The answer is unknown, but alumnae updates and directories were included in volumes through 1928 and the 1924 book was dedicated to them. Cradle rolls, listing babies born to Cookie graduates, occasionally appear, some even with photographs. The 1918 *Annual* included a letter from the first Social Director, Gertrude Beggs, who wrote,

> I am glad to be considered an alumna of the Martha Cook Building, and I think back with interest and pleasure to the times which the pioneers in its history spent there together. We are widely scattered now but an occasional letter comes with news of various members of that first group that this beautiful Building housed and the Annual will supply us with many other links in this year's history.

This suggests that alumnae as well as residents received copies, making that yearbook an extraordinarily elaborate newsletter. After

1928, there were simply too many graduates to list in each yearbook. Only one additional alumnae directory has been published, a loose-leaf binder with names organized both alphabetically and by graduation year, on the occasion of MCB's Seventy-fifth Anniversary in October 1990.

Round robin letters between Cookie friends were popular in the days before inexpensive long distance phone calls and email. A 1916 graduate indicated in the 1917 *Annual* that her class was sustaining one. Olive Chernow related a story of women from the classes of 1925 and 1926 who got together in May 1975 after remaining in touch since graduation via a round robin.[8]

Keeping records of alumnae as they moved away and changed their names has been an enormous task. The Martha Cook office maintained a card catalog of names for decades, updating as well as they could, and relying upon Cookies to send in address changes. In June 1931 Social Director Margaret Smith wrote to Governor Anne E. Shipman Stevens that a staff member "has gone to the *Michiganensian* office and to the Alumni office to compile the record of Martha Cook alumnae. Of course, these figures are not absolutely accurate, but are approximate."[9]

The MCAA of Detroit probably kept a list of its own members from its inception and may have had some addresses for non-local Cookies. MCAA and the Building sometimes joined forces, mailing invitations for the same event. Social Director Leona Diekema wrote in her monthly report that the Building sent 200 invitations to Ann Arbor alumnae and recent graduates while the MCAA of Detroit sent 400 for an April 1948 spring tea attended by 100.

During the 1950s, Diekema mailed letters to update alumnae, but whether this was done earlier is unknown. By 1955 through the early 1960s, a resident held the position of Alumnae Secretary with the tasks of keeping the card file current and sending a short newsletter. Director Isabel Quail, with assistance from the Assistant Director,

House Board President, and Alumnae Secretary, produced a more involved communique with a newsy letter, three pages of alumnae submissions, like the "Cookie Crumbs" column in the modern newsletter.[10] Unfortunately, very few of these letters were saved.

The newsletter transformed from a Building to alumnae-generated mailing during the 1970s. The MCAA president wrote a chatty, biannual letter with an invitation to the Christmas brunch or spring luncheon. It sometimes included a message from the Building Director. It also contained information on donating to the scholarship and Memorial funds. The newsletter as a paper with articles as well as invitations, RSVP and donation forms and, of course, the "Cookie Crumbs", developed further around the time of the Seventy-fifth Anniversary in 1990, to the degree that, in fall 1993, the MCAA agreed to fund up to $1000 per academic year to hire a resident to maintain the alumnae database, prepare mailing labels, and do the newsletter layout prior to printing.[11] By the late 1990s, as personal computers, photo scanning and editing, and email communication became commonly used, the newsletter grew in size and scope, first to twelve pages and then to sixteen in the 2000s.

The difficulty of maintaining up-to-date lists continued to be a stumbling block to communication until the turn of the century. Cookies' dedication to solving the problem was impressive. The October 9, 1950, MCAA of Detroit minutes relate that, "carloads of workers to check the Martha Cook files against the University alumni files were to go to Ann Arbor in October."[12] In 1951, Diekema reported that the files had about 2700 names after corrections were made the previous year.[13] The lists were updated again for the Fiftieth Anniversary, a job members of MCAA of Ann Arbor remembered taking three to four years of tedious labor.[14] In fall 1967, Maurita Peterson Holland '65, '66 spoke to the Governors and offered to reorganize the alumnae files again. By April 1968 she reported that the Ann Arbor Alumnae had twenty-five women working in the Alumni Records Office.[15] Ten years later in 1978, alumnae were at it again under the direction of Maurita Holland and Connie Amick. This list was to be computerized and hopes ran high. The Ann Arbor club tackled their end of the job, supplemented with paid assistance from two residents.[16] When this huge project was completed in 1979, the list had 4,021 names and addresses,[17] but the exasperating problem of keeping the list up-to-date over time remained.

It is unclear what happened to that list. In 1985, the association's list of "any woman who has expressed an interest in MCAA, ... women who have paid dues, have not paid dues, have contributed to the scholarship fund or are recent graduates ..." totaled 1,000 alumnae.[18] In 1988, it reached 1561[19], but *The Martha Cook Directory* of 1990 contained less than 900 names[20] and in the late 1990s, MCAA's list was approximately 800.[21] The MCB Fundraising Committee had access to a somewhat larger mailing list through the University, but it was still far from complete. A new system with a method for staying current was desperately needed.

Maurita Holland stepped in again in 2000. Using the annuals and the Building's collection of room lists, she and her secretary, Marsha Whitish, matched names with those on the University's master list now permanently maintained as a joint project of the U-M Alumni Association and U-M's Office of Development. They added a Martha Cook Activity Code onto the 4,347 Cookies they found and were done in time for the spring 2001 newsletter mailing.[22] Now, to insure that no one will ever have to undertake the job again, student names are also coded upon moving into the Martha Cook Building. While occasional "lost Cookies" still come to the Building's attention, this system, fully coordinated with the University, has worked smoothly to the present day. Lists can readily be generated for specific mailing areas, graduation years, and other criteria.

With the comprehensive list and a joint decision by the MCAA and Governors in 2003 to dispense with mandatory dues and include all alumnae in mailings, printing the MCAA newsletter (still written, compiled, and edited by volunteers) became the Building's financial responsibility.[23] The expenses are considered part of the fundraising budget as an engagement effort. The newsletter itself is now sixteen pages and contains articles from the Building Director, Governors, House Board President, and MCAA President. It also includes a "Cookie Crumbs" column to which any alumna may contribute. Event news, stories about residents, history snippets, alumnae profiles, and donation information are featured as well. It is published in the fall and late spring.

Cookies Go Digital

Marie Fox Skrobola '95 developed MCAA's website in 1999.[24] She also oversaw compiling an email list to use for event reminders and quickly sharing breaking news from MCB. She has remained the webmaster to the present, and upon becoming a Governor in 2014, designed the MCB webpage which went live in April 2015.[25] The MCAA and the residents' webpages are linked to this Martha Cook Building cyberspace portal.

The alumnae Facebook presence began in 2007 with CookieNet, organized by Lynn Zwinck '06, as an unofficial virtual gathering place unaffiliated with either MCB or MCAA due to the controversial nature of Facebook at that time. "By Cookies for Cookies" is the tagline. CookieNet began with ninety-two members in fall 2007,[26] continues to add members and has proved very useful for contacting alums with event reminders and news. In fall 2014, the U-M Victors for Michigan campaign was the impetus for an official Martha Cook Building Facebook page. Twitter followed shortly after so the Building could take part in the University's first Giving Blue Day on December 2, 2014.

Alumnae Holiday Brunch

Gathering at a restaurant or club in the Detroit area to commemorate MCB's Christmas and now Holiday Breakfast is one of the oldest alumnae traditions. While there are no records of when it began, it is safe to guess it was early. There is a reference from the *Detroit Free Press* society news section on December 3, 1934, relating that alumnae met for an afternoon tea and craft fair at the Colony Town Club and that Stevens sent a Christmas cake (just as she always did for the MCB residents).[27] The luncheon or brunch developed its own rituals which including the *Martha Cook Grace*, the Roll Call of the Classes by decade, and the Candle Lighting Ceremony. The following words are read by the President:

> When each of us lived at Martha Cook, we were influenced and enriched by the experience of traditional living, the beautiful surroundings, and the warm friendships we shared. We, in turn, added to the tradition of the building our achievements and satisfactions, which now form a common bond among all of us across the years. And so, as tradition has been a hallmark of our past, we want to carry it forward too, and once again, light these three white candles as an expression of our lives as Martha Cook women.
>
> The first candle we light in memory of those who have gone before, in appreciation of the heritage they left us.
>
> The second candle we light for the young women now living at Martha Cook with the hope they will carry on the fine traditions of many years.
>
> The third candle we light for the future, that those yet to come may find the same fulfillment while living at Martha Cook.[28]

The Building Director, Assistant Director, House Board President, and sometimes a resident or two who play instruments are invited. Some years featured fashion shows, musical entertainments, and guest speakers, but the nucleus of the event is the ceremony and conversation.

As modern lives have become busier, attendance has been a perceived problem and, from as far back as the 1950s, suggestions have been made to end it or replace it with an event at a different time of year. The Holiday brunch was replaced with a Homecoming brunch in Ann Arbor in 1995. This was not popular and after a December tea at the Building the following year, restaurant and club venues returned with varying degrees of success. Holiday brunch was not held in 2014, replaced with a well-attended January 2015 tea at MCB. The roll call of the classes and candle ceremony were showcased.

Teas

Teas are a classic Martha Cook event, and this is no less true for alumnae. The big anniversary weekends have always featured one tea and sometimes two. The MCAA has held countless teas,

63. (cjd) Golden Alumnae (fifty or more years as Cookies) were honored in 2000.

including some bridge tea parties, both for socializing and fundraising. Spring teas at the Building have been especially popular whether organized by the Building alone or with assistance from alumnae.

After a few years of alternate venues in the 1980s and 1990s, a spring tea at MCB became a traditional fixture on the social calendar with the Coming Home Spring Tea in 2000. MCAA, the Ann Arbor Chapter, the Fundraising Committee, and House Board joined the Building and Governors in organizing the event and it was a success. For the first few years the invitation was printed in the newsletter, but now formal invitations with RSVP cards and donation forms are mailed to all alumnae. Speakers, musical entertainment, and updates from the House Board President, MCAA, the Governors, and Building Director are typically included in the program.

64. (ke) A 21st century Spring Tea

New events are always welcomed, and on May 5, 2007, the alumnae held the first of three Milk and Cookies Teas. Beth Yaros Johnston '90 and Kimberly Lingenfelter Burnson '90, JD'93 organized the initial party. Held after the residents had moved out for the summer, it featured a simple, child-friendly menu, games in the garden, and crafts on the terrace. Approximately forty-five Cookies, children, and a few men attended.

Staying in Touch

Today, with the help of the alumnae address database and modern technology, the MCAA is more inclusive and connected that ever. Conference and online phone calls now make it possible for the alumnae board to accommodate members who live too far away to attend monthly meetings. The aim of MCAA has always been to connect Martha Cook women and benefit its U-M campus home. Cookies can look forward to a future of change which will continue the tradition of gathering together and returning to MCB, either in person or virtually to "guard our friendship circle ever, from year to year."

65. (a25) Illustration of Returning Alumnae by Dorothy Eggert '25

CHAPTER THIRTEEN

The Quest for Diversity

Friendship between you and me has proved that good will knows no race and color, knows no East and West.
Sui Chen Yang, MCB Resident from China, 1928[1]

A request to live at the Martha Cook Building has always been a separate act from applying to live in the other residence halls at the University of Michigan, requiring the completion of a separate application form. Today, women are admitted strictly in the order in which the applications are received, but this was not always true. In earlier times, the Social or Building Director interviewed applicants and personally chose which women would be invited to live at Martha Cook. Regardless of how a woman finally ended up as a resident, the first action was always the young woman's; she had to choose to apply, and so the population of MCB has always had an aspect of self-selection by women who want a traditional life style.

As noted earlier, William Cook thought of MCB residents as "the choicest spirits of the University." His idea of "choicest spirits," however, did not include underclasswomen, transfer students, women enrolled in the professional schools, or foreign students. Luckily, the Governors, Directors, and residents of MCB did not agree with Cook, even during his lifetime, and so these women as well as Cook's preferred "choicest American girls in the literary department"[2] have always been a part of the Martha Cook community. That is not to say that MCB has a perfect record, particularly in terms of race and religion, but the desire to be a diverse community was established early and continuing progress towards a cosmopolitan mix of residents has definitely been the norm.

Cook's Ideas on the Perfect Cookies

In a letter of July 8, 1925, to Governor Anne E. Shipman Stevens, written as the Governors were seeking to hire a new Social Director, Cook expressed his opinion of the desired qualities for a resident:

> [The Social Director is responsible] for the selection of seniors and a few juniors to live in the house. I think they should be selected chiefly for their social qualities. The building is not an educational institution. The University attends to that. If the building is to be a social centre (sic) for University live (sic), as the building formerly was and should be, it must contain girls of a high social type. That building should not aim at 'straight A' students. This has a blue stocking tang that is entirely out of place. It has or should have definite social purposes to improve the manners of the University, especially of the barbaric young men. You have had only eighty-one seniors in the building the past year .... the plan has been to have 100 seniors and ten juniors .... All professional women should be excluded .... Only a few post-graduates should be admitted and only exceptional ones at that. Nor do I think it a good plan to take in transfers from other schools on faith or recommendation except in cases of clear desirability. The transfer system drags down the University to lower levels. I don't see why those Orientals are there. That building is not a League of Nations. You can see that my idea is to gather together the choicest American girls in the literary department without regard to scholarship.[3]

His niece Florentine once said that Cook sometimes said things merely to stir things up,[4] but these comments were more than that. They described his real thoughts for in August of the same year, after the Governors had hired Elva Forncrook as the new Social Director, Cook wrote again to Stevens and suggested:

You may care to show [Miss Forncrook] my letter to you of July 8th and, in fact, you may think it well to deposit that letter in the files of the Martha Cook Bldg. for preservation, because one hundred years hence the occupants of the building may be interested in knowing what my ideas were.[5]

William Cook's ideas of the type of woman who should live at Martha Cook were shaped by prejudice, both his own and the prevailing stereotypes of the times. As his biographer Margaret Leary wrote in *Giving It All Away: The Story of William W. Cook and his Michigan Law Quadrangle:*

> Was Cook an Anglo-Saxon supremacist and anti-Semite and, if so did he impose his views on Michigan Law? The answer to the first question is a very straightforward yes. Cook like so many others of his time, held views that today make people wince. But it is important ... to know that Cook never imposed these views on Michigan Law.[6]

As far as can be determined, he also never directly imposed these views on the Martha Cook Building. Yes, he shared his opinions with the Building's Board of Governors but these women were always free to make their own decisions regarding admission policies. For several years, they tried, not very successfully, to follow Cook's request for a large senior population, but his request to exclude transfers, non-American, non-Caucasian, and professional women has been observed more in its omission.

Underclasswomen and the Honors Dorm Rumors

The first group of women to enter MCB in 1915 was comprised of representatives from all four classes and included fifty-five freshmen.[7] It was not until fall 1919 that freshmen were excluded. An article in the 1919 *Martha Cook Annual*[8] explained that it was "the donor's original desire that Martha Cook should be an honorary residence for upper-class women" although there is no existing documentation showing that Cook put any stipulation on his gift regarding either that the house should be an upper-class or honorary house. His letter of July 8, 1925, however, shows that his preference was for the house to only include seniors and a few juniors. That letter and another written in 1923 in which he stated, "Much as I value intellect I put character and womanly grace above it,"[9] demonstrate that rather than desiring an honors dormitory, Cook was opposed to the idea of a house of bluestockings. Further, there is no evidence that U-M or the MCB Board of Governors ever required applicants to be members of the Honors College or to be labeled honor student in any way. Rather, "significant scholarship"[10] was only one of several characteristics considered for admission to the Building. Nonetheless, in the days when U-M collected and posted an average grade point for housing units (residence halls and sororities), Martha Cook often ranked as the house with the highest overall GPA. For example, Diekema's reports from 1947–53 state that Cookies took the cup for highest GPA among independent women; in 1947 she commented that MCB's average of 2.91 "led the entire campus—fraternities, sororities, men's dorms, women's dorms."

The article in the 1919 *Annual* explained that MCB would exclude freshman women the following fall and sophomores a year later. Three reasons were given for the change to an upper-class house. It stated that the number of women applying to live at Martha Cook was increasing. Confining the majority of residents to a single year would give more women the chance to experience dormitory living. It was felt that by senior year the leaders who deserve the best would stand out.

The women of Martha Cook were not happy with the new plan. An article in the following year's *Annual*[11] was full of humorous pathos—"the loss of the Freshmen has been comparable to the disappearance of the sunbeams," for example. But, the article's conclusion expressed the real problem with Cook's plan, that there is "no nucleus of old girls forming a natural center of tradition."

66. (a19) Freshmen residents, 1919

Fortunately, for the continuation of MCB traditions, the junior-class was never reduced to the low levels exhorted by William Cook. In a letter to the Governors of April 4, 1929, and accompanying report on the status of applications,[12] Building Director Ethel Dawbarn requested that her quota for juniors for the following year be raised from thirty-five to forty women and that she be allowed to retain four of the current seniors as graduate students. She had ranked applicants as good, fair, or poor based on qualities such as good or poor health, age (four would-be-seniors were over age twenty-eight), personality and sorority membership. (Sorority women were not welcome at Martha Cook, see below.) A greater number of junior women ranked in the good range than did the senior applicants. Dawbarn also noted that by senior year, women had settled into a comfortable living situation and it was difficult to find women who wanted to move whereas many junior transfers were available. The Governors granted permission "to raise the Junior quota to such a point (not to exceed fifty) as to prevent the necessity of admitting inferior Seniors to fill the House."[13]

Cook relented in 1926 and agreed the Social Director could admit "ten or fifteen Sophomores next fall if she is sure they will live up to their promise to remain."[14] But, as evidenced by the annuals for the intervening years, sophomores were not admitted until fall 1934. Two freshmen were admitted in 1943 and again in 1945 to assist with the University's housing shortage.[15] In the late 1960s, U-M granted upper-class women the right to live in off-campus apartments, creating a dearth of applications to MCB, so in fall 1971, MCB accepted seven freshmen.[16] Freshmen were then admitted until fall 1976 when the number of upper-class applications increased. Following another scarcity of upper-class applications, Director Gloria Picasso wrote in the fall 1994 issue of the *Martha Cook Alumnae Association Newsletter*, "The Governors' decision to admit freshwomen has been a tremendous success and we have thirty freshwomen to form a nucleus of long-term Martha Cook residents." Freshman women have been part of the Martha Cook community ever since. While some leave after a year or two, many remain through all four undergraduate years.

Sorority Women

Although there are now no stipulations regarding rushing or pledging a sorority, for many years sorority members were not welcome at MCB. At the opening of Martha Cook, "each sorority that wished to was allowed to send two members to live at the Building"[17] but the policy soon changed and those already in sororities were excluded from consideration for admission because of limited dormitory space and "it seemed unfair for one girl to have two homes while others lived in League houses."[18] By fall 1928, women who pledged while living at Martha Cook were allowed to remain only until the end of the semester in which they pledged.

The sorority policy of September 29, 1936 was a little more moderate:

> We expect a full year's loyalty, and prefer that our residents do not affiliate themselves elsewhere. In case a resident does pledge to a sorority, the possibility of her remaining beyond the first semester becomes an individual matter between her and the social director.[19]

But by 1937–38, the policy once again firmly required the pledge to leave the building at the end of the pledging semester.[20]

Despite the policies, a few women each year opted to join sororities, sometimes earning the enmity of their fellow residents. In spring 1948, eleven Cookies pledged sororities and some of the other residents were, as Social Director Diekema expressed, "quite indignant because of the lack of loyalty and came to me to discuss the situation."[21] In 1958, House Board recommended to Social Director Margaret Blake that any woman who rushed a sorority, whether she pledged or not, be banned from MCB.[22] In both instances, cooler heads prevailed. Diekema, perhaps recognizing both the need to encourage loyalty to the Building as well as a woman's right to change her mind, changed the student handbook and correspondence leading to admission to include the phrase "it is expected that you plan to use [the Martha Cook Building] as your University home until your degree is earned."[23] Similar phrases were included in each handbook through at least 1972.

Ethnic, Religious, and Racial Considerations

In the early years, application forms requested only the student's name, address, parents or guardians, names and addresses of three friends as references, date and place of high school graduation, previous college work, date of expected graduation, specific department at the University in which the student was enrolled, and church affiliation.[24] In later years, other information was requested either via the application or at an interview with the Director. A document titled "Interviews"—undated but filed among other documents of the late 1940s—gives a list of topics to be discussed at the interview:

class
age
friends in MCB
ambition
tastes of [sic]activities, interests, and hobbies
economic status
health
   colds
   bed
   smoke
   tired
grades
sociability
   dorms
   roommates
   friends
strong and weak points of temperament
family
stock [presumably this meant ethnicity and race]
religious belief
dating
references
Why U of M
Why Martha Cook.[25]

In 1968, most of the same questions were still asked. There were no queries about race or ethnicity but other topics were added to the 1940s list: high school honors and activities, father's occupation, and experiences away from the family.[26] In 1978–79, Director Olive Chernow revised the application to exclude questions about the applicant's family financial and education status after a resident complained these were discriminatory.[27] Little is known of how individual Directors used these bits of information although there is some documentation of selection policies.

It is not known if the first applicants were interviewed by the Social Director or not, but that practice had certainly come into being before 1929, for a document dated June 1929 and titled "Selection of Residents" stated,

Miss Dawbarn saw applicants every day but Saturday and Sunday, between two and four. This seemed to her better than the previous policy, by which the receptionist gave inquiring girls an application blank, and an interview was arranged later, since Miss Dawbarn felt girls came for an arranged interview nervous and unnatural.[28]

That same report listed the qualifications for eligibility to live at Martha Cook. Dawbarn did not allow married women or affiliated sorority women. She admitted graduate women only if they were "exceptional in quality." Cookie seniors who had a good record could return for one year of graduate work provided they did not exceed two years total at MCB. Resident had to be under twenty-five and were preferably enrolled in the literary college but women could come from other colleges if there were not enough suitable "lits" and the Governors approved. The standard of desired woman was defined as "One merely takes the best material available. Miss Dawbarn tried for girls who were socially and scholastically well developed, but had to take a few charming girls with poor scholarship and a few grinds."

Religion and race were not mentioned in this policy but the 1934 policy stated, "It is wise to note how many Catholics are being accepted and it has been the policy to have no more than four Jewesses in the house."[29]

Despite Cook's biases, the Building's Social Directors continued to admit transfer students, professional students, and foreign students. The first foreign students at Martha Cook were two French women, Frida Bonan and Martha Jouard, who were admitted in 1918–19. They were well accepted by their fellow residents who understood the benefits of sharing their home with non-Americans:

> These girls, although of different nationality, fit into our daily life as though they had been here forever …. we have learned that girls are, at heart, the same the world over, cherishing similar hopeful dreams, interests, and heart flutterings.
>
> If Michigan may send the French students away with as much of true worth as they will leave behind with us, then it has indeed served the highest purpose given a University to serve.[30]

67. (a34) Graduate students and Barbour Scholars, 1934

The first Asian student to live at Martha Cook was Asha Latika Haldar MA'23 from India, who came to earn her PhD in philosophy as a Barbour Scholar.* She lived at MCB during the 1920–21 and 1921–22 school years.[31] After that year until at least 1940, at least two vacancies each year were held for Barbour Scholars.[32] Women

---

* Barbour Scholarships for Oriental Women (now known as Rackham Barbour Scholarships for Asian Women) were established in 1914 with the first of several gifts from U-M Regent Levi L. Barbour to support the studies of exceptional women from the region then "known as the Orient, encompassing the large region extending from Turkey in the west to Japan and the Philippines in the east." Recipients of the scholarship were and still are intended to use their knowledge for the benefit of their native country. The first two scholars arrived at U-M in 1918 and lived with the Barbours. Until his death in 1926, Barbour continued to provide funds so that a few dozen scholarships were awarded annually during the 1920s and 30s. Today, the income from his gift continues to support five or six women annually. (Source: "'A Cosmopolitan Tradition': Barbour Scholarships." Bentley Historical Library, http://bentley.umich.edu/exhibits/cosmo/barbour.php (accessed Feb 23, 2015).

from other countries also lived at Martha Cook over the years and it was not unusual for there to be five or six in residence in a given year. These women were as well-accepted as the first two French women and, in their turn, enjoyed living with their American counterparts. The 1925 *Martha Cook Annual*, published the same year that Cook questioned the number of Orientals, included an article titled "Our Foreign Girls" which began, "Fortunate indeed have we been to have had the privilege of association with young women who have come from across the oceans to receive an American education." The article listed quotations from the five foreign Cookies and ended with Janaki Ammal from India stating, "I have had the very good fortune ... to be a member of Martha Cook." In 1928, Shui Chen Yang from China submitted her own article in the *Annual*, "A Farewell to my American Friends", in which she wrote the teaser quote at the head of this chapter and also stated,

> Girls, I have been happy in the fellowship and friendship in this building. Sometimes I might have appeared to you as a solitary figure with a far away gaze as if I looked across the Pacific. Perhaps it is the time when I measure the height and depth of the good will and kindness of my American friends. I am happy in this building not only because it is one of the finest and most beautiful girls' dormitories in this country, but it is because I am with you.[33]

68. (a25) Dorothy Eggert's 1925 Sparking Room sketch celebrates MCB diversity.

African-American women were not mentioned in any policy, but none lived at Martha Cook until 1944. In fact, there were few African-Americans enrolled at U-M before War World War II. In 1936, there were a total of thirty-five African American students—men and women—at Michigan.[34] In their book, *The Making of the University of Michigan 1817-1992,* author Howard H. Peckham and editors Margaret L. and Nicholas H. Steneck explained the housing situation between the two World Wars for African-American women:

> A league house was available to African-American women at some distance from the campus; otherwise the women were relegated to the homes of local African-Americans, which the dean found inadequate. Therefore, a University-owned house close to the campus was fitted up for African-American women, with the enthusiastic approval of the women and of the president of the Michigan Association for Colored Women. However, during the summer of 1929, some African-American groups protested against what they saw as segregation, and the plan had to be abandoned. The situation was somewhat remedied when Mosher-Jordan Hall opened in 1930, and later a better league house for African-American women was provided. However, true inter-racial housing was still decades away for both men and women.[35]

After World War II, the US civil rights movement was in its fledgling stages and Michigan students were concerned with the plight of minority groups. "In May 1949, the joint faculty and student Committee on Student Affairs decided not 'to recognize any organization which prohibits membership in the organization because of race, religion, or color.'"[36] A reporter for the *Michigan Daily* interviewed Diekema and wrote an article on May 12, headlined "Query Covers Martha Cook Applicants", about potential discrimination at MCB:

> Mrs. Leona B. Diekema, in charge of Martha Cook, asserted that race and religion play no part in considering applications for residence. Scholarship, personality and the ability of an applicant to make a significant contribution to Martha Cook are the major factors considered in determining her selections, Mrs. Diekema declared ....

In most cases where preferences are not expressed, women are generally assigned roommates of the same religion and color, she said. She added that she would have no objection whatsoever to allowing a student to room with another of a different race or religion provided that they both requested the arrangement.

In response to a query, Mrs. Diekema said that there are no Negro women now living at Martha Cook. She declared, however, that "there are absolutely no restrictions against Negro women," citing the names of three who resided there in 1944 and 1945. Since that time not a single Negro coed has applied for residence, Mrs. Diekema said, adding that she could not account for their failure to apply.

Perhaps with this article in mind, Diekema, in her March 1950 report to the Governors, spelled out the characteristics she considered in carrying out admission interviews that year.[37] She indicated that she chose individuals "to round out a group picture as much as for the individuals themselves." She said she considered substantial scholarship, an interest and established record in either or both campus and dormitory activity, and an ability to enjoy working and living with other women to be important individual characteristics. She strove to accept women who would form a cosmopolitan group "typical of the University and its democratic spirit." She further explained that the cosmopolitan characterization meant that she chose women

> from as many different places in Michigan as possible. Girls from different states in the Union and from foreign countries. There are no racial or religious lines. It further means individuals from as many of the University's schools and colleges as possible. The overall aim is to make a versatile and as interesting a group as possible.

Although most residents over the years have been receptive and welcoming to others of different races and cultures, some women come to Martha Cook with prejudices. Usually, the sharing of living spaces and cultural events leads these women to a greater understanding of others. But, occasionally, intolerance rears its ugly head. In January 1994, for instance, at least one resident carried out incidents of harassment, threats, and intimidation.[38] At the same time, a campus radio program made allegations of racism at Martha Cook.[39] A concerned group of Building residents, worried that the situation could escalate, met with the Board of Governors both that January and again in April 1995 to suggest that MCB hire a Minority Peer Advisor to serve as counselor and educator, a position already in place in the residence halls managed by University Housing.[40] In the second meeting, they explained that some residents were concerned about whether or not the Building should concentrate on one group but the overriding issue was that some women—both African-American and international students—did not feel welcome. The Governors took the suggestion very seriously and established a new student staff position for fall 1995. Because MCB's problems crossed several cultural lines, the Governors chose a broader title than Housing and designated the position Multicultural Peer Advisor, a position still in existence today. The first MCPA was LaTonya Sutton, an African-American with cerebral palsy who not only developed education programs for the entire house and met every Saturday with the twelve African-Americans then living at MCB but also brought an awareness of physical disabilities to the diversity discussion.[41] In February 1996, Building Director Gloria Picasso reported that following MCB's lead, Housing had broadened its job description and adopted the job title, Multicultural Peer Advisor.[42] The Housing designation has changed over time and is now Diversity Peer Educator. MCB's MCPA must now meet all the requirements of a DPE, but MCB holds onto its own title in respect for its history-making impact on the University.

Recruitment of Residents

William Cook was very much in favor of actively recruiting women to live at Martha Cook. As he wrote to House Director Mack in 1923, "Yost selects his football team from the best of the University – I consider the elevation of women more important than the elevation of a football team."[43] He was even more specific in his letter of July 8, 1925, to Anne E. Shipman Stevens where he wrote:

> It is a mistake ... for the social director to think it undignified to send for a desirable girl and ask her to come to the building. It was formerly the custom for the social director to do this and that custom should be resumed .... If necessary in order to secure the best it may be well to arrange with choice sophomores to enter the building when they become seniors or with a few choice freshmen to enter when they become juniors.[44]

In actuality, MCB has never done any kind of recruiting other than that which may be termed soft. The Building has participated in the occasional housing fair at the Michigan Union[45] and alumnae have been encouraged to recommend the Building to relatives and friends.[46] Generally, however, a simple announcement each spring in the *Michigan Daily* that the "Martha Cook Building is now receiving applications"[47] and a similar notice on the outside door of the Building are all that have been required to attract those women who enjoy MCB's traditional living style.

Current Application and Admissions

Today, women are accepted in the order their applications are received. There is no required interview although the Building Director often meets with prospective residents to describe the Building and its community. The current application form[48] requires only name and address, basic education information (e.g., institution and year of graduation), and emergency contact information. It also asks three essay questions:

> Why would you like to live at the Martha Cook Building?
> What contribution do you think you could and would be willing to make to the building and our community?
> Describe your ideal roommate.

In addition, there are a few questions for roommate matching, such as whether the applicant is a morning or night person, whether she prefers to follow a regular or irregular schedule, whether she plans to study in her room, her views on male visitation in the student rooms, and whether she is messy, casual, or neat.

69. (as) "New Women," at the dinner in their honor, 2011

Recent events within the US are causing its citizens to re-evaluate the degree to which racial, religious, and ethnic differences are accepted in our society. At Martha Cook, acceptance and inclusivity have been hallmarks but the community must be constantly vigilant to ensure these qualities remain the standard. If the future follows the past, progress may not be perfect but it will continue to move positively. Cookies will be able to say, as Joyce Collins Tucker '54 did in 1990,

> Though the residents ... came from different parts of the country and from various ethnic and religious backgrounds, we became as one family. We had periodic informal meetings at which we took turns telling about our personal religious beliefs, home towns .... I frequently ... remember how we taught each other socialization skills which prepared us to treat other people with more tolerance and understanding.

CHAPTER FOURTEEN

In Loco Parentis:
Rules and Rebellion

Beds are to be made after breakfast or surely by noon. Close room door in the morning if bed is unmade.
Rules, September 1937[1]

Under pressure from the U-M Board of Regents to provide some kind of supervisory authority over women, President James Angell established the Office of the Dean of Women in 1895 and appointed Dr. Eliza Mosher to be the official substitute for parental authority for female students at Michigan.[2] All matters related to women were under the guidance of the Dean of Women until the dissolution of the office in 1965. With her approval, the Women's Judiciary Council determined the rules for the hours women could be out and about and when and where they could entertain male guests.

These University rules applied to women living at Martha Cook. In addition, Cookies were subject to the influence of the Building's donor, William Cook, who felt women needed to learn the social graces to a greater extent than they might learn them at home and so rules were devised to teach these. Changing social mores, new technologies, and desires and demands of the Building's residents have also played a role in determining rules and lessened the authority-imposed constrictions but, at least for the first fifty years of MCB's history, U-M and MCB served as parent proxies.

Early Rules of Etiquette

Although there are no extant copies of very early rules specifically designed for Martha Cook, an early rules document does exist at the University level. Labeled *Uniform House Rules for Fall, 1916*,[3] it stated the rules of the Judiciary Council of the Women's League for all organized houses (at that time, the Martha Cook Building, Helen Newberry Residence, League Houses, and sorority houses). The document stipulated that girls leaving town must make arrangements and leave addresses with the head of the house, all houses would close each evening not later than 10 or 10:30 PM, and "Girls finding it necessary to be out later than the closing hour (Theater, exclusive of moving pictures and dances) must make arrangements with the househead, landlady, or chaperon (sic)." It further "suggested that girls do not go to men's rooming houses or fraternities either for dinner or calls, unless assured a chaperon (sic) will be present. Girls are also advised not to go to hotels unchaperoned." But romance was not totally outlawed as "Engagements for boating shall terminate at 9 PM unless the party consists of more than two, in which case, 10:00 shall be the limit." The 1916 rules prohibited mid-week dances and attendance at moving picture shows on Sundays, confined engagements lasting past midnight to weekends, and stipulated that freshmen were limited to three evening commitments per week with only one allowed on a weekday.

Still extant are *Etiquette Suggestions* specific to MCB for 1933-34 and 1934-35[4] which list rules that were probably in effect from the earliest days of MCB. Women were given instructions to rise when the directors entered the room, introduce guests to the directors, and know general dining room procedures such as "Seat yourself from the left, and rise from the right of the chair." Other rules included admonitions to "close curtains on the Law Club side whenever at all necessary" and "Have guests call for you at the desk, do not allow them to call or whistle from below."

The rules of etiquette were eventually collected with other policies and placed in handbook format, informally referred to as the *Blue Book* because of its blue cover. The 1969 rule booklet was titled *Regulations, Constitution and By-Laws of Martha Cook Building.* Today, the handbook is simply called *The Martha Cook Building Handbook* and is available online at a website that is the property of the Martha Cook Student Organization.[5]

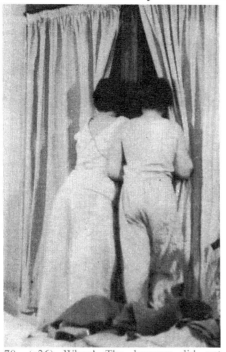

70. (a36) Whoa! The lawyers did not observe the same curtain rules as MCB. (1936)

Hours, Signing Out, and Lateness Penalties

For many years, all U-M women's residence halls, including MCB, closed when the front doors were locked at 10:30 PM on weekdays and 11:30 PM on weekends. The rule to be in the Building by that time was referred to as "having hours."[6] As late as 1926, all freshman women were required to be in their houses by 8:00 PM, and no freshman was permitted to be out after hours except Friday, Saturday, Sunday, or on a night before a University holiday. Over the years, the limits on hours became less restrictive. In the spring of 1934, seniors were allowed to stay out until 1:30 AM on Saturdays. In

1942, the closing time was set at 12:30 AM for Friday and Saturday nights.[7] In November 1958, U-M's Women's Judiciary Council revised women's weekday closing time to 11 PM for freshmen, midnight for all others and on November 22, House Board approved those hours for the Martha Cook Building.[8] By 1969 women's dorm hours were changed to midnight on weekdays, 1 AM on Fridays, and 1:30 AM on Saturdays.[9]

Today, MCB's front desk shuts down at 10 PM, except on Sundays when it closes at 8 PM. The Building's doors are continuously locked and women are given keycards so they can enter or leave at any time. Prior to 1962, however, any woman who needed to be out of the Building beyond closing time needed special permission and had to request a special key from the Building's director. The Social Director could provide late permissions for concerts, lectures, and other campus engagements on any day of the week as well as similar types of engagements or overnight visits if they occurred on weekends. For other types of events or overnight visits that occurred on a weekday, permission had to be obtained from the Dean of Women before seeking a key from the Social Director.[10] (In 1929, girls were allowed twenty minutes after the closing of a campus engagement to return to the Building.[11])

Any lateness, whether it be missing the 10:30 PM closing or arriving home later than expected after a special permission, was subject to penalty, according to a very detailed plan based on number of minutes late and number of times the student had previously been late. A first time lateness of up to five minutes subjected the resident to a warning; more than five but less than fifteen minutes required the resident to remain home on the following Thursday night. For second and third lateness greater than five minutes, the woman would be confined to the Building on the following weekend. University probation took over at the fourth lateness if longer than five minutes and for any fifth lateness. Any infraction greater than fifteen minutes required referral to House Board which would determine sanctions.[12] On the night a girl was required to remain in house, she signed a document at the front desk at the beginning and end of the time period; she was required to spend the entire time above stairs with no visitors although she could receive telephone calls.[13] Lateness penalties became a thing of the past when the University granted all women the right to "no hours" in 1968.

Women were required to sign out of the dormitory if they were going to be out of the residence hall in the evening and, of course, sign in on their return. At Martha Cook, even a stroll on the Building's terrace, attached to the east side of the Building, required the completion of a sign-out slip.[14] No matter how long a woman would be out, she had to include the address of her destination, and for excursions other than to University events, she had to indicate her hostess' name.[15] The University tried to require sign-outs as a safety measure after it granted "no hours" in 1968, but it was a futile effort. In fact, the reminder to sign out was included in so many minutes of all-house meetings from as early as February 11, 1952, that it is safe to say that despite rules and penalties, sign out was often practiced more in omission than commission.

"No Hours" and Keys to the Front Door

Beginning in fall 1962, U-M granted all senior women the right to determine their own hours and House Board was thrown into a tizzy on how that would be implemented at Martha Cook. Although University Vice President for Student Affairs James A. Lewis was opposed to building keys being distributed to women in most residence halls, he approved this idea for Martha Cook women due to their past record of leadership and responsibility on campus.[16] House Board discussed the topic at twelve different Board meetings that year[17] and at a special meeting of seniors on October 2. To its credit, the Board was concerned with safety issues, both for the woman staying out after hours and for all residents should one woman lose a key. But moral issues also raised their heads. House Board considered recommending the hiring of an elderly woman to act as night porter at the door, checking seniors in and out, but realized this was not realistic, at least from a cost standpoint. In the end, House Board decided that the Martha Cook honor code would induce the residents to be careful with their keys and to respect the policy. House Board presented a proposal to the Building's Board of Governors. That body (with its caveat that the policy was not absolute and could be changed if situations warranted) approved the policy which included the statement,

> A senior, losing her permanent key, will automatically lose her five dollar key deposit. Upon payment of a new key deposit of ten dollars, she will be issued another permanent key. If this key is lost, the senior will then revert to the use of the key permission for special events.[18]

Junior women at the University were allotted "no hours" privileges on Friday and Saturday nights beginning in fall 1964. Minutes of six House Board meetings indicate that "junior keys" were discussed.[19] The proposal sent by the House Board to the Board of Governors stated,

> With their parents' permission, Martha Cook Juniors will be issued keys to use on Friday and Saturday nights automatically, or with permission on week nights .... Sophomores may sign out keys with permission from Mrs. Quail, Mrs. Scott, or [the judiciary chairwoman].[20]

The Governors accepted the proposal with the proviso that all girls must still sign out. They also stipulated the issuance of special occasion late keys, which had been the purview of the Building Director, could no longer be granted by the Director unless she had a parental covering letter in her file.[21]

By the time campus-wide sit-outs and other protests in 1967-68 gave all women, with parental permission, the right of "no hours" seven-days-a-week and access to building keys,[22] Martha Cook women apparently felt they had already talked out potential problems of key distribution because the campus fervor elicited no mention at all in the House Board or all-house meeting minutes. And, by 1970, all MCB residents were required to have late keys.[23]

Male Visitation

If to us, fifty years later, the amount of time spent discussing building keys seems excessive, it was nothing compared to that spent conferring over male visitation hours, an issue that resonates even today at Martha Cook, although all other University dorms have allowed twenty-four hour male/female visiting privileges since 1973.[24]

Legend passed down through generations of Cookies claims that male visitors were not originally allowed into the Building proper, but were required to stand between the two sets of doors of the vestibule. There may be some truth to this rumor, at least for certain times of day. A U-M document titled *House Rules for Undergraduate Women*, dated July 1941, states that "Calling hours for men shall not begin until 3:00 PM, except on Sundays, and the hostess shall be responsible for seeing that afternoon guests leave the premises at the dinner hour."[25] It is doubtful, however, that men were excluded from the main floor parlors at allotted calling hours. In 1904, Dr. Myra Jordan, U-M Dean of Women, had negotiated with Ann Arbor landladies for "parlor privileges" at the all-female League Houses so that the women could entertain male callers[26] and it is likely that this practice continued after the openings of the Martha Cook Building and the Helen Newberry Residence in 1915.

Beginning in 1930-31, open houses allowing men above stairs, were held once or twice a year for two hours on a Sunday afternoon.[27] Pauline Putnam, House Board Vice President for 1937–38, reported that Social Director Mary E. Gleason obtained special permission from the dean's office and explained that "A conscientious chairman is needed to appoint monitors for each floor—these must check unostentatiously on open doors." Leona Diekema mentioned an "open house" in several of her reports to the Governors in the 1940s. In her May 1948 report, she wrote of the May 9 event:

> The residents held "Open House" in their respective rooms, playing bridge, listening to records and serving their own refreshments. In many instances, the girls combined forces and received together. Saturday, all day, and Sunday morning the house resembled an ant hill as the business of house cleaning, brass and furniture polishing went on apace .... It is a decidedly popular form of entertainment. From the housekeeping angle, especially, it is popular with the directors.

The term "open-open," used to describe an open house where the whole house was open to visitors, first appeared in House Board minutes on November 19, 1953, when House Board discussed having more than one per year. Suggestions were made to allow visitors above stairs every Sunday afternoon or at least twice a semester but the approved plan allowed one such event per semester. December 13 was designated as the first open-open. In May,

71. (a41) More than "three feet on the floor": Residents and guests play bridge in a student room during a 1940-41 open house.

Leona Diekema announced that an open-open would follow parents' dinner[28] and House Board minutes of September 14, 1954, announced an open-open would be held on Homecoming Weekend.[29]

By 1960, the desire to allow men upstairs more often was taking on a life of its own. Discussion at an all-house meeting in April again brought up the idea of holding open-opens on Sunday afternoons and the next fall the residents voted in favor of approaching Dean of Women Deborah Bacon for permission to hold them every Sunday afternoon. Dean Bacon's response was to ask the women to wait until University Housing determined which residence hall, Helen Newberry or Betsy Barbour, would become an upper-class house. Then both houses could approach the Assembly Dormitory Council together.

At the all-house meeting on September 30, 1963, House Board President Jan Zehnder '64, MPA'87 reported that the Governors and the Office of Student Affairs had approved holding open-opens each Sunday from 2–5 PM for a trial period of one month. At the close of the trial month, the residents voted to extend the events until May 1964, with the stipulation that the motion would have to be re-voted the following fall.[30] The addition of nighttime open-opens was raised at a House Board meeting in April 1964 but the

> general consensus ... was that the Sunday afternoon open-opens were enough and the nighttime ones might be a) embarrassing to those wanting to take showers or b) anticlimactical (sic) after all those Sundays. It was proposed, however, that we might have one after a football game, just to spice things up a little.[31]

Rebellion against "in loco parentis" erupted on U-M's campus in fall 1967. Students at some residence halls—although not at MCB—refused to comply with dress codes and rules on curfews and visits by members of the opposite sex. On January 19, 1968, the University's Board of Regents agreed that individual houses could set their own visitation hours without requiring University approval.[32] At MCB on February 12, it was announced that, "The Red Room will be open after hours on a trial basis, for quiet talk."[33]

The issue of male visitation hours at MCB heated up in fall of 1968. In September, the women were told that Sunday open-opens now ran from "the time Sunday dinner ends until buffet starts at 5:30 PM."[34] Then, at the all-house meeting on September 9, President Vicki Bergsma '69 introduced a proposal to extend the hours of open-opens. A proposal to open the house on every Saturday afternoon failed as did a proposal to have open-opens on Saturday nights. But, the women agreed to open hours on football Saturdays from after the game until supper. Unsatisfied by the results of the meeting, residents circulated a petition calling for a referendum to hold Saturday night open hours from 10 PM to 12 AM on three specific Saturdays. The vote was held on Tuesday, October 8.[35] The tally of the vote was not recorded, but the referendum passed for the November 6 minutes reported that November 9 would be the last trial nighttime open-open.

The proposal to make 10 PM to 12 AM permanent open hours on Saturdays was discussed at the Monday, January 20, 1969, all-house meeting and speaking limitations were set ahead of time with one woman from each side designated as the primary speaker. The subsequent referendum passed 85-55.[36]

Open-opens were again on the agenda at the first all-house meeting of the 1969-70 school year.[37] This time there were three proposals: to allow open hours on Friday and Saturday, to open the house every afternoon and evening, and to have unlimited open hours at a resident's discretion. The two most liberal proposals were defeated but the Friday and Saturday option passed and open hours were now observed from 9 PM to closing on those nights.[38] Over the next five years, open hours were gradually broadened so that they began at noon on each of Friday, Saturday, and Sunday.[39] The public spaces on the main floor and the basement were opened after hours to guests escorted by residents in spring 1974.[40] Thursday nights from 7 to 11 PM were added as open hours in November 1975.[41]

After a period of relative calm, open-opens were again a point of contention in 1978 and 1979. By now, the purpose of male visitation hours had gone beyond just entertaining a guest. Women used the open hours to meet with male lab partners or study groups which included males and females. The residents felt more open hours were needed to accommodate these new needs and in March of that year, 124 residents sent a petition to the Governors requesting that 7 to 11 PM on Monday, Tuesday, and Wednesday be added as open hours during the next school year.[42] The Governors heard speakers from both sides of the issue, but denied the request for the current year because the residents had not followed the referendum procedures spelled out in their constitution. The Governors suggested the residents present a request following proper referendum procedures the following fall.[43]

The minutes of the next year for both House Board and the Governors portray a saga of passionate politics. An early fall referendum, held by the residents, approved the extended hours but was followed by an accusation of coercion by at least one resident. The Governors and residents representing both sides of the issue held multiple meetings. Building Director Chernow expressed a preference for the status quo and the Governors were concerned that the addition of open hours might increase the cost of liability insurance. (It didn't.) Discussions both among and between the two Boards included justifications for and refutations of the status quo which was seriously out of step with University Housing policy. Privacy and feminine tradition were also part of the conversation. But, miscommunications and misinterpretations on the parts of both House Board and the Governors, over whether the Governors' February approval of the new hours were intended as additions or replacements to existing hours, led to heated exchanges and sixty-one residents refused to sign leases for 1979–80 unless the open hours included both the old and the new hours. The issues were resolved by the end of March and all open-open hours, old and new, were now the law of the house.

Since then the Governors have been willing to consider all proposals regarding open hours but, because emotions run high on both sides of the issue and privacy and safety are paramount at Martha Cook, the Governors have opted to allow cautious increases in the hours. They have consistently kept the early morning hours closed so that residents may feel at ease taking showers or roaming the halls in their pajamas. Open hours for the bedroom floors have gradually broadened to today's hours of 10 AM to 2 AM on Fridays and Saturdays and 10 AM to midnight on the other days. The public rooms on the first floor and in the basement are open for guests at any time.[44]

To further ensure the safety of residents, it has always been a policy that all guests be escorted at all times by the Cookie they are visiting. This includes trips to the men's room in the basement.

Public Display of Affection (PDA)

Nestled under the front staircase to the upper floors is a small alcove, set between the two main parlors on the first floor. This room is known to Cookies as the Sparking Room, a sobriquet which might cause one to think that affectionate displays are an authorized practice at Martha Cook. A June 1929 report titled *Policy Concerning "Necking"* written by Social Director Ethel G. Dawbarn might further increase one's idea that making out is de rigueur at MCB. It reads,

72. (a28) Three feet on the floor? (Sketch by Anne Schell '29)

> No legislative attempt to control necking was made this year—on the theory that it is a recognized student custom, and that an attempt to screw down the lid in the building would just drive the "neckers" to movies and park benches, not to mention parked cars. Furthermore, the majority of girls in the house are engaged, or settled down to one "boy friend" (sic), a practice I think a bit unwise so young, but which at least keeps these demonstrations from being promiscuous.
> ... the snuggling and hand-holding I condoned was, of course, a violation of adult taste for behavior in public places. It is done here so frankly and so entirely without shame, however, that I think it silly to attempt to suppress it entirely.[45]

However, if one thinks that all was or is libidinous at Martha Cook, one would be wrong. The policy on public display of affection has been far more conservative, if difficult to enforce, than Dawbarn's "girls will be girls" attitude. An undated list of rules which, because it mentions House Director Sara Rowe, can be placed between 1932 and 1949 states, "The student body considers it poor taste and out of keeping with the standard of the Building for the residents to display undue affection in the drawing rooms, corridor and lobby—or outside the front door."[46] The 1969 *Blue Book* used the same wording but added the lobby and TV room to the list of inappropriate places for PDA. Today's handbook does not specifically mention affectionate behavior.

In 1949, many of the residents were displeased with flagrant violations of the PDA policy and, without pressure from the Building's management, drew up a "Decorum Pledge." The pledge, which 100 women signed, promised that a woman would refrain from public displays inside the Building. Diekema was interviewed by *Time* and the *Michigan Daily*. The latter included a strong tinge of ridicule in its article, but commendations were called to the Building by readers.[47] In January 1950, Diekema reported that "Decorum in our social rooms has been much improved—and the girls think it is due to last year's famous 'Decorum Pledge!'" Behavior outside the front door had not improved, however.

Dress Code

A glimpse at any older *Michiganensian,* U-M's yearbook, reveals that until the 1960s women at Michigan wore skirts to class and for most other activities, although casual dress gradually became more acceptable for non-academic events. In her memoir, *My Years at the Martha Cook Building*, Olive Chernow told of her student days, "In 1945 Mrs. Diekema ordered us not to wear jeans to any meals at MCB, to class, or on campus except for picnics."[48] In 1952, however, Diekema allowed jeans to be worn within the Building on Saturdays but she specified they could not be worn in the Blue Room.[49] By the mid-1960s, women had begun to wear slacks to class and, in dorms other than Martha Cook, could wear slacks at breakfast and lunch but not dinner. The dress code at the University began to change in 1967 when U-M's Student Government Council removed the oversight of dormitory policy infractions from a campus-wide judiciary council and gave it to the individual residence hall judiciary committees.[50] The council at Blagden House of Mary Markley Hall was the first to do away with the "skirts at dinner" rule. Other dorms soon followed. Rules were a bit stricter at MCB. Slacks in the dining room were officially off-limits until 1968, when the Governors announced in March that "In view of the change of dress regulations on campus, the Board felt that starting in August, casual dress would be permitted at lunch and breakfast." On September 3, 1968, it was reported at an all-house meeting that "culottes may be worn to dinner and in the Red and Gold Room as long as they look like skirts and not shorts." At an all-house meeting a week later, it was further announced by the House Judiciary Chair that "slacks could be worn to dinner on cafeteria nights if those girls so doing ate outside on the terrace," an allowance not practical in the Michigan winters. In March 1970, however, the Governors gave approval for slacks to be worn at all cafeteria meals, adding Friday and Saturday dinners to the approved list.[51] Skirts were required to be worn at sit-down dinners until 1972, when it became possible for residents to wear coordinated pants suits to dinner.[52] Rules were lightened further in January 1973 when

> anything is permitted [at dinner] except for the following: Anything with denim (blue jeans, green jeans, white jeans, etc.), sweat shirts, T-shirts, shorts, slippers, and grimy corduroys. No grubbies of any kind are permitted.[53]

Today, with a more relaxed meal schedule, jeans are permissible at dinner but wearing skirts or dress slacks is required for all "special" dinners, including faculty dinners, Dinner for New Women, and Dinner for Graduating Women.[54]

Even as slacks were allowed in the dining room in 1968 for breakfast and lunch, women were still required to wear skirts in the two main floor parlors. In fall 1968, permission was granted to wear

73. (mcb) A 1960s tea in the Gold Room

slacks, not jeans, in the Red Room after closing.[55] Then in October 1969, the Governors approved the residents' request to allow slacks in the Red Room at all times. It was not until September 1971 that House Board minutes reported, "The ban on slacks in the mighty Gold Room has been lifted. Poor lost souls can float in and out of there in comfort."

Within the last five years, Martha Cook alumnae have enacted what is becoming a new Building tradition, wearing hats to the Spring Tea, an annual event that brings alumnae back to the Building. The recent trend is not completely new. Alumnae appeared en chapeau at the Twenty-fifth Anniversary Gala Tea in 1940. But hats were not always considered appropriate indoor wear. A photograph in the 1919 *Annual* lampooned tea at MCB, displaying Cookies in hats and gloves dining under the watchful gaze of *Venus*. And a June 1930 document entitled *General Information* found in the Social Director's notebook included the statement, "It was found that there was a tendency for guests to wear hats in the dining room, especially for Sunday night tea; even some of our own girls occasionally appeared in their hats. The house felt that the tradition of 'no hats' in our dining room should be continued."

74. (a19) Mock tea, 1919

Room Inspections

"Make your bed. Clean your room." These phrases, beloved of most mothers, were rules at Martha Cook until at least June 1956, when Diekema retired.

In 1919, Social Director Grace Greenwood addressed the annual meeting of the National Education Association on "The Scoring of Rooms in Residence Halls."[56] She described the system inaugurated at Martha Cook in 1917 which allotted to each resident, on a weekly basis, ten possible points to nine different categories of room cleanliness:

order of the room
aesthetic aspect of the room in general
care of surfaces (i.e., absence of fingerprints, ink, dust, defacements)
care of drawers
care in making the bed
condition of the bed's "clothing"
order of the closet
care in hanging of clothes
ventilation

75. (mcb) Students were expected to keep their rooms neat and tidy.

An additional five points each were awarded to the cleanliness and appearance of the washbasin. To assist the young women in meeting the requirements, instructions were given in the Blue Room on the proper way to make a bed and the rearrangement of an actual room "according to the standards of good taste" was demonstrated. Greenwood indicated that the inspection was not always done on the same day of the week and this uncertainty along with the novelty of "being definite about what had hitherto been vague" (i.e., what constituted a tidy room) and the embarrassment of being unprepared helped maintain order in student rooms. There is no indication in her speech about the types of penalties to which girls with deficient scores were subject.

In the mid-1930s, there was a rebellion of sorts among the residents as evidenced by instructions from the Board of Governors to Social Director Kathleen Codd. In November 1935, she was asked to see that all beds were made by two o'clock. In May, she was given the time of 12:30 as the limit for unmade beds. The *Martha Cook Annual* for that year joked about the rules: "Feb 9—Board of Governors heard in the hall during exams: It doesn't seem to be so much a matter of who doesn't make their beds as of who does."

Inspections were carried out by a committee of residents under the direction of a House Chairman. In October 1952, Diekema told the Governors, "Room care which is considered inadequate is reported to the [committee] chairman and a note is left for the offender. The Director comes into the picture only in the case of continued and stubborn infractions." It is not clear if the committee used the same score card introduced thirty-three years earlier by Greenwood or if a new system had been devised.

Although the residents were expected to make their beds and keep their rooms tidy, they were ably assisted in the latter as weekly maid service was provided to the students until 1976 and then bi-weekly until fall 1977 when it was eliminated, with student approval, as a cost-cutting measure.[57] The 1969 *Blue Book* described the duties of the resident in preparing for the weekly cleaning as "clearing dresser tops, desks, bookcase tops, tea tables, and floors. Soiled linen should be placed outside the door." The soiled linen consisted of one pillowcase and one sheet each week, the idea being that the top sheet did not get soiled so could become the bottom sheet for the following week.

The Director as Housemother (or not!)

The role of the early directors certainly included characteristics of a mother—enforcing rules, monitoring behavior—but they were not referred to officially as housemothers. William Cook defined[58] the role as one who teaches, not one who mothers. He also stated that the women of Martha Cook "will learn even more by example than by suggestions," thereby defining the role as mentor. Nonetheless, the 1923 *Annual* states "Miss Clark ... has been a real mother to us."

Today's Cookies would probably not refer to the Building Director as mother, opting for more descriptive terms such as counselor, guide, advisor, mentor, role model, wise woman. Her sensibility to their need to be independent endears her to residents while her maturity and common sense, and just the fact that she lives in, appeals to their parents. The rules have changed; the spirit to nurture in the best way possible remains.

CHAPTER FIFTEEN

Scholarships: Room, Board, and Encouragement

I want to thank you ... for making it possible for me to enjoy living in Martha Cook this year. The people here and the traditions we have mean more to me every day and I am so glad that I can make them part of my life. The receipt of the scholarship also made me feel that I am contributing something to Martha Cook and that I have a real share in the responsibility and joy of living here in the Martha Cook spirit.
Nina Jean Knutson '36, November 1935[1]

This note, included in the 1935 Governors' minutes, represents the untold number of thank you letters written by residents over the last 100 years. Scholarships and loans are a Martha Cook priority that goes back to William W. Cook's 1914 deed of gift in which he stated,

> the remainder [of surplus revenues], if any at the end of each year shall be set aside as a fund to be used in the following year to give lower or free rates in the building to such under-graduates or post-graduates as the President of the University and the Dean of Women may designate from time to time.

Financial assistance, along with paid student jobs, has been provided throughout the Building's history but the sources of money and system for awarding scholarships have altered and modified over time.

Choosing Recipients

In practice, the U-M President has never been consulted in scholarship and loan decisions which have been the purview primarily of the Board of Governors and the Social Director or, in more recent years, of a Scholarship Committee consisting of representatives from the Governors and from the MCAA. The Dean of Women, however, was directly and keenly involved until that position was abolished in 1964. Dean Alice Lloyd (1930–50) in particular is referenced in the Governors' minutes and Director's reports as regularly attending meetings, approving decisions, and sending letters with her own choices for MCB scholarships. While the majority of scholarship recipients have been current residents, Dean Lloyd sometimes submitted names of women she wanted recruited to Martha Cook or even the University with a room and board offer. In 1933 there was enough money for two scholarships. One went to a current resident recommended by the House Board and the Social Director and approved by the Dean of Women; the second was "for a non-resident, on campus, recommended by the Dean of Women." Any additional surpluses were to be used for student aid as needed.[2] In a May 10, 1935, letter to Governor Florentine Cook Heath '17, Dean Lloyd mentioned applications she had received and said that the Social Director Kathleen Codd had vouched for them. Dean Lloyd also wished to continue providing free room and board to a music student she felt was making good progress with her studies. She reported offering half room and board to a possible transfer student who was deciding between U-M and the University of Chicago. She concluded, "I cannot begin to thank the Board enough for the privilege of awarding these scholarships. They fill a very great need …."[3]

Subsequent Deans of Women did not regularly attend Governors' meetings. They did, however, consult with MCB's Social Director regarding admissions and financial aid, and continued to give formal approval to scholarship choices.

The Governors and Social Director were always the most directly involved with providing assistance during these early years. The Social Director could contact the Governors by phone or mail with special cases requiring a timely decision. For example, on December 12, 1928, Ethel Dawburn wrote to Governor Anne E. Shipman Stevens of one student:

> [She] seems to be in financial difficulties. She has been supporting herself.... She is working in the building this winter, but is getting, in my opinion, dangerously near the limits of her nervous strength. She has asked me if the building could lend her about $150 ... and personally I sincerely hope it will be possible to arrange it.[4]

Similarly, in 1939 Social Director Mary Gleason wrote to Governor Grace Campbell Bruce about a Chinese student whose family was in dire straits due to the war in China. The student's contribution to the Martha Cook community was put forth as the most important reason to offer the necessary aid:

> She has received no money from home for months, and of course is anxious to make her funds last throughout the summer. Personally, I feel that the Building is going to lose a great deal with ... [her] withdrawal .... She is an outstanding person and has a great deal to contribute to the other students .... We all feel that the foreign students bring a great deal of interest to our life in the Building.[5]

Clearly, there was money in the budget for emergency purposes and the MCB administration involved themselves in finding ways to meet residents' needs. The criteria have historically been need, character, and service or somehow enhancing the MCB community. Even the Dean of Women's choices followed these guidelines. It is also important to note that graduate students were assisted as well as undergraduates. In later decades, it was sometimes put forth that MCB scholarships were historically meant only for undergraduates but that was not the case.

Multiple scholarships were typically awarded each semester from MCB's beginnings until the present. Social Director Leona Diekema wrote to the U-M Scholarship Committee in December 1939 to say,

> We desire to call attention to the fact that the number and type of scholarships at the Martha Cook Building vary each year since the Board of Governors and the Dean of Women determine the same each successive year according to the needs of each particular student group and the finances of the Building.[6]

Alumnae were taking part in the process of awarding Building scholarships at least by the 1950s. In 1956, arrangements were made to add an alumna to the Scholarship Committee to work with the Director and Dean of Women.[7] From at least this point until 2000, the Governors do not appear to be directly involved in the process. Specific documentation of the roles played by the Governors, Directors, and alumnae are not spelled out until the mid-1970s when Building Director Olive Chernow's reports and her autobiography verify that alumnae, usually in the person of the MCAA president or designate, assisted the Director in making choices each semester. When Chernow wrote that an alumna was appointed to help her and the ARD with applications in January 1974, she added, "We were glad that the Detroit group wanted to be more involved in the selection process ...,"[8] implying that this had not always been the case. She only refers to reviewing applications, never conducting interviews. In 1979, she wrote in her *Director's Procedures Manual* that the MCAA committee decided the number of scholarships and the amounts, but they met with the Director and ARD to review and discuss applications.

In April 1981, two alumnae met with Director Josette Allan and the ARD to choose recipients. Applicant interviews had begun at least by 1985 because the interview date is listed on a memo Director Rosalie Moore provided to residents.[9] The Director facilitated the process but was no longer involved in the decision-making by this time. She distributed applications, provided copies to alumnae interviewers and scheduled the appointments. The Governors reassumed direct involvement early in the 2000s when the entire system was revamped and codified following a major gift to the scholarship fund.

Sources of Money

The sources of student aid money have changed significantly from the pool of Building profits Cook first envisioned. The Social Director's notebook lists three financial aid sources in a June 1929 entry: the House Loan Fund, in the hands of the House Director with permission from the Governors; the Alumnae Loan Fund; and loans from the Office of the Advisors of Women.[10] Many of the early awards from MCB revenues were loosely considered loans and in several documents the resources are referred to as loan funds. Some loans were repaid, but the Building did not consistently keep records or go to any lengths requesting repayment. In March 1930, House Director Alta Atkinson, having attempted to sort out the accounts, wrote to Governor Anne E. Shipman Stevens:

> Unfortunately no further record than this has been kept. I have kept detailed accounts of payments which have been made since I took over and would be able to make up a fairly complete record of the loans made within the past two or three years and the partial payments which the girls have made since. The procedure has been to return the cancelled note and keep no further record of the transaction. It seems to me that in years to come it will be very interesting to know just how many of our girls have availed themselves of the privilege of this loan fund.[11]

Permanent records of awardees have never been kept, but Atkinson was correct in thinking that it would be wonderful to know how many women have benefited over 100 years.

In a 1935 letter to U-M Vice President and Secretary of Business and Finance Shirley Smith, Governor Florentine Heath brought up the possibility of the University sending notices to students for repayment of MCB loans but went on to say:

As you know there is a substantial profit each year at the Martha Cook Building and this money can only be used for the building or its residents. Therefore we wish to continue a very liberal policy as far as deserving students are concerned. It may be best to abandon the whole loan scheme.[12]

The residents themselves sometimes added to the House Loan Fund. "The Student Board decided to dispense with the May Faculty Party and to give instead, four fifty-dollar scholarships," wrote Social Director Margaret Ruth Smith to Governor Vera Burridge Baits in May 1933.[13] The 1947 spring formal profit went toward scholarships. In the late 1950s, revenues from a cigarette machine in the basement were designated for the scholarship fund.[14]

Early on, MCB's alumnae desired to be part of Cook's vision of making MCB affordable for all Cookies and established their own scholarship and loan fund in 1924.[15] Stevens kicked off the fund with a gift of $100. In addition "the girls of '16–'22 have contributed about $100; the class of '23 is raising its quota and that of '24 has already brought in its offering …. the interest in this fund [will] be the tie that binds us all together …" wrote Social Director Zelma E. Clark in the 1924 *Annual*. The alumnae's awards were usually in addition to those made by the Building and at least by the 1950s,

76. (kgm) *The Scholar*, portal of Martha Cook Building

they chose their own recipient based on ratings supplied by the Social Director.[16] Since then, they have continued to raise money for the Building's scholarship fund and have established their own funds, the MCAA Memorial Fund and the Minority Merit Award (see below).

The Anne E. Shipman Stevens Scholarship Fund

For more than twenty years, Anne E. Shipman Stevens, one of the three original governors, personally contributed to the Building. Known as Martha Cook's fairy godmother for her gifts of library books, scrapbooks, candy, and cakes even after her multiple terms ended, she also donated scholarship money. In addition to her support for alumnae fundraising over the years, she donated another $500 from her late husband's estate for student financial aid in January 1936.

The concept of a formal scholarship fund named for Stevens was first mentioned in the December 1936 Governors' minutes. Governor Florentine Cook Heath had already suggested the idea informally to Stevens and she was amenable. The plan was to raise an endowment to be managed by U-M; the income would cover scholarships. Money already in the current loan fund, which included gifts previously given by Mr. and Mrs. Stevens as well as alumnae and residents, was to be transferred to the endowment. The minutes record that the Detroit alumnae group and future graduating classes were likely sources for future contributions and the Governors suggested a direct mail solicitation.

The Governors formally voted to proceed with the new fund on January 30, 1937. The March 21 minutes state that,

> $1,100 and further gifts go into the Ann Arbor Savings and Commercial Bank and the account to be known as the Anne. E. Shipman Stevens Fellowship Fund.* A balance of $67 and any

---

* It is now called the Anne E. Shipman Stevens Scholarship Fund (AESS).

payments on outstanding 'loans' are to remain as the Martha Cook emergency Scholarship and Loan Fund.

The named scholarship, then totaling $2,073.50, was officially announced at the June 1937 Regents meeting.[17] On June 22, 1937, after a conference with Dean of Women Alice Lloyd, the first AESS scholarship was awarded to Barbara Lovell for the 1937–38 academic year, and the Governors voted to supplement interest from the account so that the scholarship would completely cover expenses for the coming year. MCB now had an official scholarship program in addition to an emergency fund.

The Martha Cook Building's first surviving solicitation letter was mailed to alumnae March 15, 1939, less than two weeks after Stevens' death and signed by Governor Marguerite Chapin Maire '20. It said in part:

> You will recall that two years ago we established the Anne E. Shipman Stevens Fellowship fund in honor of Mrs. Stevens. We are happy that she has already had the deep pleasure and satisfaction of knowing two splendid girls who have been recipients of this fund.
>
> The fund has been growing steadily but we still have not reached our goal of $10,000. It seems to us that this is a very appropriate time to call to the attention of all Martha Cook alumnae and friends this memorial to Mrs. Stevens whose devotion to Martha Cook was so constant and so deep for many years.[18]

Stevens' daughter, Winifred Stevens Kirby, sent $1000 in her mother's memory later that year.[19] Cookies have enthusiastically donated and raised money for the fund ever since. Some alumnae left bequests to the AESS fund long before fundraising became a part of regular mailings. The Governors' minutes of April 18, 1970, record that Building Director Thelma Duffel had recently discovered that a gift of $20,000 had been deposited in the AESS fund in September 1968 from the estate of Margaret Henkel '17.[20] Some recipients have chosen to repay their scholarships when they were able.

Even after the AESS fund was established, the Building continued to provide scholarship and grant-in-aid assistance from a separate pool of budget surpluses. These were referred to in the Social Director's reports in the early 1940s and in a 1946 letter from Heath to Dean Lloyd:

> Since 1933 when a good many of our girls would have been forced to leave school unless they had help, the Martha Cook Building has had partial room and board scholarships. These have gradually grown until this year we have six besides the Anne E. Shipman Stevens scholar. At the September meeting it was voted that because of present building finances we would abandon all our partial scholarships for the year 1947-48. Mrs. Diekema felt that not one of the girls now enjoying these grants would have to leave school if she did not receive it and I gather that the general picture of need is nowhere near as great as it was in 1933.[21]

The letter went on to explain that the Building profits were now much lower due to making back payments to the employees retirement accounts and paying for repairs and replacements that could not be done during WWII. This may be when the Building ceased to use income for student aid. It also further illustrates that student need was the core priority for scholarships at Martha Cook.

The number and size of scholarships, disbursed from the investment income, has varied over the AESS fund's history, depending upon available resources, which vary with the stock market, and resident need. Sometimes one or two full-semester awards were allotted and sometimes several partial awards. It is heartwarming to learn that when the AESS expendable account was $15 short of the necessary award amount in 1949–50, Social Director Diekema made a personal gift to fill the gap. [22]

Elizabeth Thompson's Bequest and the Modern Application Process

The scope of the AESS Scholarship Fund increased significantly after an unexpected bequest from the estate of alumna Elizabeth Thompson '30, who passed away in April 2000 at the age of 92. Governors' minutes from February 19, 1963, reveal that she had enquired about bequest procedures and she was referred to the University for assistance, but this was long-forgotten by the time attorneys contacted MCB some thirty-seven years later. The fund received $822,152[23] and the Building's ability to meet resident needs was transformed.

77. (cjd) Fall AESS Scholarship recipients during Welcome Week, 2011

The substantial amount of money now available brought the lack of a written policy to the forefront. The Governors appointed a committee to research the scholarship's history and another to recommend formal policies.* This was completed in 2001. The policies and application form are regularly updated and refined. Scholarships are awarded on the basis of financial need, service to MCB and the community, scholarship, the application essay, and a

---

* Governor Catherine Walsh Davis'70, MM'76 and MCAA VP Kathy Graneggen Moberg '79 researched scholarship fund history. The scholarship policy was developed by Governor Beth Yaros Johnson '90, MCAA President Phyllis Taylor '91, and Kathy Moberg.

fifteen-minute interview with a team of two or three alumnae. At least one Governor must be present. The Building Director's involvement consists of making the application available to residents, answering questions and arranging interview time slots. Awards are announced at the Holiday Breakfast in December and the Dinner for Graduating Women in April. The number of awards is flexible, depending upon investment income and the number, needs, and qualifications of the applicants. In recent years, approximately $35,000 has been available each term. Any money not awarded is held for the next semester but is also available for emergency student aid. Applicants must live in the Building for one full term and may reapply for any semester in which they plan to remain in MCB as full-time students.

MCAA's Memorial Fund

In addition to raising money for the AESS fund, the MCAA awarded additional scholarships from its own coffers for many years. In 1971, after learning that a $3,407.32 bequest from the Hildegarde Beck '25 estate was forthcoming, the alumnae group decided to launch a formal account with the University and call it the Martha Cook Memorial Fund. This expendable account was established with the University with $1000 in 1971. The Beck estate money was received in February 1972. By late 1973 the MCAA Board decided it wanted the fund to be more flexible, allowing gifts to the Building in addition to student loans and scholarships. Chernow assisted the Board, and by spring 1974, they awarded one scholarship in honor of Leona Diekema and paid $1000 toward a steam kettle for the kitchen[24]. Records show that one loan and four one-semester room and board scholarships were awarded by 1977.[25] Some scholarships were awarded in the 1980s, too, but the fund has been used primarily for gifts to the Building which have ranged from buying kitchen equipment, repairing the silver teapots, purchasing embossed silverware, reupholstering furniture, donating new dining room chairs, and assisting with fundraising-related expenses.

Requests are often made to open special funds in honor of specific people, but this has the problem of creating too many small funds to manage whereas pooled resources can do greater good. For this reason, the Memorial Fund is officially described as, "An expendable fund to honor any and all alumnae and house directors, created and overseen by the Board of Directors of the Martha Cook Alumnae Association and used for Building and resident needs."

The Minority Merit Scholarship

The Martha Cook Alumnae of Ann Arbor voted to establish a Minority Merit Scholarship on June 27, 1987. It was endowed in 1993. They wrote:

> The Board of Governors has expressed a concern at the lack of Black and/or Hispanic girls at Martha Cook. We need to help in active recruiting of girls to give a broader cultural environment among those living in the dorm. At the 1987 summer salad luncheon, Sally Burden introduced a motion which was passed unanimously to establish an endowment fund of a minimum of $2000, the interest of said fund to provide room and board support for such a minority student. Those present felt this would be an excellent way to celebrate the building's anniversary.[26]

The scholarship was intended to aid a student member of a minority group designated as underrepresented by the University, and the amount awarded was the difference between the cost of a double room in another U-M residence hall and MCB. Applicants were required to be American citizens and demonstrate merit and financial need. There was an application form, and interviews were held during winter term. The award was for both semesters of the next school year, and recipients could reapply each year. A committee of two read the applications, conducted interviews, and made the decisions. When the Ann Arbor club formally disbanded in

2006, it chose to merge its scholarship into the AESS fund, and this was accomplished in 2007.[27]

A Custom that Encourages Connections

The Martha Cook Building and all its alumnae can be proud of their nearly century-old tradition of consistently assisting fellow Cookies to live in the Building and reach their educational goals. It is an MCB custom to encourage one another and changes to the scholarship policies have supported that end. The residents themselves suggested a scholarship fund in 1917 and wrote in the *Martha Cook Annual*, "The establishment of a scholarship would not only help a needy student, but would also do much towards making Martha Cook alumnae feel that they still have close and vital connection with the Martha Cook Building." They were wise young women. This tradition continues to link Cookies to the future.

CHAPTER SIXTEEN

Food and Fellowship

Who will ever forget that memorable first meal?
Martha Cook Annual, 1919

Meals are integral to the Martha Cook community's robust sense of identity. From hurried breakfasts before eight o'clock classes to cafeteria lunches to teatime, sit-down dinners, and special occasion repasts, the dining experience has consistently provided an atmosphere of kinship in addition to physical nourishment. The Dining Room is where Cookies from all the floors connect on a daily basis. Alumnae remember these meals fondly and even model gatherings in other venues along the lines of their common MCB mealtime experiences.

Meals are not simply a time to relax with friends over food. They are also opportunities to share information relating to the community. Cafeteria meals begin with walking through the Cookie Corner, a small hall area between the main hallway and the pantry in which the cafeteria is based. The area is tiny but the walls are covered with bulletin boards on which Building and campus announcements as well as the week's menu are posted. Standing in line or waiting in the hall for the dining room doors to open for sit-down dinners is a time to socialize with one another. During sit-

78. (a23) Standing in the "bread line," 1923

down dinners, announcements are made between the main course and dessert. These can be anything from reminders for all house meetings, upcoming special events and schedule changes to news of graduate school acceptances, engagements, and birthdays.*

Seating charts were in effect to varying degrees from MCB's beginnings until their complete demise in the 1970s, with the exception of seats at particular tables reserved for the Director, Chorister, President, and ARD for sit-down dinners.† The President's Report for 1947–48 states that the observance of the seating chart was conscientious during the first half of the year but collapsed after Christmas.

> This seating chart is designed and enforced for the noble purpose of encouraging and facilitating a wide acquaintance among the girls of

---

* Announcements are preceded by the clinking of spoons on glasses to gain everyone's attention. This has been the tradition for decades, but has not always been the case. The 1920 *Annual* refers to how "... the musical tinkle of Miss Greenwood's tiny bell at the head table immediately brought quiet to the dining room."
† Other live-in staff members have had special seats over the years including House Director, Dietician/Food Service Manager and Night Chaperone.

the house. It is for this reason that it should be enforced effectively, although I understand, it is a perennial problem ....

We would like to suggest also that some concession be made, such as relaxing the seating chart at weekends and allowing the girls to sign up for their own tables for several of the two-week periods in which the seating chart is in force.[1]

The seating chart was a component in the traditional Name Game,[*] and it was also important during the years when the women were expected to use the same napkin for several days in a row. The Director's summer letter for 1957 states that the chart was prepared weekly and posted in the office and "lunch line bulletin board" and it was to be followed Monday through Thursday. "At your assigned table you will find a linen napkin with your name on the envelope. You can reserve a table only when you have a guest."[2] In 1960, the cloth napkins were replaced twice a week.[3]

Sometimes it has taken extra effort to keep the kitchen, and hence the meal schedule, running smoothly and Cookies and staff have worked together. World War II brought many challenges to MCB's high standards. The Social Director's Report for March, 1943, relates,

> The girls have been helping in the kitchen mornings. They are 'good sports' and willing to go along with any and all suggested programs. I hear no complaints. So far, we have been most fortunate. Miss Rowe continues to maintain the accustomed standards and only she knows 'What Price Maintenance'![4]

Several decades later, Building Director Olive Chernow, Food Service Supervisor Barbara Foote Shingleton, and the residents worked together to keep up standards during the AFSCME employees strike from February 24 to March 19, 1977. At first, they could not get their food orders from University Food Stores and so Shingleton ordered from several different sources while Chernow drove around to pick things up. "I remember driving to a trout farm

---

[*] See Chapter 18, Tradition: Phantoms of the Past.

in Dexter to pick up fresh fish she had ordered," wrote Chernow in her autobiography.[5] Shingleton did most of the cooking with the help of paid students. (Students also assisted with general maintenance, such as cleaning bathrooms.) One morning, Shingleton surprised residents with homemade honey bread for breakfast. The recipe became a Martha Cook favorite.

MCB provided twenty-one meals per week (in addition to regular teas and special, food-oriented occasions such as football open houses, exam snacks, and parties) until 2001 when they decreased to nineteen.[6] They decreased again to the current eighteen. Which meals are offered can change slightly from one year to another.

An undated letter from Gertrude Beggs to Grace Greenwood, presumably to smooth the transition between Social Directors prior to fall 1917, states that during the first years, breakfast was held between 7:15 and 8:15 AM; lunch was from 11:45 AM to 12:45 PM; sit-down dinner was at 6 PM.[7] The trend, which picked up speed over the years, has been toward expansion of meal hours. Sometimes to accommodate specific outside events, such as the fall football Saturdays or particular MCB occasions such as a party or alumnae weekend, a particular mealtime may change as needed. Even as far back as the 1950s (and very likely earlier), meal hours could not accommodate everyone and brown bag options, early, and late dinners were made available by special permission. These alternatives were so popular with a portion of the Cookie community that Social Director Diekema wrote in 1956 that early dinners were "becoming a racket."[8]

Attendance at meals was required in MCB's earlier decades and few if any individual dietary adjustments were provided, although at some undocumented point, substitutes for pork became routinely available, and by the 1990s vegetarian options were regularly available. In 1998 vegetarian entrees were offered at every sit-down as a standard option and residents no longer needed to sign up for them ahead of time.⁹ 2001 saw the addition of a vegan entrée to the daily lunch menu.¹⁰ But back in 1935, the Governors' minutes state that a resident who required a special diet, which is not described, would be asked to leave because the Building could not serve her needs and, "not coming to meals is unacceptable."¹¹

Waitress, cafeteria, and kitchen jobs have been a Martha Cook mainstay from the beginning when Cook felt strongly that women from all economic levels should be able to live in his building. Waitresses wore uniforms for several decades until 1993 when they, "complained about the uniforms, saying they looked like servants' uniforms and were demeaning."¹² The Governors agreed to dispense with them in favor of street clothes and aprons. A drawing of waitresses in the 1925 *Annual* shows that uniforms were not an original requirement, as the women are wearing assorted casual

79. (a25) Sketch by Dorothy Eggert '25

skirts. The 1941 *Annual* has a photograph of the waitresses in street clothes with matching white aprons. By the 1950s however, uniforms were de rigueur. In the early 1960s, they were stiffly starched yellow dresses. These were replaced by yellow polyester, tumble-dry uniforms around 1970, and by the mid-1970s, waitresses wore blue polyester uniforms with white trim.¹³ A new dress with a red bodice appeared in the 1980s. Today, the MCB waitresses wear street clothes and black aprons when working at casual meals. Black pants, white blouses, and white aprons are worn for special dinners.

Breakfast

Sunday breakfast, held in the second and third floor kitchenettes, was one of MCB's first distinctive mealtime traditions. Social Director Gertrude Beggs is credited with instituting the custom which continued from 1915 until the 1990s. Coffee, juice, and easy to serve foods such as doughnuts and sweet rolls were brought up to the kitchenettes on carts by residents who took turns doing the job as their semester house duty. Cookies, wearing night clothes and robes, arrived with their own cups and plates to serve themselves, and either congregated in the adjacent libraries and hallways, or returned to their rooms.

80. (a24) From the *Martha Cook Annual*, 1924 (artist unknown)

81. (a24) From the *Martha Cook Annual*, 1924 (artist unknown)

In 1964, the House Board voted to change the schedule so that Sunday breakfast was served from 8:30 to 9:30 AM on the second floor and 9:30 to 10:30 AM on the third, beginning the next semester,[14] but this experiment ended by the mid-1970s. The tradition is documented through lists of house service assignments into the early 1990s when it was eliminated.

On the other days of the week, breakfast has been a cafeteria meal. The 2004–05 school year established a deluxe continental breakfast, a simpler meal requiring a smaller kitchen staff while allowing the dining room to remain open longer. In 2014–15, breakfast was available Monday through Friday from 6:30 AM until 9:45 AM. A typical menu included eggs, steel-cut oatmeal, muffins and breads in addition to cold cereal, toast, and the usual beverages.

Lunch and Brunch

Lunch is traditionally another cafeteria meal, with the exception of special brunches when buffets are set up in the dining room such as the formal Thanksgiving brunch offered the Sunday before the holiday. The chief modifications have been expanded hours and new equipment which increased meal options. A refrigerated salad bar with a sneeze guard was installed in the pantry during the 1976-77 school year.[15] In the early 2000s, an improved and expanded salad bar and a panini maker were installed in the dining room, enhancing menu options, and in 2010 a soft serve ice-cream machine was added.[*] Of course, this equipment also affects cafeteria dinners.

The 2014–15 plan provided lunch Monday through Friday from 11 AM until 1:30 PM. Soup, sandwiches, entrees, a large salad bar, and desserts as well as vegetarian and vegan choices were offered. Brunch was served on Saturday and Sunday from 10 AM until 1:30 PM.

Dinner – Sit-Downs, Buffets, Cafeteria-style, and Sunday Tea

The Martha Cook Building's first dinner was inauspicious. Marie K. Horning '19 recounted that first day in the 1919 *Annual*, saying,

---

[*] According to the Governors' minutes, Food Service Manager Jan McCrath received the Governors' permission to rent an ice-cream machine for four months in fall 1993. Surprisingly, it was not used much by residents at lunch, but Dining Services used it a lot for pies and other desserts. The lease was terminated in December.

> ... who will ever forget that memorable first meal? With all due respect to Miss Walmsley, the dinner gave us a pang of homesickness, with its spare ribs, so very spare, followed by burnt pudding. Several girls rushed to their rooms to bewail the pies that Mother made, while the braver ones gathered in the living room to play.

She went on to say that things quickly improved.

82. (bh6) Dining Room, ca 1915

The sit-down dinner is a signature MCB tradition. Prior to 1974-75, residents gathered in the Gold Room until the head waitress announced dinner, and then followed the directors into the dining room. That fall, the system changed after some discussion and a poll, and residents entered the Dining Room together and stood until the Head Waitress ushered in the Director, ARD, and any special guests who had been waiting in the Gold Room.[16] Traditionally, the Chorister led everyone in singing the *Martha Cook Grace*. The Chorister position, which came with a designated seat near the center of the Dining Room, fell out of practice in the 2000s but is poised for a comeback in fall 2015.[17] Arriving on time has always presented occasional difficulties for students. *Dining Room Procedures* lists from the 1930s include directions for excusing oneself to the Social Director when late to a sit-down, a formal practice that continued at least into the 1980s.

83. (as) A sit-down dinner, 2011

Residents who work as waitresses bring platters and bowls to the tables and food is served family-style. Diners place spoons above their plates in special code: first, facing up for one glass of milk and turned for two, and again before dessert the spoon is up for coffee and tipped for tea, so the waitress or Cookie pouring knows at a glance what is needed.

Every night except Sunday and some special occasions was a sit-down during MCB's first decades. As student schedules grew busier, early, late, and sack dinners became inadequate for the numbers who could not attend sit-downs and fewer were slated. Saturday night sit-downs were the first to go, originally due to football. "Because all games were called at three this year ... Saturday night dinner on game days had necessarily to be turned into buffet supper," wrote Social Director Diekema in the fall of 1942. In 1950, she recorded, "During foot-ball season, we took to serving cafeteria dinner at noon.

Open houses run so late that they interfered with the serving of dinner. Moreover, the food at Open House took the edge off many an appetite."[18] Then in September 1966, the House Board minutes state, "Saturday night dinners will be cafeteria style from 5:30 – 6:15 PM," and that became the norm. Friday night was the next sit-down to be cut and the others eventually followed.

It is somewhat ironic that Sunday night dinner is the one remaining sit-down in 2015, for it was the first evening meal to be less formal. Called Sunday Tea in 1915–16, it was Beggs' inspiration to provide a simpler meal, presumably to overcome the difficulty of procuring enough staff to cook and serve a sit-down that evening. For decades it was customary to sing *The Yellow and the Blue* at its conclusion. (This tradition was followed at least through 1970 when it was sung following a midday Sunday sit-down, but gone by 1975 when a buffet brunch was on the schedule.) Residents assisted in serving Sunday Tea. The 1929–30 President's Report discussed this, saying that the chairman "must get someone to serve tea each Sunday. Only seniors and graduates are asked. Make the girls realize this is a privilege, not an obnoxious duty."[19] House Director Sara Rowe put forth extra effort to maintain Sunday Tea through the challenging WWII years. She wrote, in an undated essay describing her duties,

> One semester every other Sunday with the help of one woman in the kitchen I took care of the teas in order that we might continue to have our traditional Sunday night teas. In the other dormitories at dinner the girls were given a bag lunch for their supper and the Union and the League closed up on Sunday afternoon.[20]

Martha Cook's evening meal plan has recently been redesigned. In 2015, Monday through Thursday dinners are available between 4:30 and 7 PM while on Friday the kitchen closes at 6:30 PM. There is no dinner Saturday. Sunday, when modern students are less likely to have activities or classes, the dining room doors open at 5 PM and sit-down dinner runs from 5:15 until 6:30 PM.

The seating charts of MCB's first decades are gone. The dress code, once pertaining to the entire first floor, is only activated for special "tablecloth" dinners and consists of no jeans, sweatpants, or flip flops. The cloth napkin each resident used all week, carefully replaced in an envelope with her name on it, has thankfully gone the way of the Dodo bird. However, good manners, interesting conversations, friendship, and mutual support are still shared every day in the dining room, helping to make the Martha Cook Building not just a residence hall, but a true home on the University of Michigan campus.

Sunday Night Tea
Mary Esther Oakes '20, from the 1917 *Annual*

In the hall the lamps are lighted,
Glowing candles, fairy-wise,
Gleaming bright in hanging clusters,
Light the sparkle of young eyes,
As the girls come in to dinner,
Laughing, talking, trooping down,
Pious saint and charming sinner,
Each in silken Sunday gown.
Some aloof, some friendly, teasing,
Stranger, pause a while and look,
Saw you anything more pleasing?
Sunday tea at Martha Cook.

CHAPTER SEVENTEEN

"Our Innumerable Cups of Tea"

More fun! We sit on the floor, drink tea, and chat – so cozy – and every day, too! Men and all!
Martha Cook Annual, 1926

If there has been one constant over MCB's first 100 years, it is afternoon tea. It began as a daily affair when the Building opened and was meant to be a mechanism for teaching social skills to the young women of the Building. While it may have done that too, the young women of the Building chose to make the affair their own and determined it would be a respite from the cares of the academic world and a community builder within the house, or as it was put in the 1924 *Annual*, "[it] gives a cozy atmosphere that promotes closer understanding and fellowship." The 1927 *Annual* concurred, referring to "the happy associations of our building" which included "... our innumerable cups of tea, and the not so innumerable cookies consumed ...,"[1] and in 1932 a resident wrote,

> There's always a bright spot in the day, anyway. Bluebooks may come and bluebooks may go, but tea at three-thirty is satisfyingly stationary. It's positive balm to the soul to drift into the Blue Room, with the fire blazing cheerily, get a cup of tea, steaming with

hospitality—and fresh-baked hermits. Perhaps even three, if the supply is surprisingly large.²

Daily Tea

While special teas have always been held on the first floor, daily tea was originally an informal affair in the second floor library. The residents would gather there, "... about four o'clock for a cup of tea and a wee chat."³ This changed during the 1925–26 school year when, according to that *Annual*,

> The informal teas which we have enjoyed every afternoon have been served in the Blue Room, thereby breaking precedent. But we who have indulged in that pleasure can safely say that the others do not know what happiness they have missed.

84. (a24) From the *Martha Cook Annual*, 1924 (artist unknown)

Casual teas have been regularly held on the first floor ever since.

Organizing and serving daily and Friday tea has been done by the residents for most of Martha Cook's history, either informally or as a house duty. Tea Chair was usually a standing committee post, sometimes shared, but at the turn of the twenty-first century, Tea Chairwoman became an elected House Board position, reflecting the importance of tea within the Building. While tea is a segment of the Building's food budget, some of the more elaborate teas are supplemented by the residents' dues.

Some Social Directors had the custom of regularly holding intimate teas for small numbers of residents in their apartment. Margaret Smith, for example, had a private tea each Tuesday where they talked about everything: "books, the theater, tennis,"[4] or sometimes, "... about the place in which some of these out-of-state, and even out-of-United States girls lived. They were interesting, and you had better bases for friendship ...."[5] She placed invitations in mailboxes, set her guests at ease, and provided special delicacies. "We wonder if we'll ever be able to pour tea so poisedly as Miss Smith. Here's hoping."[6]

Daily tea continued apace, even through the financial upheaval of the Depression and into the new decade of the 1940s. Then, in her September/October 1942 report to the Governors, Social Director Diekema wrote unsettling news about the daily tea hour:

85. (a41) Tea in the corridor, 1941

> This very pleasant and distinctive feature of life in the Martha Cook Building, like Lucky Strike Green, has gone to war. The tea shortage made this change imperative although the sugar shortage also precludes home-made sweets for such uses. It may be that during January and February we may be able to revive this custom.

In May 1943 she wrote,

> The regular daily tea hour has been missed. I hope this can be resumed. It makes a very real contribution to friendliness in the house, and one of the things the girls talk about as a choice custom. The house officers voted to raise their dues for next year and to finance one tea weekly from their treasury as part of their social program, if nothing else is possible.

Alas, it was not to be. Afternoon tea did not return to Martha Cook until the fall semester 1944 when, still due to rationing, it was only served on Fridays[7] which remains the custom today. But, like the first generation of Cookies, each group of residents has tweaked the ceremony. Some years it was a simple tea and cookies event and others have seen creative themes with inventive menus. The principle idea, however, has been to share tea with others in the University community and to call some fetes "special teas."

Special Teas

A special tea means the spread of food is more elaborate than at a routine tea and it may also mean a specific group of people such as campus organizations, clubs, University staff, or faculty has been invited as guests. For example, members of the Women's War Council, Women's Judiciary, and all sorority and dormitory presidents were invited to a Friday tea in April 1944[8] and the heads of campus organizations were typically invited during Diekema's tenure. She wrote in her November 1951 Report:

> This has become a very pleasant traditional affair. It was an expansion of a regular Friday tea. The girls, however, had extra refreshments and flowers which they paid for out of their funds .... There is quite a bit of work connected with it as the list of approximately 125 people had to be prepared and written invitations sent.

In the pre-World War II years, a special tea was often a tea dance, sometimes, as at the first Lawyers Tea in 1934, with male guests.

> The house invited the members of the club as a group. A joint committee of the two houses planned the affair. Cutting was the privilege of either sex. Successful, we thought, and everyone seemed to have a good time. But the return invitation that had been hinted at was never formally extended ....[9]

Men were not always in attendance at tea dances, however, and they were listed regularly on the social calendar as entirely in-house parties. Pauline Putnam '38, House Board Vice President in 1937-38 recounted in her year-end report that the first tea of the year, a tea dance in honor of the Building's new women, was "a strictly girls affair"[10] and that an outside pianist provided the music for dancing. Sometimes, a small orchestra was even hired. In 1929 for the first get-acquainted party, "The Blue Room rugs were rolled back, and the davenports arranged along the sides of the room. Here and there vases of tall flowers added color and charm." [11] It was held on a weekday, and residents came home from class and joined in the dancing and tea, which was served in the Alcove, between the Blue Room and the Dining Room.

86. (tw) Cookies welcome U-M President Mark Schlissel to tea September 26, 2014.

New U-M presidents have been invited to a special welcome tea, at least since 1996 when Lee Bollinger began his tenure. The cast and crew of the Royal Shakespeare Company were invited during their fall 2006 U-M residency. Nearly thirty members came to MCB for tea, scones, and American brownies.[12] In October 2012 the custom was even televised when the Big Ten Network's *Tailgate 48* show included a feature on the Martha Cook maize and blue-themed tea held the Friday before the Michigan vs. Michigan State football game![13]

The desire to invite large portions of the University community to share tea crosses the generations (and would please William Cook) but the means of doing that has been different over the years. In the pre- and immediately post-World War II years, University guests were sent individual invitations to a Garden Party Tea or Lawn Party

87. (mcb) Garden Party Tea, ca 1928–30

held near May Day. On April 29, 1917, residents entertained faculty with a spring tea, serving sandwiches in festive May baskets made of colored paper. From 1928 to 1930, this party grew into an Old English Festival or Robin Hood-themed extravaganza with upwards of 500 faculty guests and residents resplendent in elaborate costumes of medieval court ladies, gentlemen, archers, and even a horse. The Social Director wrote to Governor Cora Strong Bulkley on April 29, 1929, to say, "The house is humming like a factory these days. Term papers are due, and every typewriter is working hard. Furthermore work has started for the May Party. Some seventy costumes are to be made in the house."[14]

88. (mcb) Old English Festival costumes, ca 1928-1930

The women resumed wearing party dresses or "chiffons" in 1931. The fete was canceled in 1942 due to WWII, but returned in 1944 when more than 400 people were present. In 1945, 981 guests were invited; 600 attended. A typical menu from the 1940s included ice cream, molded in a brick and sliced, cupcakes, and salted nuts.[15] Only once was inclement weather recorded, and that was May 15, 1938. The party was to be held outdoors between 4 and 7 PM. Nearly 430 of the 750 invited attended, and the Martha Cook Building carried on graciously despite having to move the party inside. Diekema only records the change in venue in her monthly report with a stiff upper lip and no complaints.[16]

Large, campus-wide tea receptions were also held to honor and welcome new social directors. November 11, 1934, was the date for a special evening soiree for Kathleen Codd, with over 400 invited. The residents entertained guests by playing the piano, violin, and harp. Male guests put their coats in the cloak room, guest room, or Codd's apartment. Women's wraps were placed in rooms on the Front Mezzanine where maids were stationed all evening. The guests then went through the receiving line in the Red Room and chatted in the Blue Room before being guided to the Dining Room as space became available for refreshments. Residents, "... were careful to rise as soon as the plates were taken away so that the guest would not stay in the Dining Room," and once in the hallway, guests were introduced to a Corridor Committee member who, "escorted guests from the Dining Room to their wraps and then to the door."[17] Perhaps this sort of event occurred to the Governors because Codd was the widow of George P. Codd, former Detroit mayor, US Representative, judge, and U-M graduate. However, a similar formal reception, described in the 1937 *Annual* as a "simply colossal affair, involving hundreds of people," was held November 17, 1936, to welcome Mary Gleason when she became the new Social Director.

International Tea

The MCB International Tea celebrates diversity in a grand way but has humble origins that go back to the Building's beginnings. Martha Cook residents have always exhibited a deep and lively interest in diversity and the world beyond US borders. Tea for the Cosmopolitan Club, U-M's first international student organization, was a regular event in MCB's early social calendars. As described in the 1926 *Annual*, "Almost every nation was represented—very interesting. After tea we sang patriotic songs of different countries." Another event that year was a tea with Russian food and music, "to honor Miss Forncrook's Russian friends."

International dinners to honor foreign students in the house were held regularly over the years as seen in House Board minutes and social calendars. There was even an International Chairwoman in 1959-60 whose job was to help make MCB's foreign residents feel at home, to represent the Building at the International Committee of the

Women's League, and to plan a special dinner and take charge of United Nations Week* activities in the Building.[18]

The first recorded tea that could be called International Tea was held in November 1947 and in terms of complexity was a far cry from what it is today. The residents decided to participate in the campus's International Week by inviting foreign students to the regular Friday tea. Diekema reported,

> Much to our surprise, about sixty men came swarming in, and one woman. Fortunately, there was a large supply of cookies and 'while there's hot water, there's tea.' Apparently the guests enjoyed the episode because at ten minutes of six (despite the tea hour 3:30 to 4:30) there was still a large group gathered around the piano.[19]

Cookies continued to regularly honor international students at mixers, dinners, and an annual Friday tea. By fall 1983, they began to add information booths and entertainment.[20] The first time the minutes indicate that the event was an open, community-wide affair rather than invitation-only was October 1985. "See the World from MCB! Invite Friends, Teachers, Family, Acquaintances, People off the Street," declare the House Board minutes. A detailed description of the 1989 tea, held in January, sounds even closer to the current International Tea.

89. (a05) International Tea, 2005

> The International Tea should prove to be an enriching and educational experience for all. Remember that this is a campus wide event so spread the word to your friends!!! ... There will be a traditional high tea comprised of bundt cake, scones and clotted

---

* UN Week was a U-M campus event at that time.

cream, and cucumber sandwiches. There will be people performing cultural activities from other countries ...

Residents had display tables, but there is no mention of ethnic foods at these booths as is the current tradition. The event was growing in size by 1990 when the minutes say,

90. (a90) Booth at International Tea, 1990

> Yes folks, it's right around the corner on Friday, February 9. I want all of you to consider doing a booth for this great event. This might mean displaying a costume or garment from a certain country, giving a little history of your chosen county, or performing a song or dance.[21]

The event continued to be successful and grow more elaborate, and today, the International Tea is one of the premier events on campus and the largest on the MCB social calendar. International Tea is funded by House Board and the Residence Hall Association. The doors are opened to the community between 3 and 5 PM and hundreds of University students, faculty, staff, and passers-by throng through the Building,* partaking of traditional treats set up on tables in the Gold Room with displays depicting fifteen to thirty countries. Many residents wear traditional garb. Some years there are musical or dance performances by the residents and their friends.

The Abiding Tradition

Through the years, Martha Cook women have adapted a beloved tradition to meet their own needs while maintaining the same dedication to building and preserving a strong community. Teas may be formal or informal, with or without entertainment or guests, and with simple or extravagant food. No matter how a tea is presented, it remains central to the MCB ideal of gracious living and is always an enjoyable respite from the stresses of college life. Each woman who has lived at MCB can agree with Henry James, "There are few hours in life more agreeable than the hour dedicated to the ceremony known as afternoon tea."[22]

91. (avr) Silver teapots and china cups and saucers are still used regularly.

---

* Over 400 guests attended in 2015.

CHAPTER EIGHTEEN

Tradition:
Songs, Goals, and a "Ghost"

The greatest and finest tradition of Martha Cook does not lie in the tangible things we do but in the intangible spirit that hovers in the building itself.

Martha Cook Annual, 1925

Tradition, by definition, is the "established or customary pattern of thought, action, or behavior,"[1] often expressed through shared participation in an activity. Sometimes a special event becomes a tradition, but not all traditions are events. Rather, traditions sometimes take the form of shared tasks, a shared ethos, a shared group identity and a special camaraderie. At Martha Cook, traditions such as songs, goals, ideals, and "in" jokes help create the foundation for what Martha Cook women have called their friendship circle for 100 years and counting.

MCB Songs

The most significant community-building activity from MCB's beginnings to the present day has been the singing of the *Martha Cook Grace*, composed during the first school year by Ellen M. Sargeant '16 with words by Hilda Hagerty '19. More than anything this grace has unified Cookies across the generations as it is not only sung at every sit-down dinner at the Building but is also the opening ritual of every alumnae brunch or dinner. The nondenominational lines celebrating friendship resonate deeply with Cookies. Nothing is known about the original impetus for composing the song, but it was considered important enough to copyright April 3, 1916.[2]

> Oh Power of Love, all knowing, tender, ever near:
> Our thanks for bounty now we render, gathered here.
> Oh, guard our friendship's circle ever,
> See that naught its firm bands sever,
> From year to year.

Early Cookies fostered camaraderie through singing. Governor Anne E. Shipman Stevens purchased song books for the residents. Booklets of MCB and other college songs were also produced in-house into the 1970s. The earliest, *Martha Cook Songs,* compiled by Edna R. Doughty '22, was a thirty-two page booklet containing nine pages of MCB song lyrics, followed by U-M songs including selections from the Junior Girls' Play and "Other Songs Comic and Otherwise." The *MCB Grace* is not included but *Martha Cook, Our Building, Our Dormitory Dear* is, conveniently dating it between June 1918 when *Portia* was installed "o'er the doorway" and 1922. This song, sung in the dining room between courses to the *Skinimirink* tune (a 1910 song with lyrics by Felix F. Feist, music by Al Piantadosi) was accompanied by "percussion"—clinking water glasses with spoons. It was traditional until shortly after 1980 when it abruptly went missing from the repertoire.

> Martha Cook, our building, our dormitory dear (clink),
> We (clink) love (clink) you (clink).
> To you tonight we raise a song with voices loud and clear (clink),[*]
> We (clink) love (clink) you (clink, clink).
> With Portia o'er the doorway,
> And Venus in the hall,

---

[*] By the 1970s this line was replaced by a repetition of the first line.

And Prexy in the sparking room,*
No harm can e'er befall; Oh
Martha Cook, our building, our dormitory dear (clink),
We (clink) love (clink) you (clink, clink).³

Many Martha Cook songs have been written over the decades, typically set to popular melodies of their day, but sometimes residents composed original music as with *Oh Happy House of Golden Memories* by Bernice Cornell '27 (lyrics) and Grace Glover '28 (music). The poem was first included in the 1926 *Annual*, set to music later, and remained in the Cookie repertoire for several decades. *Martha Cook Serenade*, with words by Adele Hager '51 and music by Carol DeMond '50, has been rediscovered in the Gold Room music case a few times since it was written. A few humorous songs are documented in more recent MCB history, too. Stephanie Takai '88 penned a Cookie-themed version of *Thanks for the Memories* in the 1989 *Martha Cook Cookbook* which includes the lines, "Thanks for the memories/ Of singing grace off-key!"⁴ A special take-off on *My Favorite Things* was written by Rachel Mathews '05 and performed by the Cookie Chorale at the 2004 Messiah Dinner.⁵

A song that fell out of use during the early 1970s but kindles fond memories in older alumnae is the *Engagement Song* with which Cookies traditionally serenaded the recently betrothed at dinner. It is credited to Katherine Wright '33† and is referred to in the 1935-36 Chorister's report.⁶ A later but undated MCB songbook says the tune is *Mighty Like a Rose* (a 1901 song with lyrics by Frank Lebby Stanton, music by Ethelbert Nevin).

---

* A photo of the U-M President traditionally hung in the Sparking Room until the 1990s.
† An undated songbook from at least 1940 actually credits Katharine Weight, but no one of that name lived in MCB. Katherine Wright does appear on the room lists for 1931-32 and 1932-33.

> Someone whispers, "Do you?"
> Someone says "I do!"
> 'Tis the happy moment that a girl looks forward to!
> We love (so and so)
> And someone stole her heart.
> Now we hope that happiness and
> (Girl's first name) never part.

By the late 1960s the first lines had altered to "Someone said 'I love you'/ Someone said 'I too.'"

A completely new engagement song was written by Jean Crawford '40 to the tune of *Here Comes the Bride* and was included in the most recent songbook of the day, but it did not catch on:

> Someone's engaged,
> Whom do you guess?
> Look at _____ _____
> She may confess.

Yet another engagement song was written as part of a contest in 1970, but not only did it not take hold, the tradition itself faded away.[*] Also going out of fashion during this period was the pinning song, a take-off of *Skinimirink* and sung when a resident was "pinned" by her fraternity boyfriend. The long-time tradition of singing U-M's alma mater, *The Yellow and Blue,* following Sunday tea or dinner also ended in the 1970s.

The Chorister led group singing in the Dining Room. In the beginning, she was elected early in the first semester.[7] Her duties included leading *Grace*, songs between courses, *Happy Birthday* on appropriate days, and *The Yellow and the Blue* on Sundays. The position, which had its own designated seat in the dining room, went empty in the early 2000s but is being revived in fall 2015 as a new House Board position titled Arts Chair.

---

[*] The *Engagement Song* made a reappearance at the 2015 MCAA winter tea when the gathered alumnae were asked to serenade a newly engaged resident.

In February 2015, Carrie Ramseyer, then a junior, brought the idea first to the Governors, who were enthusiastic[8], and then to an all-house vote which passed. In her words,

> The Arts Chair is responsible for cultivating an appreciation for the fine and performing arts in the building. It is one of her duties to begin grace for sit down dinner, or to find a suitable replacement in the event of her absence. She will be in charge of planning music for Messiah Dinner, starting songs during the Holiday Caroling, and working with alumnae regarding music at Spring Tea.

Liaising with the Tea Chair, organizing in-house performances, and planning field trips to shows and museums are also in her domain.[9]

The Martha Cook Annual

The residents created an annual the very first year. It was a simple, eight by eight and one-half inches blue book bound with a yellow string and embossed with the title and MCB logo. It contained photographs, candid and formal, pen and ink drawings, descriptions of the year's events, jokes, editorials, and advertisements. While sometimes very serious, the young women exhibited humor, too. The Board of Governors page, for instance, is titled *The Powers Behind the Throne*!

The format changed slightly in 1919, increasing to seven by ten and one-half inches. Cook and Scrantom were involved in the printing process that year, and wrote several letters back and forth regarding the prints, color of ink, and other details. Cook's motivation was to provide a more impressive volume. He did not censor or suggest content.[10] In 1924 the string was gone and the book had a hard cover with an elaborate, deeply embossed logo. This format continued through 1932, although some covers were red or brown rather than blue.

The *Annual* was simplified in 1934, due to Depression-era constraints. It was paper bound, typed rather than printed, with snapshot prints individually attached. There were far fewer photos, too. The books for 1935 and 1936 were similar. It was during this period that the Board of Governors committed to publishing a special memorial volume, later titled *A Booklet of the Martha Cook Building at the University of Michigan: A History of the First Twenty Years*, and some of MCB's resources were dedicated to that project. Governor Heath first brought up the subject at the December 20, 1934, meeting where, "It was agreed that we begin to gather together materials from all possible sources."[11] Marion Slemons, a graduate student in medicine, was chosen for the undertaking which was completed by May 1936 when she was paid $50.[12] The hardbound book was printed on high-quality paper with large, black and white photographs, and is still an excellent resource for MCB history.

The 1938 through 1940 yearbooks were typeset and printed on higher quality paper. The 1938 issue was partially financed by what was dubbed a radio dance.

> We inaugurated this sort of dance in order to pay off the debt on our Annual. Not only was it successful in a financial way but it suggested the possibility of similar parties in the future if informality is desired or if another debt emergency should crop up. Our phonograph was lent to us and we rented our records resulting in a net profit of thirty odd dollars. A girl was paid two dollars for changing the records all evening.[13]

Life and Times in Martha Cook Building, the 1941 yearbook, was a step up with a more elegant paper binding, glossy paper, and quality printing. It featured some MCB history and reported upon the Silver Jubilee, as it was meant to highlight the Building's first quarter century. A combination of publishing costs and a desire to use their finances to aid the war effort convinced the residents to discontinue the *Annual* in 1942[14] and, with the exception of *The Cookie Press*, a compilation of monthly dorm newsletters in 1945–46, the 1941 edition was the final book until MCB's Sixtieth Anniversary. This 1975–76 volume was printed on good quality paper, stapled down the center, and had black and white photographs.

The *Annual* finally became a regular tradition again in 1989–90. It was black and white and stapled. The first full color volume was 2001–02 and had a spiral binding. The digital age made the books easier and less expensive to produce. They are coordinated by the Building Historian, an elected House Board member. Extra copies are kept in the Sparking Room.

The Cookbook

Not the same as an annual but still a delightful piece of memorabilia, especially since food plays such an important role in the Cookie community, MCB cookbooks have been produced with varying degrees of regularity over the years, possibly beginning in the 1950s. The Building has never made a serious effort to collect them, so it is unknown when they began or how many have been compiled.

Sara Rowe received a letter in 1946 from an alumna who mentioned wishing she had copies of the recipes she remembered so fondly,[15] especially the molded salads, so presumably there was not a recipe collection for residents in those days. Small recipe booklets were sometimes made available during the 1950s and 1960s, but there are no examples in Building files. Circa 1970, the cookbook was a few mimeographed eight and one-half by eleven inch pages, stapled and presented to seniors at Graduation Dinner. The 1978 and 1979 volumes were photocopied portrait-style on white paper with seventeen pages of recipes. The 1980 version, however, was completely revamped. It was twenty-five pages long and titled *Venus and Friends in Foodland Presents Martha's Cookin'*. It had drawings on every page with comical, anthropomorphic food and the recipes were clearly divided into categories. The cover was yellow paper. The book also contained a few MCB song lyrics.[16] Another was compiled in 1989. It was five and one-half by eight and one-half inches with a spiral binding, cardstock cover, and forty-two pages counting dividers between food categories. The recipe collection dedicated to the 2002–2003 graduating seniors has a few more pages and a clear plastic cover-protector.[17]

A number of recipes from women with early ties to MCB were printed in the *Blue Book of Cooking: a collection of favorite recipes of University of Michigan alumnae throughout the United States*, a 1938 cookbook compiled by the Ann Arbor Alumnae as a fundraiser.[18] Former Director Grace Greenwood Reeves, soon-to-be director Leona Diekema, Governor Grace Campbell Bruce, and the Martha Cook Building itself (probably courtesy of Sara Rowe) submitted recipes.

What's in a Name? The Term "Cookie"

"Cookie" has been the residents' term of choice when referring to themselves for much of MCB's history. The residents have also typically referred to themselves as "the girls." Through all the documents, "Martha Cook girls" is a standard reference. The Governors and Directors also regularly used the term girls until the 1970s when women started to become the preferred term.

The 1916 *Annual* does not use the name Cookies, but has one reference to a Cookite. A poem in the 1918 *Annual*, titled *A Fable, or a Cookie's Complaint*, is the first use in print. The 1920 *Annual* has, "poor, tired little Martha Cooker." There are no Cookies in Edna Doughty's 1922 compilation of MCB songs, but the nickname appears again in the 1923 yearbook in a poem called *Informal Dances*:

> Listen my Cookies, and you shall hear
> Of the dances we held in November drear,
> After the football games were won,
> And our hearts were full of pep and fun.

From this point on, Cookie occurs routinely, although it is never the sole appellation used and it turns up between one and a handful of instances per volume. Sometimes it is randomly placed within quotation marks. *The Cookie Press* (1945–46) which has a more casual tone than the annuals, is brimming with references to Cookies, however.

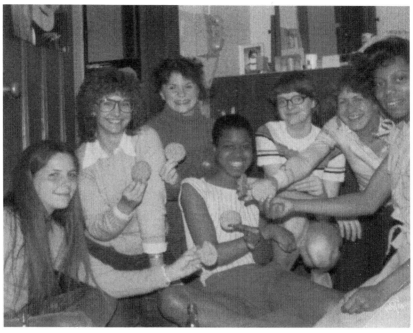

92. (kgm) "Cookies" with cookies, 1979

The term seems to have fallen out of favor in the 1950s and many alumnae from that period dislike it. They are more likely to think of themselves as Cook girls or Cook women. In the "Cookie Crumbs" column of the fall 1992 *MCAA Newsletter*, an early 1960s era alumna asked, "Am I the only one who hates being called a 'Cookie'?" There must be a less condescending label for us."[19] However, the next issue included a response from Joan Gassaway Berndt '58 who wrote, "You can blame the 'condescending' (?) title of "Cookie Crumbs" on me as it was my idea when I was on the

Board in the late 60s-early 70s."[20] Martha Cook women, as they do for a great many topics, have a variety of opinions on the subject! Cookie has been the accepted name for residents from the later 1960s to the present day.

An assortment of terms has been used for the Martha Cook Building itself over 100 years. From the very start, the initials were a handy moniker. MC was incorporated in the original logo with the M above the portal and the C below. M.C.B. was used at first but quickly simplified to MCB. The initials appear in the early annuals and some of the first songs. Cook, simple and direct, has also been common. In the twenty-first century, Martha and Marth became popular. Also, for the full 100 years, residents, staff, and the Governors have called MCB the Building, with the "b" capitalized. This sometimes confuses outsiders and even for Cookies it creates editing conundrums. The rule is that if one is referring simply to structural elements, the writer should use a lowercase letter b as in, "the building's heating system", but the whole structure or the actual home is the Building, a proper noun. This is due to both traditional usage and the fact that the full, formal name (carved in stone above the front door) is the Martha Cook Building.

The Building often seems mysterious to the campus at large and numerous misconceptions and fallacies are common, including gloves being required at tea, men never being allowed inside, and residents all being wealthy. For several decades, MCB's nickname has been the Virgin Vault, generally causing residents and alumnae to roll their eyes.

Honor Code

In the student government structure at Martha Cook, the individual residents have been responsible for their own conduct under an honor system. Board President Luanne Cevala noted at a House Board meeting on May 8, 1962, "that the honor system was not specifically mentioned in the *Blue Book* until the 1958 edition."[21] But some form of an honor code existed before that because Diekema mentioned "our honor system" in her April 1949 report to the Governors when she described the Decorum Pledge.* By 1969, the Honor Code's opening statement read,

> Those who live here are given a great deal of freedom and a correspondingly large amount of responsibility for their actions with the hope that they will emerge from this rather unique experience in group living with independence and maturity. Inherent in the responsibility is an attitude of consideration and respect for each member of the group.[22]

The Honor Code published in the 2014 Handbook begins with essentially this same phrase. Both the older code and the current code require that residents obey University and MCB rules, that they serve the Building in some capacity, and that they respect certain courtesies—considerate use of the showers, TV room, and refrigerators, for example. The major difference between the 1969 and current version is that in 1969 women were expected to turn themselves in to the Judiciary Chair or Building Director if they violated a rule and, if witness to another's infraction, to remind the offender to report herself. Today's resident witness may still choose to remind another resident of her responsibility to report her own violation but may, if she'd rather, directly report an infraction to the Building Director or one of the student staff members. This difference is probably due to a change in the seriousness of actions considered to be violations of University rules and their resultant consequences. However, the policy ends with a statement in bold capital letters,

> It is understood that, by applying for residency at the Martha Cook Building, residents have voluntarily chosen to accept and abide by the policies of conduct of the Building. Therefore, it is anticipated that the above guidelines will not require enforcement.[23]

---

* See Chapter 14, In Loco Parentis: Rules and Rebellion.

Idealism

Martha Cook women have been giving back for a century. They volunteered time and money during the two World Wars and raised money for Martha Cook scholarships. They have supported needy children and children's hospitals and have participated in University-sponsored ecology programs. The causes and Cookies' responses have altered with the decades and are described throughout this book. The underlying idealism and sense that Martha Cook women should collectively step up and volunteer is a well-established tradition. Perhaps knowing that a generous donor made their college home possible helped to set the precedent, and of course, the University of Michigan community has a long, lively history of public-minded idealism. Cookies fit right in.

The "Ghost" of Martha

While checking out the fourth floor storage areas shortly after becoming Building Director, Marion Law discovered a burgundy dress designed to replicate the one in Martha Wolford Cook's Red Room portrait. Law wore it for Martha's Birthday Dinner (there is a photo in the 1997-98 *Annual*) and a few other events, including a comedy sketch at one of the resident talent shows held in Lydia Mendelsohn Theater.* The ARD wore it to another Birthday Dinner. Governor Margaret Leary donned the dress during a 2014 summertime event when MCB hosted the Ann Arbor Rotary Club. According to Marion, "Margaret situated herself in the second floor library and surprised the guests. Margaret answered questions as if she was Martha Cook and was totally convincing (if a bit slimmer than the real lady)."[24] The dress made an appearance at the 2015 International Tea at a Martha Cook table, and again at the 2015 Alumnae Spring Tea, worn by House Board President Amy Pestenariu.

---

* See Chapter 20, Tradition: Phantoms of the Past.

Building Director Rosalie Moore (1981–92) was, in fact, the originator of the "Ghost of Martha" costume which she topped off with a wig for Halloween one year. She is thought to have made it herself.

Some residents and one security guard have reported actual ghostly encounters in the Building. Music is typically associated with this benevolent, female apparition. The Martha Wolford Cook costume has had many more documented appearances!

93. (rpj) The Ghost of Martha at Spring Tea, 2015

Spiders

Spiders in Cookies' rooms are such a long-standing complaint that they must be deemed a Martha Cook tradition. The 1925 *Annual* mentions the unwelcome residents on a humorous page titled the "Third Floor Weakly":

> Victim Recovers
> Miss Blanche Hull had a bad case of spideritis as the result of seeing a terrible monster, an eighth of an inch in diameter, jump from one of her galoshes as she was about to put it on. Hearing her screams, her friends dashed to the rescue. She is improving slowly.
> The spider died of fright.

The spiders were still in abundant evidence when Stephanie Takai wrote the following in 1988:

> Thanks for the memories
> Of showers clogged with hair,
> Guys sneaking up the stair,
> Laundry carts and broken hearts,
> And spiders everywhere![25]

This wide-ranging collection of traditions, by its very variety, is a testament to a healthy, vibrant community. Humor, camaraderie and seriousness are well represented. Martha Cook women are engaged with each other as well as the world around them.

CHAPTER NINETEEN

Tradition: Parties and More

Our girls know that play has its place in our education as well as lectures and textbooks and laboratories, nor have we neglected study in our effort to attain joy and avoid dullness.
Martha Cook Annual, 1917

The Martha Cook Building has cultivated its sense of community and home from its first year to the present through shared routines and special events. While coursework and studying are of paramount importance in students' lives, residents and staff, encouraged by the Governors, have filled "between times" with traditions to foster unity, create happy memories, and provide breaks from academic pressure. A large percentage of these traditions revolve around meals, as sharing food is a hallmark of cultural identity. Some of MCB's traditions, such as Holiday Breakfast and dances, have continued in one form or another for 100 years. Others fell out of fashion and were replaced by new customs and rituals. The Social Calendar has never been determined by rote.

Martha Cook traditions have a lively history and still draw a houseful of young women to select this residence hall over U-M's other choices, and many remain for multiple years. What follows are the stories of current MCB customs. Some are new twenty-first century events while others are several decades to a century old, having stood the test of time, freshened by new ideas but easily recognizable to all alumnae.

Halloween

Halloween revels have been a constant at Martha Cook for a full century. The diversions of dress-up and spooky make-believe are good antidotes to serious studying, paper-writing, and test preparation. Costumes and decorations (frequently involving the statue of *Venus*) are the only constants. The 1941 *Annual* even comments, "... the manner of celebrating Hallowe'en has changed almost every year."[1]

MCB's first Halloween was complex and creative. It seems to have helped set the tone for community building, long before the more modern advent of Welcome Week. The festivities were described in detail in the 1916 *Annual*:

> The girls of the fourth floor decided that on Hallowe'en it would be very novel to give a party to the rest of the house in order that the girls might become better acquainted. The entire fourth floor was given over to the project. One room was called the Chamber of Horrors and contained many bloodcurdling sights. The most distinctive feature was Bluebeard. The heads of his wives were hung on a portion of the wall making the combination of long hair and blood present a gruesome sight. Margaret Hurst took the part of Bluebeard .... Standing at the door with a treacherous sword, "alias" butcher-knife, she bade all cowering spectators enter.
> The gypsy fortune teller, Beatrice McKnight, afforded much amusement and satisfaction of curiosity, and in some cases she actually told things that were really true .... The main feature of the evening was the "eats." Large doughnuts, apples, and cider were served .... Ghosts, witches, and pumpkins lanterns were prevalent everywhere and everyone left with a feeling of great satisfaction.[2]

The 1928 *Annual* refers to the "Ladies from Hades" walking the MCB corridor and decorating the dining room in spectacular fashion. All hundred and eighteen residents were given horns at dinner, causing an immense racket and following the meal was "the stunt, furnished by the laggards of the name contest. Then there was

94. (a29) The 1928 Halloween costume contest was won by this line of Cookie convicts.

dancing, and finally cider and doughnuts."

Wearing costumes to dinner has often occurred and Halloween was frequently the night the losers of the Name Game[*] performed their skit. The 1936 *Annual* describes their event: "October 31— Wild Night! Masquerade dinner. Sang engagement song to *Venus* who donned black lace for the occasion." Dances, teas, and pumpkin carving contests are typical entertainments, with dances being the favorite choice in recent years.

Welcome Week

Special get-acquainted activities at the start of each new academic year have probably always occurred as the women devised ways to

---

[*] See Chapter 20, Tradition: Phantoms of the Past.

get to know each other. The 1924 *Annual* mentions, but unfortunately does not describe, a "Progressive Get-Acquainted Party" on September 29 and an afternoon party for new girls in February. In 1934, "In the midst of unpacking trunks ... we take time off ... in the Blue Room ... in gay pajamas ... fluttery negligees." Fireside sings in casual and bedtime attire, sharing food (spreads), and playing games were popular and are mentioned in the annuals. Social Director Mary Gleason and House Director Sara Rowe are reported to have played Blind Man's Bluff with residents at a September party in 1938.

Welcome Week, as the elaborate multi-day affair the Building carries out today, first began in the early 1930s as part of the University's Orientation Week. Many of the Building's events were originally aimed at students new to the University, which at that time at MCB meant transfer students rather than freshmen. Like all new ideas, it took some time to work out the bugs involved with the week-long undertaking. In the beginning, some of the returning women were designated as advisors to specific new women but did not always return to Ann Arbor in time to meet their advisee's arrival. In September 1939, Social Director Leona Diekema, new to the Building herself, recommended in her monthly report that "better organization that first week can do much to make a happier situation" for the new girls. She recommended that for the next year, all the advisors should arrive on a certain date and an organized house program should begin after that point. In fall 1941, she further recommended that there be a more careful selection of advisors, a planning meeting be held in May, a summer letter be sent to the residents by the Director, a fuller social program be planned for the weekend, afternoon tea be served on Wednesday as well as Thursday and Friday, and the dining room should open on Sunday at the end of the week instead of Monday, the first day of classes. That the women of Martha Cook took her suggestions to heart is evidenced by the fact that most of Diekema's suggestions are still in effect today.

House Board and the Orientation Week advisors planned such a spectacular "Get Acquainted Party" during fall 1948 that it was given special mention in Diekema's report to the Governors:

> The "Get Acquainted Party was very clever .... Lionesses met the new girls ... and romped with them to the elevator for a trip to the moon. On the fourth floor, a group of "Martians" in costume took over and piloted them about the Building to introduce them to the various public rooms. In the music room, there was a "mad musician" playing and singing .... The costuming was nothing short of amazing! After the aerial trip, all came to the Blue Room to see the biggest one ring circus ever. Yours truly was the ring master. The most outstanding portion of her "get-up" was Gratia Boice's pair of red tights. Popcorn and pink lemonade finished the performance.

September 1950 saw the first Orientation/Welcome Week picnic on the terrace, held on Thursday evening, giving the women a break from the "customary foraging about town for food which they had been doing for several days."[3] For this event, House Board paid the cost of the food and the "old girls", as they called themselves, each paid twenty-five cents to help defray the costs. The cook made potato salad and coffee and the girls cooked their own hotdogs in the

95. (kgm) Bar-B-Q on tennis court for Welcome Week, ca 1999

serving pantry. It's not clear when full meal service during the week was added.

Modern Welcome Weeks, now geared at all Cookies and not just those who are new, continue the idea of building camaraderie at MCB but the choice of activities is more eclectic. The Dining Room now opens for meals on the first move-in day and parents are invited to join their daughters on that day for the first lunch of the new

96. (a90) Welcome Week 1989 included croquet in the Garden.

school year. The women join together during the week for craft-making and excursions to Stucchi's for ice cream and Angelo's for breakfast. A Girls' Night In, complete with manicures and pedicures has been held several times in the Gold Room on one of the Welcome Week evenings. Alumna Ashley Erdman Miguel '04 remembers that Cookies tried to "paint the rock" at Washtenaw and Hill Streets in 2002 but "only a handful of us showed up in the middle of the night and we grossly underestimated how much paint it would take to cover the Rock."[4] In 2006, Cookies again attempted the feat, this time with more success and it has been repeated several times. Various games—from tag to tea pong—have been held in the

Garden and in fall 2013, the games took a new turn when an inflatable water slide and bounce house were installed for a day.

97. (kgm) Bounce house on the lawn, 2013

Dances – Formal, Informal, Mixers, and Others

Dances have been a Martha Cook social calendar staple from the beginning. The first reference is in the 1917 *Annual*: "The residents of the Martha Cook Building have established the custom of giving two dancing parties during the year," with the first in early December and the next in late May with dancing on the terrace. The 1918 volume, however, referring obliquely to the United States' entry into WWI, states that only simple parties were felt appropriate that year. Several informal dances called corridor dance parties were held in addition to four "Blue Room dances," which were presumably dressier occasions. The formals were back again, at least by the 1920s, and have continued to the present, with a notable hiatus throughout most of WWII and occasional years when residents opted for something a little different. For example, in 1955 the spring formal was dispensed with in favor of a western-style dance on the tennis court.⁵ In April 2015 Martha Cook residents joined together with South Quad, Betsy Barbour, Helen Newberry, and Fletcher for a "dormal," a Casino Royale-themed formal dance at the Michigan Union with a DJ, dancing, casino games, photo booth, mock-tails, and snacks. The MCB Social Committee under the direction of Quinn Fischman was in charge of decorations.

98. (a18) Sketch by Helen Osband '19

Typically, formals have been held in December or early January and again in the spring. Often in recent years, a Halloween dance, complete with costumes, has been a better fit, since December is heavily booked with Messiah Dinner, Holiday Breakfast, study days, and exams. Winter dances held during WWII were toned down affairs. In 1942 the Director's Report states, "It was ... decided to simplify the Christmas dance and turn the proceeds to the Bomber Scholarship Fund." The same was done in 1943 when Diekema noted that few dances occurred on campus at all with the exception of USO parties.⁶

The dance returned in 1947 but food shortages kept it scaled back. However, the following year residents pulled out all the stops. Diekema wrote in her log that the terrace lanterns which, before the war, had been a time-honored tradition dating to at least the 1920s, were back on the terrace and in addition, trellises covered with lilacs closed all of the doorways except the center Blue Room door, and all the windows in the Red and Blue Rooms. A real rock garden with a pool and three live baby ducks occupied the center of the ballroom floor. Needless to say, its attraction was colossal ....

The profit from this dance went to the Anne E. Shipman Stevens Scholarship Fund. In 1959, invitations were sent to all of the new women who would be moving into MCB that coming fall as well as local alumnae from the past two years.[7]

Until the U-M calendar changed from two semesters to three terms in the 1964–65 academic year, the spring formal was a late May occasion, taking advantage of Ann Arbor's typically balmy

99. (bh6) Spring formal with the traditional lantern lighting, 1935

weather. The party spilled from the Blue Room into the corridor and onto the terrace. The new academic calendar shifted the spring formal to March or April when it had to be held indoors. Creative themes and decorations abounded. Some of these included a Spring Fly Away Dance in 1990 with proceeds going to SAFE House;

Enchantment Under the Sea in 1992; another western theme in 1994 at Martha's Saloon with the Sparking Room turned into a "jail" with black crepe paper bars and old western movies playing on the TV; and Old Hollywood in 2007 complete with residents' hands outlined in chalk on the sidewalk outside the Building for a "walk of fame."[8]

In addition to tea dances,* to which men were not always invited, many other less formal dances have been held over the years. Radio dances were a simple and inexpensive Saturday night entertainment in the 1940s. One was held during Orientation Week of 1943 and the Director's Report states that it

> was attended largely by servicemen and thus did double duty as a "mixer" and U.S.O. affair. The men served punch and washed the dishes, having made themselves especially welcome in these days of help scarcity.

Square dances were occasionally held on the tennis court. One was planned as part of Orientation Week in 1958. Blind dates were arranged with Frederick House in South Quad and hay was imported for authentic decoration.[9]

Mixers with an open invitation to campus men have been held, but not frequently. Although several are mentioned in the 1940s, in 1960, the Vice President's Report states, "It is a Martha Cook policy not to have mixers."[10] They were back on the Social Calendar in the 1970s, during the years when the legal drinking age was eighteen, and kegs were available. One was held each semester during the 1974-75 school year. The fall 1975 mixer was disastrous by MCB standards. According to House Board Minutes,

> The fire alarm was pulled by a prankster and no one evacuated the Building. Housing Security was called to break up a disturbance and one of their men was jumped outside the building. This caused the Ann Arbor police to be called and a police report to be filed on our mixer.

---

* See Chapter 17, "Our Innumerable Cups of Tea"

Apparently previous mixers had incurred problems, too, and Building Director Olive Chernow announced that campus-wide mixers were no longer allowed. The minutes go on to say, "Only half the residents attended and several left in disgust of the crowd's antics. Others had a great time and helped to maintain order." Nonetheless, future plans were to invite smaller groups of men such as law students or particular fraternities so Cookies could maintain closer control over who attended.

Christmas/Holiday Breakfast and the Mothers' Christmas Party

The Holiday Breakfast (called Christmas Breakfast until the late 1990s or early 2000s*), with its candle-lit caroling procession through dark halls before dawn on a December morning, began in 1915 and continues one hundred years later. Originally held on the last day before winter break, it shifted when U-M's academic calendar changed in 1964, first to final day of classes and then, in 1975, to the beginning of Study Days. The idea is credited to Anne E. Shipman Stevens who usually attended, even after she was no longer a governor.[11]

100. (mbs) Holiday Breakfast procession, 1979

---

* The first reference to MCB using the word holiday in place of Christmas to be more inclusive of all residents' traditions is in the November 16, 1970 House Board Minutes which state, "the Christmas Function will now be referred to as the Winter Function by suggestion of Ruth Stock."

Song books and candles (later, flashlights or electric candles) were distributed the night before. In the morning, a bugler played *Reveille* to wake the residents and overnight guests in time to dress before the procession began. Other instruments have been used and today, the caroling alone begins the procession. The Social Director and Chorister led the way with Governors, staff, and any guest participants following. Beginning on the fourth floor, everyone proceeded downward through the Building, singing carols and lighting the candles of women waiting in the lower hallways. In 1929, Social Director Elva Forncrook wrote that "Mrs. Stevens likes to begin with *Adeste Fideles*. It's best to leave the more difficult songs until we get down to second floor where there are more girls present."[12] They wound their way through the Red and Blue Rooms, and took their places at decorated tables in the dining room and down the corridor. In the early days, singing continued at the table. Forncrook reported, "After breakfast it is usual to sing *Martha Cook Our Building*; *Five Hours More to Vacation*, and Mrs. Stevens likes to have *The Yellow and the Blue*."[13] The 1922 *Annual* describes how the residents and their invited friends lighted the small candles that decorated each place, "… one by another all around the long tables. This symbolized the flame of friendship." In 1931 however, Social Director Margaret Smith's report alarmingly noted, "Caution, be watchful for fires on the table. There is much crepe paper and many small candles."[14]

The 1924 *Annual* makes the astonishing claim that, "… a procession of about three hundred Martha Cook girls and their guests marched through the spacious rooms of the first floor." A January 1928 letter from Forncrook to Cook recounts that year's breakfast was larger than previous years with approximately 110 guests: mothers; faculty; two Advisors of Women; and two Governors, Stevens and Sargent.[15] In 1935 and 1936, President and Mrs. Ruthven attended.[16] Archival footage of the 1938 breakfast is available on YouTube, depicting residents and their mothers coming down the stairs and women seating themselves at the table near *Venus*. The Social Director, Mary Gleason, is recognizable and there is a white-haired woman who may be Anne E. Shipman Stevens.[17]

Guests must have been a part of the festivities very early in the event's history because the 1919 *Annual* states that due to the influenza epidemic, "... Christmas Breakfast was a purely family affair .... And feeling not so much on our best behavior we even danced at breakfast with a pine branch in our hair." While it is unknown exactly when mothers were first invited to spend the night before the breakfast with their daughters, the first Mother's Christmas Party, where residents hosted their mothers for dinner and late evening merrymaking, was in 1926.[18] The Building closed at 10:30 PM and a pajama party[19] was held in the Blue Room. A special Christmas cake, provided by Stevens, was shared by all. Following the performance of a play or, as in 1937, a tableaux depicting the Christmas story,[20] starring residents, the women of the Building presented their mothers with wrapped toys to be opened and admired, then packed into a large box to be sent to the pediatric unit at University Hospital.[21] In 1935 the hospital was more in need of money, so the women stopped donating "dime-store gifts" and instead each girl contributed ten cents.[22]

The last year mothers, older sisters, or older female relatives (college girlfriends were against the rules) were invited was 1941, after which the entire Christmas Breakfast event went on a wartime hiatus.[23] World War II, with its gas, food, and staff shortages, caused the only break in this tradition.[24] The residents voted to hold a special Christmas dinner in 1942, with the Dean of Women as a guest and holiday music afterwards in the Blue Room. Winifred Stevens Kirby sent a fruitcake, candy, and flowers in honor of her mother who died in spring 1939 (she also sent a cake in 1939 and 1940 according to the Social Director's reports).[25]

The January 1946 entry in *The Cookie Press*, an informal stand-in that year for an annual, happily states that, "the traditional Christmas breakfast was resumed this past holiday season to make the vacation send-off especially gay for all Cookies." Mothers were not invited that year and Diekema wrote in her monthly report that, "Miss Rowe and I both felt that it might always be desirable to arrange this affair for ourselves only and give a mothers' house party either at the time of Mother's Day or in conjunction with the May Festival."[26] However, the party for mothers never returned. Diekema commented

101. (kgm) Christmas Breakfast, 1978

again two years later that the Christmas Breakfast, "... has lost none of its impressiveness despite the fact that we no longer have guests on this occasion since the Messiah Party takes care of that, and on a much larger scale."[27]

Christmas Breakfast reports in the 1950s and 1960s focused upon the menu. The Dean of Women was the only traditional guest until the office was eliminated in 1962.[28] Without throngs of guests, the hallway tables were no longer needed and the residents decorated the dining room the night before. Red apples with birthday candles inserted were put at each place. Grapefruit halves, sweet rolls, eggs, bacon, and candy canes were typical fare,[29] served by the resident waitresses, just like a sit-down dinner. In the 2000s the spread became a sumptuous breakfast buffet with eggs (scrambled or Benedict), bacon, hash browns, vegetarian choices, and sometimes a French toast bar with fruit, chocolate chips, syrup, and more. Hot chocolate is commonly available in addition to juices, coffee, and tea.

Permission to wear pajamas on the first floor (always a special treat for Cookies!) began when the date changed to the beginning of Study Days. The change in day was instituted by Building Director Olive Chernow in 1975 so that the breakfast need not be rushed for residents with 8 o'clock classes.[30] Another change early in Chernow's tenure was eliminating the December senior dinner, recognizing the prospective graduates at Christmas Breakfast instead.

Martha Cook scholarships have long been announced at the event, originally near the end of the meal, but today they are announced in the Gold Room prior to breakfast. Another recent addition to the festivities is a resident, dressed as Santa or an elf, reading Chris Van Allsburg's *The Polar Express* aloud. Some years all attendees are given a silver bell, significant in the story, as well as candy. Secret Santas are revealed at this time, too, if the residents of a particular year opt to carry out this practice.

A holiday buffet dinner held the night before to celebrate the last day of fall term classes is a modern innovation. This is a University-wide tradition which MCB follows with the Building's own unique flair. It is an elegant replacement for the long ago Mothers' Party. Stevens would probably be delighted.

Faculty Dinners and Entertainments

Entertaining University faculty is a time honored MCB tradition, ranging from teas (both large and intimate), to a community sing in 1918, to dinners. The first mention is in the 1917 *Annual* where it states that two Sunday evenings a year were scheduled for the faculty in addition to a grand tea in the spring. While faculty dinners have usually been held two or three times a semester, there has been a wide range in frequency, and in the twenty-first century, faculty teas have often been held in their place.

The invitation procedure, now and in the past, allows residents to sign up for a turn to invite a professor and usually his or her spouse and to choose which friends join them at the table. Some years, the dinners were very elaborate with themes and entertainments, but more often they were special sit-down dinners with tablecloths and an enhanced menu. The 1931 *Annual* states, "The residents of the Martha Cook Building make this truly their home by being frequent hostesses at dinner to faculty members and their wives."[31] It is noteworthy that professors were expected to be male in those days!

Food rationing put a stop to faculty dinners during WWII. Diekema wrote in 1943 that rationing "has made necessary an edict of no more guests for meals until further notice. This has eliminated our informal faculty Thursday nights."[32] The dinners did not resume until late March, 1946.[33] The winter term social calendar in 1977 included five dinners. Ten invitations for a faculty member and spouse were allowed per event and each resident was allowed one professor per term.[34]

Some of the most elaborate faculty dinners occurred in the 1950s with large, themed events and guest lists of forty to seventy-five people. The 1951 April Fool's Day Circus party reportedly had seventy faculty guests. There were clowns in costume, animal crackers for pre-dinner nibbles, and the dining room was filled with balloons and stuffed animals standing in for circus animals. The residents provided cabaret-style entertainment during dinner and an after-dinner skit and community sing afterwards.[35] The 1952 party was titled Farmers' Picnic and Political Rally and included a farcical skit about a rally for a dog-catcher election. The 1955 theme, 20,000 Leagues Under the Sea, included a lengthy program of skits and songs and the 1959 dinner featured appetizers in the corridor and a Beat Generation theme.

Dinner for New Women

The first Dinner for New Women was held in early fall 1926 and described in the *Annual:*

> This year, for the first time a very lovely ceremony was added to our number of traditions. That was our initiation service in which every new girl was given a foreshadowing of the beauty and strength of this building, adequately symbolized by the entwined rose and oak leaf which it was now her privilege to share.

Several pages later, it is mentioned again:

> One Sunday afternoon witnessed our formal initiation. All the girls were in light fluffy dresses .... It was the time when we new girls were taken into the inner circle of Martha Cook, the time when we all pledged ourselves to uphold the honor and traditions of this building that was to mean so much in our college life.

During this first year and possibly the next couple of years, the ceremony took place before the evening meal and it is unknown if the dinner itself was special, but over time, it did develop into the first formal dinner of the school year.

The rose and oak leaf have continued as the symbols for this event, and still stand for beauty and strength. In 1929, the House Board President said in her speech,

> We have chosen as our house symbol, the oak. The oak has been a sacred tree among primitive peoples, the Greeks, the Romans, and even our own ancestors, the peoples of Northern Europe, associated their highest god with this tree ....[36]

However, even in the far-more ethnically prejudiced 1920s, not all Cookies hailed from Northern European backgrounds, so by 1931 the genealogical reference was omitted from the speech, and a penny was added to the mementos.

> The reason for the penny is to be found in those three Latin words at the top on one side—E pluribus Unum. From the one many ... For Martha Cook can be neither greater nor less than our combined personal interest in it .... May the penny remind you of the interest of the house over individual and may it bring you, each and everyone, Good Luck![37]

The ceremony began with a grand march from the Red Room to the Blue Room where the new residents, wearing white dresses, stood along each side of the room and the "old girls" in formals, stood in front of the north fireplace. Music was played throughout. A soloist performed the MCB song *Oh Happy House of Golden Memories*, the House Board President spoke, and the Directors gave out corsages. The new girls then marched in pairs down the center of

102. (a90) New residents with their roses, 1989

the Blue Room, out through the Red Room and, escorted by the "old girls," into the Dining Room for Sunday Tea.[38]

The tradition was little changed in 1950, although at that point the name became the Cook Memorial Service, everyone wore "afternoon dresses and heels", and more Martha Cook songs were featured. The meal was still Sunday Tea.[39] Ten years later, more revisions made it less formal and less religious (no records have been found documenting what the religious aspects were). Quail spoke about the Building and its history and yellow roses were used in place of corsages.[40]

The 1970s, 1980s, and 1990s usually featured a receiving line with the House Board President, Dietician/Food Service Manager, Director, the Governors, and the U-M President's wife. The House Board President read a speech and presented a yellow rose or carnation, oak leaf, and the *Gold Book* (a description of MCB history and traditions) to each new resident. The tradition continues in 2015. Immediately following a special dinner, there is a receiving line in the Gold Room where the new women are given the time-honored gifts, and the House Board President reads the customary speech.

Dinner for Graduating Women[41] and Turnover Dinner

The Senior Dinner of the early 1930s was a festive, lighthearted affair held the night of the University's Senior Swing-Out.[*] Juniors pinned corsages on the seniors and dancing, sometimes with a three-piece orchestra, occurred later in the evening. In 1932, the juniors wore "kid clothes" and dinner had a school room theme. The 1934 theme was a captain's farewell dinner, complete with invitations that looked like passports, ship centerpieces, a ship's log with humorous couplets for each senior to read, and all was followed by singing and dancing. Seniors wore caps and gowns to Senior Dinner in the 1940s,

---

[*] Senior Swing-out was a University tradition celebrating the first wearing of graduation caps and gowns. It was discontinued in 1934.

and humor continued to be central to the tradition. Undergrads signed up to write a funny verse to a popular song about each grad. Corsages were creative and meant to bring laughter in 1948 when they were fashioned from "everything from Kleenex to bottle caps." The juniors wrote a Senior Will in 1953, with each junior writing a verse about a senior and then acting it out in costume in the Dining Room. That same year, the outgoing House Board sat together as did the twenty-one summer brides. The 1960 Activity File contains a mimeographed copy of the *College Bored Exams: MCB Achievement Test* which was presented as the entertainment. Witty senior wills have been popular on and off for decades. The Senior Dinner report for 1964 notes that they should be kept to one side of a five by eight notecard. That year, they were mimeographed for memorabilia.

The tradition had a near miss in 1950 when it was inadvertently left off the social calendar. "However, mistakes do happen in the best of families—so they say!" wrote chair Doreen Collins. The dinner did still occur, without a skit but with a "coke-tail hour" prior to dinner.

The custom since at least the 1970s has been to present each graduating senior with a rose and a Martha Cook cookbook. One student reported being offended by these in 1993, saying they reflected a time when women left the University to become wives and mothers. Director Gloria Picasso asked House Board to consider alternative gifts, but the Board voted to continue the tradition.[42] The 1993 Dinner for Graduates was unique in that it featured a time capsule, placed in the attic with directions for it to be opened in 2015.[*] Those receiving the Anne E. Shipman Stevens Scholarship for the upcoming fall semester are announced at the Dinner for Graduating Women, as is the Outstanding Resident award recipient.

---

[*] Opening the time capsule is on the schedule for the 100th Anniversary Gala in October 2015.

The tradition has continued. Graduates are recognized individually and given a Martha Cook cookbook and a special keepsake, paid for by House Board. In 2015, graduates received compacts, engraved with the MCB logo.

Turnover Dinner, when the current House Board passes the torch to the newly elected Board and committee chairwomen are officially honored, was frequently combined with the graduation dinner. Silver spoons were the traditional gift for outgoing board members until the 1970s when small, engraved silver bowls were presented. Early in the 2000s, the gift changed again to necklace charms, engraved with the MCB logo. Because of recent changes in the U-M residence hall election cycle, the dinner now occurs in February rather than spring.

Dessert for New Women

Welcoming new residents the spring before they move into Martha Cook is a longstanding tradition originating with Grace Greenwood, the second Social Director, and continuing to the present day. The tea or, as it has been called since at least the 1970s, the Dessert for New Women, is among the keys to the Building's community ambiance. The women are formally invited to attend. At the event, they are greeted by current residents, introduced to one another and served tea in the Gold Room. They are taken on a tour of available rooms and participate in a second tier room draw (current residents choose their rooms first, based on seniority). Leases are signed.

In the earliest years, however, rooms and roommates were chosen by the Building's administration. The 1925 *Annual* recounts, "Those of us who had the privilege of attending that occasion," meaning the first tea for new women, "remember the thrills when Miss Clark gave each one a slip telling what room she would occupy."

For many years, the event was casual, as was the 1947 Cocktail Hour for the New Girls which featured punch, cheewees, pretzsticks, and popcorn.⁴³ Coke parties were traditional in the 1960s and early 1970s and these were often, but not always, separate from room draw. In 1961, the residents held multiple events for the new women beginning with an informal Study Break Party in May at 9 PM when House Board officers and the Director explained about living in Martha Cook. Coke and pretzels were served, followed by group singing around the piano. The prospective Cookies drew numbers for the upcoming room lottery. They were invited to the regular Friday tea two days later and then at 7 PM the next Monday for the official room draw. In both 1965 and 1967, a mid-March Coke Party featured getting-acquainted games, choosing roommates, and picking rooms.

By the 1970s, the Dessert for New Women tea, held in the early evening, became the tradition. In the 1990s, mothers began accompany their daughters, making the party a much larger undertaking. Women who cannot attend or who commit to MCB later in the year may tour available rooms with the Building Director individually or even make all arrangements via phone and email if they are not local.

Birthday Dinners and Martha's Birthday Dinner

Finding ways to celebrate the birthdays of all residents, including those born in the summer months, is a challenge readily taken up by Cookies. In the Building's first year, the Helen Club (informally composed of the fourteen residents named Helen and called Martha Cook's first "inner unit" in the 1916 *Annual*) made a point of seeing that all members' birthdays were observed in some special way, sometimes by arranging for the club to sit together at dinner.⁴⁴

Individual birthdays were regularly commemorated during announcements at sit-down dinner. *Happy Birthday* has been sung countless times. Some years, a monthly dinner was held to recognize birthdays. In 1950, for instance, Diekema wrote,

> One night of each month the committee in charge ... invites all of the residents whose birthdays fall in that month to sit together at the big table in the dining room. The table is always decorated with something ingenious but inexpensive. The pastry cook provides a decorated cake and there are usually favors such as paper hats or something similar.[45]

But in the later 1950s it became the custom to have one big party to celebrate all birthdays at one time. Individual tables were bedecked with symbols for each month of the year and residents sat at the appropriate one. In 1954, the party was arranged to fall on Diekema's birthday.[46] The House Board minutes for March 17, 1958, also favor one all-inclusive party for practical reasons: "The Building has one big annual party for everyone so that the waitresses and people with classes aren't held up throughout the year."[47] This also covered the problem of recognizing summer birthdays. The themes were clever. The 1957 dinner featured an Alice in Wonderland un-birthday party and 1963 had a Zodiac theme with balloons, a "mad astrologer to read horoscopes and seating arranged by the residents' signs."[48] Nonetheless, a special party for summer birthdays has often shown up on MCB's social calendar. In 1974, a paper cake was wheeled into the dining room by the busmen and a busman popped out! The files state, "Carried things a bit far by chasing waitresses with whipped cream."[49]

April 1, 1975, appears to be the first year the summer birthday event merged with April Fool's Day[50] and it went on to become a traditional celebration called Martha's Birthday Dinner (not to be confused with Martha Wolford Cook's actual birthday of September 7, 1828). Costumes were de rigueur for several years. Rather than spooky Halloween regalia, these ranged from silly to edgy. A group of pseudo punk rockers attended the dinner in 1979. In 1980, the Building's three fifth-year residents dressed as grumpy old women. *Venus,* fully draped in a bedsheet, mimes, and a killer bee were among the other dinner attendees. The 1985 party witnessed the infamous and reprehensible food fight which took over two hours to clean up and caused residents to re-think the event.[51]

By the 1990s, themes were the order of the day, such as the 1920s Speakeasy in 1994. The concept of Martha's Birthday Dinner has relaxed over time. Today it consists of a special birthday buffet dinner on April 1, and in 2014–15, Martha's Birthday was celebrated with a Girl's Night In party with residents wearing pajamas on the first floor, watching movies, and doing other typical sleepover activities.

Dining Al Fresco

Dining al fresco has long held appeal in MCB in the early fall and especially in the spring following the long, cold Michigan winter. The beautiful terrace and garden easily lend themselves to meals outdoors. Lunch on the terrace in good weather has probably always occurred informally, as it is so easy to carry a tray out the side door.

Casual outdoor dinners have taken place too, although not many made their way into the Governors' or House Board minutes. On May 28, 1941, the Director's Report recorded that, "the residents indulged in what has come to be the perennial lawn picnic. Instead of eating dinner in the dining room, the girls dressed in picnic clothes and took picnic suppers on trays to the terrace and garden ...." The meal ended with a baseball game between the juniors and seniors.[52] In 1955, Diekema reported the innovation of a picnic supper at 6 PM followed by community singing, games and other entertainments until 8 PM, and culminating in a square dance from 8 PM until midnight. In modern times, barbecues are organized on the tennis court with the staff grilling hamburgers, hot dogs, and veggie burgers.

Messiah Dinner

Messiah Dinner, the elegant, formal event following the final performance of *Handel's Messiah* by the University Musical Society

(UMS),* has been held every year since 1945. The UMS President, Conductor and the four soloists are invited along with the U-M

103. (a90) UMS President Ken Fischer. Messiah Dinner, 1989.

President, Regents, Vice Presidents, Deans, and other high-ranking U-M officials as well as spouses, former MCB Governors, MCAA Board members, other alumnae volunteers, and special friends of MCB. The University President unfortunately has had to send regrets since the 1990s because an event for Big Ten officials has taken precedence. Residents spend weeks planning the invitations, decorations, menu, and entertainment. Once RSVPs arrive, a seating chart is arranged. Residents wear formal gowns. The House President, Messiah Dinner Chairwoman, Building Director, and Governors stand in the receiving line and guests go through with their resident hostesses. Following dinner in the Dining Room (some years additional tables were set up in the corridor), guests traditionally returned to the Gold Room, where additional seating

---

* The Chorale Union first performed Handel's *Messiah* in December 1879. The University Musical Society, which included the Chorale Union, was established a year later in December 1880.

had been arranged during the meal, for a musicale. Residents performed on instruments, sang, danced, or presented short skits. The evening wound down with the Cookie Chorale leading everyone in carols. In recent years, the musicale has not been held, but in 2014 entertainment returned with a spectacular rendition of "Be Our Guest" from *Beauty and the Beast* by several residents in the Dining Room.

Diekema set the first Messiah Dinner in motion when she invited her friends, UMS President Charles Sink and his wife, Alva Gordon

104. (a90) 1989 Musicale

Sink, to dinner at Martha Cook. Alva Sink sent regrets, saying they already had plans that evening to take the guest soloists to dinner following the Sunday matinee of Handel's *Messiah*. Diekema suggested they bring the soloists along, invited President and Mrs. Ruthven and a few others, and a University of Michigan tradition began. Diekema described the event in her December 1945 Director's Report:

Christmas Party, December 16: this took the form of a supper and dessert party on Sunday evening following the Messiah Concert. Twenty-five faculty guests were invited for supper at six. Hostesses met them at the door, took them to dispose of wraps and then brought them into the Red Room where they were introduced to their supper hostesses, who in turn went with them into the Blue Room. There they met more of the girls and chatted until supper was announced. The house wore a gay Christmas air with its huge Christmas tree, and with every window showing a large green wreath, resplendent with its red bow. Mistletoe in all of the doorways served as an excellent "ice breaker."

A committee had decorated the dining room sideboard, mantel and tables with Christmas greens, red bows and white paper angels which they had designed and made. One course was served in the dining room whereupon all adjourned to the Blue Room where seventy-five guests of the girls joined the party for dessert. It was served from a large table in front of the south fireplace. Harriet Risk arranged and presented a charming Christmas program of music and readings which included the story of "The Nativity" with background music which was hummed in harmony by the chorus of thirty voices. It was most impressive! Following the program, Harriet led the entire group in carol singing ....

We all think this is one of the best parties we have ever had and recommend its adoption as a tradition. We regretted that circumstances prevented the Board of Governors from enjoying it with us.[53]

The Governors have been attending ever since. In 1946, the total number of guests for the combined event was a jaw-dropping 305 and in 1950, 350. Inviting additional friends for the dessert portion of the evening was discontinued during Director Isabel Quail's tenure in the 1960s.[54]

Sara Rowe, who planned the meals for the first Messiah Dinner, continued to attend as a guest after she left MCB in 1949. For many years she was included in the receiving line as the event's *grand dame*, but the Messiah file for 1975 states that she asked for that to be her final year to stand.

While every Messiah Dinner has been a lovely and grand event, a few stand out as unusual. In 1948, the residents were asked to reprise their musicale for radio station WHRV on the Tuesday following

Messiah Dinner from 10:30 to 11 PM. "Permission to be out late was secured from the Office of the Dean, cars were borrowed for transportation. After the broadcast, we all had cokes and listened to the recording of the program at the station."[55] The 1964 theme was a Canterbury Christmas and featured a procession through the Dining Room with a boar's head and yule log![56] The first vegetarian entrée

105. (jm) Waitresses just before the 1981 Messiah Dinner

choice was offered to residents and guests in 1993. The 1999 dinner, chaired by Alexandra Berardi '00, Leslie Calhoun '01, Sheila Davis '00, and Meredith Hockman '00, was an especially elegant gala, celebrating the new millennium (or "odometer roll-over" for purists who pointed out that the new century really began in 2001) with a white and silver color scheme. Most memorable of the decorations were the 600 white helium balloons with long silver strings hung from the Gold Room ceiling. The effect was stunning! The Dining Room table decorations sparkled festively. No one guessed at the time, but the shiny objects serving as decorative "rocks" in the bowl-shaped vases were several pounds of baby carrots, spray painted metallic silver. The after dinner entertainment "included comedy skits, vocal, instruments, and dance performances, bound together through the theme *A Retrospective Look Forward.*"[57]

The 2002 Messiah Dinner stands out as an anomaly, the only time the dinner took place on a Saturday and was held prior to the performance. Hill Auditorium was undergoing a massive, eighteen-month renovation which necessitated performing *The Messiah* in the Michigan Theater, the beautifully restored 1927 movie palace located on Liberty Street. Performances occurred only on Friday and Saturday evenings at 8 PM with no Sunday matinee. The House Board, Governors, Director, and UMS staff thought long and hard about how to proceed, and canceling the dinner was seriously considered. However, rather than break the tradition, it was decided to hold the event on Saturday, December 7. A sumptuous early evening buffet was laid out in the corridor by *Venus*. The soloists and conductor were unable to attend, the after-dinner musicale did not occur, and some guests had to dash out the door before dessert to arrive at the performance on time, but it was still a beautiful and impressive party, much appreciated by those who attended.

Director Rosalie Moore wrote the following undated note (probably 1990) to residents regarding the importance of Messiah Dinner in the MCB Social Calendar and in residents' lives that still rings true:

> But on to the more general question as to why we have Messiah Dinner at all. The Governors and I feel that a forty-five year tradition which gives residents a chance to meet one on one with the administrators of their University is a tradition to be cherished .... It is one chance to do something for the University, all the while we sharpen our skills and increase our pride in MCB for being able to put on an event which no other housing unit has the desire nor the resources to provide. I guarantee that the organizational and social skills you learn by participating in events such as Messiah Dinner will stand you in good stead as you go out into the world beyond the University. [58]

Exam Snacks

It is unknown when the tradition of providing late-evening exam snacks during study days and exams began, but it was well established in the 1940s. In February 1941 when daily tea was still part of MCB's routine, the Director's Report states, "For relaxation from study, afternoon tea was served as usual and at ten in the evening, crackers and milk were available in the kitchenettes." The same offerings are mentioned in 1948. In spring 1965, exam snacks were served in the dining room for the first time and a screen was placed across the hall so residents could wear pajamas![59]

The Dining Room remains the favored venue and this has made more elaborate menus possible. The nocturnal spreads are held three times each exam period. Ice cream socials have made regular appearances, at least from the mid-1970s. Today in addition to ice cream, trail mix, make-your-own yogurt parfaits with fresh fruit, vegetables and dip with hummus, and chips and salsa are typical offerings. Current chef, Gary Marquardt, sometimes provides homemade gingerbread for residents to decorate and consume for the December Exam Snacks. Residents help with the planning and the regular first floor dress code does not apply, so pajamas are allowed.

Girls' Night In

Girls' Night In, a Cookie-only evening party revolving around traditional slumber party activities such as movie-watching, getting manicures and pedicures, doing hair, experimenting with make-up, playing games and music and, of course, indulging in snacks, was first documented in the 2000 *Annual*. It has been a tradition ever since and is among the rare occasions when pajamas may be worn on the first floor. It is usually a fall Welcome Week activity, but can be held at any time during the school year, and sometimes occurs during the winter term, too.

Harry Potter Week

March 2009 saw the inaugural Harry Potter Week at MCB, combining floor bonding and raising money for charity with the wildly popular book series the current generation grew up reading. It is still going strong in 2015. For a week, the Martha Cook Building becomes Hogwarts Castle, the novels' magical boarding school, with each of the floors taking on the identity of one of the school's four houses (the mezzanines join with the first floor). The Dining Services staff sets the bar high with a special Harry Potter Buffet dinner. One evening is a movie night in the Gold Room with themed snacks, crafts, and Harry Potter films. Residents decorate, wear Hogwarts house colors, devise floor passwords, and compete in the Penny Wars. Each "house" has a jar. Pennies are positive points, while paper and silver money (donated by rival houses), result in negative points. The floor with the most positive or least negative points at the end of the week wins the House Cup and all money goes to a charity such as Ronald McDonald House, Relay for Life, or Dance Marathon.* Everything culminates in a rousing game of Quidditch in the garden on Saturday. The rules to this game change from year to year, but nerf balls, hula hoop goals, and Cookie charm are staples, and the prize is a stash of pennies.

A list of Martha Cook traditions is always a work in progress. Customs change, disappear, and sometimes even return again. New traditions emerge. They are freshened each year by the enthusiasm, creativity, and whimsy of the women who call MCB home. The

---

* Since 1997, Dance Marathon has been a U-M campus institution, raising over $5 million to support children's programs at Mott Children's Hospital in Ann Arbor and Beaumont Hospital in Royal Oak, MI. MCB is active in the organization.

Cookie community is the constant and alumnae from any era will always find a familiar aura when they return to visit.

CHAPTER TWENTY

Tradition: Phantoms of the Past

During these twenty years that the Building has been open many splendid activities have been evolved. Some have served their temporary purpose and disappeared.
                                                             Marion Slemons[1]

In *The First Twenty Years*, Marion Slemons whimsically referred to MCB's lost and abandoned practices as phantom traditions. Eighty years later, the list has grown longer. These events, which occurred for short periods or ended long ago, provide a window into enthusiasms of other eras. They also demonstrate that, as tastes change, Cookies have always been open to trying something new. The Martha Cook Building is not a museum for early twentieth century ideas and events are not continued simply because "that's how we've always done it." And who knows—future residents may read about a phantom tradition and creatively find a way to bring it back to life in a modern context.

The Name Game

Cookies who lived at MCB prior to 1973 remember—some fondly, others with horror (whichever emotion is felt is probably directly related to how well one scored)—the Name Game. During the first few weeks of sit-down dinners each fall, residents were assigned a different seat in the dining room each evening so that they met virtually each fellow Cookie. Some years they also wore name tags. Then, they were tested on the names. In most years, those with the ten lowest scores were required to perform a skit at a later all-house party, usually Halloween, but sometimes it dragged on until December or did not happen at all. The test began in 1915 as a game played in the Blue Room when each and every girl stood in turn to be recognized. Some years, residents could attend with curlers and robes, making it more difficult to recognize them. Another year, they came dressed for a beach party, "to give the affair glamour and interest ...."[2] In 1940, the game changed to a dining room activity. It was held as the opening to an all-house meeting in 1958. By fall 1968, it returned to a dinner event with only ten randomly chosen women standing to be named.

House Board spent several weeks discussing whether to eliminate the contest in 1955, although nothing came of it.[3] The name challenge continued with varying degrees of enthusiasm until it simply disappeared from Cookie life in 1973 with no mention in House Board minutes, Directors' reports, or Governors' minutes.

Laying a Wreath on Martha Cook's Grave

On October 8, 1915, the Governors voted to establish the tradition of laying a wreath on Martha Wolford Cook's grave in Hillsdale each April 16th as a way of honoring both the Building's namesake and benefactor on the latter's birthday.[4] It was still an annual ritual in 1935 when the Governors' Minutes state that a wreath was to be sent

June 4th, the anniversary of Cook's death.[5] No further references have been found.

Vespers and Senior Vespers

Vespers were conducted on Sundays following the evening meal during MCB's second and third years. Senior Vespers, held near Commencement, was one of Governor Anne E. Shipman Stevens' ideas and began in 1916. Originally, all U-M senior women were invited to tea on the terrace, but by 1918, the gathering was a tea in the Blue Room for residents and their guests. When held very close to graduation day, parents attended. Senior Vespers was not as popular as Mrs. Stevens' Christmas Breakfast inspiration, and it ended in 1935 by a vote of the residents.[6] It was unequivocally religious and included area ministers. Mrs. Stevens herself read scripture or, as in 1918, from *The Contented Heart* by Lucy Keeler.[7] By rule, the elevator was off limits during the service as the noise was distracting.[8]

Scholarship Dinner and Silver Spoons

The first Scholarship Dinner was held March 14, 1917. It was a rollicking affair. Some residents wore costumes which included President Hutchins and a Dean whose moustache would not stay in place. The Building's highest academic achievers were presented with a gold bar pin, engraved with the University insignia, resident's name, the letter "A" (recognizing the woman's A average), the date and MCB.[9] In 1934, the token changed to a desk set with an onyx base and engraved gold plate.[10] During World War II "the perennial pen sets were not available …. sterling silver charm bracelets were purchased and bangles were made for them, on one side of which was the Martha Cook crest."[11] War bonds with $25 maturity were the gift in 1945,[12] and in 1949, silver spoons engraved with the MCB logo and recipients' initials were given to the ten straight-A women.

"They were as pleased with the spoons as with the bonds," wrote Diekema. "If they were disappointed there was no evidence of it."[13]

106. (a17) The first Scholarship Dinner, 1917

The silver spoons had already been the traditional end of year gift to House Board for some time. When Diekema reported on the 1949 House Board recognition dinner, she commented that, "the silver spoons—souvenirs of their work for the house—proved most acceptable as always."[14] In the 1950s it became customary to award spoons to a larger number of residents. "Since the Building stresses activities as well as scholarship, these awards are also made. The same silver spoons which are used for the Scholarship Dinner are used for [Graduation Dinner] occasion, too,"[15] noted the 1950 Activities Chairwoman. Over the next several years, spoons were given to the nurse, chorister, head waitress, night chaperone, outstanding seniors, and, in 1959, to Pakistani resident Viquar Quadri.[16]

Silver spoons continued to be presented into the early 1970s at the turnover and graduation celebrations. Why the tradition ended is unknown. The Scholarship dinner was discontinued in 1968 when University policy changed and grades were no longer publically disclosed.[17]

Ivy Day

According to Slemons, "Ivy Day was started by the seniors of 1919 who planted English Ivy along the north side of the Building as a living memorial. The custom was continued only two or three years for it was found impossible to get the ivy to grow on the grounds." Ivy was planted again at a later, unspecified date, and while it took root and climbed the walls, it was completely removed in the early 2000s because of the potential for damage to the brick.

President's Dinner

The long Messiah Dinner tradition had a forerunner with the President's Dinner and Formal Dinner with the Deans. Invitations were sent weeks in advance and the seating chart was arranged so guests were spread throughout the dining room, involving as many residents as possible. The event is documented several times in the 1930s and 1940s, usually in November or December, but occasionally in the spring. The 1939 President's Supper was even held following the *Messiah* concert. Building Director Leona Diekema described it:

> President and Mrs. Ruthven were the guests of honor at a Christmas supper party. More than fifty members of the administrative faculty including the wives accepted our invitation. Guests were seated at tables in the candle-lighted dining room where a delicious two-course supper, suggestive of the Christmas season, was served. The large overflow was cared for in the corridor adjoining. After dinner, Christmas music in the Blue Room added charm to the occasion which, it seemed to me, went beautifully. The girls were enthusiastic hostesses and the guests responded most genuinely to their efforts. If the guests reacted as the girls did, it can truthfully be said that it was a successful party.[18]

An amusing glitch happened at the 1944 event, proving that even the best laid plans do "gang aft a-gley." According to the Social Director's Report,

> President and Mrs. Ruthven had also been invited but through some error, they had appeared unexpectedly on the preceding Sunday. We thought it part of diplomacy not to reinvite them especially since we

had pulled an excellent impromptu party for them 'out of a hat' as it were – with a program of music after dinner and everything.[19]

The Martha Cook Building has long been proud of its ability to make an occasion special, even at very short notice!

Football Open House

The football open house, commonly featuring cider, coffee, and doughnuts, was a popular, casual event until the 1980s when the advent of more frequently televised games with varying kickoff times made it inconvenient to plan the parties. The increased popularity of tailgating at other venues also contributed to the demise of football open houses. MCAA attempted to revive the custom in October 2001, but it was so poorly attended, they never tried it again.[20]

Informal dances were common following games in the 1920s according to the annuals. The even less formal open houses were first documented in the Social Director's Report of 1935, although they may well have begun earlier. Sara Rowe wrote to Governor Marguerite Chapin Maire in October 1938 to report that over 200 guests had attended that week's open house.[21] Open houses were held after all home games during much of the 1950s. Inviting West Point cadets to MCB following the U-M vs. Army game was tried occasionally, either for an open house or for dinner. Records from 1963 indicate that three open houses were held that year. In the mid-1970s, the Building held between five and seven open houses per football season for residents, their friends and parents, and alumnae. The chairwoman wrote in her 1975 report that extra amounts of food were required for Homecoming and the Ohio State game. She added that a table should be set up at the end of the corridor in front of *Venus*, with food, napkins, dishes, and a trash can. The chair needed to leave the game a few minutes early to be sure everything was ready in time.

The open houses have been replaced by special Friday teas to "kick off" Homecoming weekend or other important football games. Maize and blue abounds and the dining staff bakes appropriate treats, such as block M cookies with blue or yellow frosting.

Away Game Football Lotteries

Beginning in 1925, residents contributed a small amount of money early each fall to the lottery. The proceeds were enough to send one or two residents to an out-of-town football game, and names were drawn in the Blue Room with suitable fanfare.[22] As explained in the 1929 House President's Report, "One girl is always sent to out-of-town football games, provided they are not too far away. The lottery system has proved successful. Expenses there and back are paid by the House."[23] Presumably enough other students on campus also went to the games to provide company and make the trip fun. In 1942, however, "they collected money, bought two $18.75 bonds and drew lots for ownership, instead of using the money to attend the Ohio Game."[24] Diekema referred to the tradition being revived in 1946, with four residents having their expenses paid to attend the Ohio State game, "via a special train leaving Ann Arbor early in the am and returning late at night." It is unknown when this was discontinued.

107. (a28) *Bridge* by Anne Schell '29

Bridge Tournaments

Bridge tournaments were extremely popular in Martha Cook at one time. Six were held from the late 1920s to the 1931–32 school year. According to Marion Slemons in *The First Twenty*

Years, the Blue Room was reserved for bridge on Tuesday nights for several weeks and a Grand Prize was offered at the end. Unfortunately, the prize is unknown. In September 1926, a bridge party was one of the first get-acquainted activities of the year, followed by a six-week tournament.[25]

May Day Flower Basket

Cookies used to celebrate spring by presenting the University President (who has always been considered a Martha Cook neighbor) a May basket filled with flowers, sometimes at 10:30 PM on April 30 and sometimes during the day on May 1. The women serenaded the President, too. Slemons does not mention it in *The First Twenty Years*. Perhaps Cookies were too busy preparing for the grand May Day teas in that earlier era. The May basket tradition is cited in the 1936 *Annual*, however, with the ditty, "Under the stars and the lawyers' eyes, We greeted the Ruthvens with a happy surprise." By 1961, it was described as an old MCB tradition where "the President and the Vice President will deliver a May basket to the Hatchers from the Martha Cook Student organization."[26] The custom ended in 1964 when the academic calendar changed and winter term was completed in late April instead of June.

108. (a37) Flowers for the Ruthvens, 1937

The Fresh Air Camp Party

Fresh Air Camp, located about twenty-five miles from campus, has been affiliated with U-M since 1921 and began as a camp for underprivileged children. It later specialized in camping experiences for handicapped children. Apparently, it was available as a venue for campus groups to hold social events during the off season, for a picnic at Fresh Air Camp was an early 1950s Cookie tradition. The first was held October 12, 1951 when it replaced the fall informal dance. Residents chartered University buses which picked up Cookies and their dates at 5:30 PM. The cost of the residents' meals was covered by House Board money and the women paid for their dates. The MCB dining staff packed the food which included frankfurters, potato salad, relishes, buns, cake, and coffee. "With the help of the escorts, the coffee and frankfurters were prepared out there in the club house," according to Leona Diekema, who chaperoned with House Director Sara Rowe. Square dancing followed the meal. She continued, "It really was a barrel of fun and will doubtless become a perennial affair."[27]

Knitting at Sit-Down Dinner

Late 1950s through mid-1960s House Board minutes record that knitting was allowed during dinner from November through December with the exception of Sunday and Faculty Dinners. This was typically announced at a house meeting.[28] Presumably, a high percentage of Cookies' nearest and dearest received scarves and sweaters for Christmas in those days!

Wine Tasting Parties

The legal drinking age in the state of Michigan was lowered to eighteen on January 1, 1972, raised to nineteen on December 3, 1978, and then raised again to twenty-one on December 21, 1978, During this period, kegs were allowed at campus mixers. Green beer was sometimes served in the Martha Cook Dining Room on St. Patrick's Day and a half keg of Stroh's Light beer was on the menu for a German dinner in February 1976.[29] Wine was a choice at a French-inspired international dinner. And then there were Building Director Olive Chernow's wine and cheese tasting parties!

She got the idea after completing a wine tasting course through Walter Rosenberg, a Detroit-area wine merchant and a U-M graduate. The first party was in January 1974. Four were held during Chernow's six years as Director.[30] They were very successful. Different wines and complimentary cheeses were arranged around the dining room and Rosenberg provided humorous educational commentary for Cookies and their dates.

Residents' Talent Show

To benefit the Martha Cook Building's fundraising drive to finance a new slate roof, the residents held a talent show titled *Raising the Roof* in Lydia Mendelssohn Theater the evening of Spring Tea in April 2007. Residents staged a variety show featuring song, dance, musical instruments and skits. Cookies, their friends and families, and alumnae attended and were delightfully entertained. A similar show was performed in February 2008. This one was called *You Can't Stop the Beat* and was also held in Mendelssohn. The wintry weather affected attendance. One more show was held March 27, 2010, at UMIX (a series of late night activities sponsored by U-M's Office of Student Life) in the Underground at The League.

The 1990 *Annual* commemorates a "No Talent Show" where residents took a break from studying and gathered in the Gold Room for an evening of sublime silliness. Skits, music, and a chorus line of dancing onions were part of the residents-only entertainment.

Hot Water Ditty

Generations of Cookies remember the ditty attached to all toilet stall doors in Martha Cook prior to 1998 when, at long last, plumbing improvements made it unnecessary:

> Hot water burns with a mighty power
> So before you flush, please call "Shower!"

If a fellow resident was showering when it was time to flush, loudly calling "shower" first was required, as the water would become dangerously hot for a few moments. The woman showering responded, "thank you," stepped aside (fortunately, MCB's shower stalls are generously sized), and flushing could safely occur. While many women undoubtedly feel nostalgic about the poem and can recite it verbatim long past graduation, no one is sorry the problem has been corrected and the tradition has died.

Each of the traditions included in this chapter existed over multiple years and affected many women. Other customs were special to specific years at the Building or were personal to small groups of friends. Many experiences were not recorded and so are phantoms of a different sort. But all, officially recorded or not, are part of Cookies' shared history and bring a smile when recounted.

CHAPTER TWENTY ONE

Coming Home: Alumnae Reunions

Thy great doors will swing wide to welcome me,
And Portia's calm face almost seems to smile
Bernice Cornell '27[1]

William Cook wanted the Martha Cook Building to be a college home, not simply a residence, and that goal has been achieved year after year. Not only do Cookies make lifelong friends as residents and even as alumnae, but they return to the Building itself, singly, in pairs, with families, and for reunions, in droves.

1919 Reunion and the First Alumnae Gift
The class of 1919 considered itself special because it included the first "four-year girls" who had lived in the Building their entire college career. They held a class reunion at MCB in October 1919, a mere four months after graduation, demonstrating the propensity of alumnae to come back. They also demonstrated the tradition of giving back to their college home with the first recorded alumnae gift to Martha Cook. It was a high chair, presented with fanfare and complete with pink and blue satin ribbons, which was carefully chosen to be a good match for the dining room furniture.[2] The high

chair does not seem to have been used often but as recorded in the 1925 *Annual,* the residents continued to have hopes for it:

> the high chair which was presented by the class of 1919 looks lonesome as it stands unused in the back hall. Let us hope that one day we may have a tradition of an annual baby party when all the new 'cookies' of our cradle roll may be royally welcomed.

The chair was never mentioned again.

Reunion Weekends

From 1926 until 1938, a series of alumnae reunion weekends were major events on the residents' social calendar. Held the weekend of the Junior Girls Play, a popular campus event which by the 1920s was raising funds for a Michigan League building,[3] upwards of one hundred women returned to MCB for meals, tea, bridge parties, and the play. Astonishing to modern sensibilities, the alumnae stayed in the Building for the whole weekend. Cots were set up in the guestrooms, library and music room, as well as in the student rooms. Some residents vacated their own quarters for the weekend. MCB must have been wall to wall with women! All reports indicate that everyone considered this great fun.

The 1932 Social Director's Report spelled out the schedule. A few women arrived on Friday to stay the night, but the majority came on Saturday for bridge, tea, dinner, and the Junior Girls Play which was followed by a skit back at the dorm. This was presented by the residents and typically related to the play. Alumnae joined in the traditional Sunday morning breakfast served in the upstairs kitchenettes, and later in the day there was a musicale. In 1926, according to the *Annual,* Governor Anne E. Shipman Stevens sent candy and prizes for the "most splendiferous bridge party" on Saturday afternoon and after the alums were "snugly tucked in their beds, they were serenaded by the girls on the terrace side ...."

The House Board President commented in 1933 that next time there should be a $1 registration fee to divide between the Building and those residents "forced to take their meals out," as MCB could not accommodate everyone and the alumnae guests came first.⁴ The weekend event was not held in 1933 due to finances, and 1938 was the final year, interest having run its course in combination with restrictions brought on by the Depression. The Vice President wrote in her 1938 report, "... the whole idea seems to be passé as far as the alumnae are concerned, because not enough enrolled to make it worthwhile. If it is to be continued at all, it might better take place every two or three years."⁵ The House Board President suggested replacing it with a dinner or tea.⁶

A May 28, 1946, letter from Frances Osborn Gibson '39, who experienced the last of the weekends as a junior, provides a glimpse from a resident's point of view: "When I lived at the building I remember how funny I thought it was during alumni week when a gray haired lady popped out of the elevator at each floor and bellowed down the halls, 'Where is the class of 1919?!' Now I'd like to do exactly the same thing myself."⁷

25ᵗʰ Jubilee, Saturday October 12, 1940

MCB's Twenty-fifth Anniversary was celebrated with panache. Thelma James '20 was the chairwoman and Leona Diekema, only in her second year as Social Director, was in charge of arrangements on campus and in the building. The Governors authorized covering many of the expenses, including paid help to check addresses against the University Alumni Office. The 1941 *Annual* was more elaborate than the previous few to commemorate the occasion in style and related,

> Martha Cookies of previous years began to move in on Friday afternoon and every available room in the building was occupied by an extra cot to take care of the large influx of guests. By Saturday noon, almost seven hundred alumnae were present.

All of these women did not stay under the MCB slate roof. Diekema's October report states that seventy-seven women stayed in the Building.

The weekend's instructions[8] for residents were elaborate, filling three typed pages. Women were expected to give up their beds to guests. The rules for the Saturday tea were headed by, "WEAR LONG DRESSES and BE ON TIME," and further admonished, "Please do not eat while you are serving (it gives an undignified appearance)." The instructions conclude, "Each of us has a high standard of perfection to live up to for the parties here at the Martha Cook Building have always been spoken of with admiration and delight as 'a visible expression of gracious living.'"

There was a massive reception Saturday afternoon from 3:30 until 5 PM, attended by almost twelve hundred persons.[9] Tea, cookies, nuts, and ice cream molded in the form of a pair of silver bells were served in the dining room and residents worked shifts as hostesses.

The Jubilee banquet, with a blue and yellow color scheme, was held in the Michigan League Ballroom and attended by 500, including residents. A waiter is the only man visible in the photo in the '41 *Annual*. Thelma James, Diekema and representatives from ten classes were the speakers,[10] and following dinner was a style show featuring *Things We Used to Wear and Music We Used to Hear – a Panorama of the Clothes and Music of Twenty-five Years* with a commentator, models, and an accompanist.[11]

A multi-page newspaper titled *Jubilee Bells*[12] was compiled for the Twenty-fifth Anniversary. It contains articles about the Building, Anne E. Shipman Stevens, and many submissions from alumnae covering everything from their careers to their hobbies, families, and travels, providing a wonderful insight into the lives of U-M women graduates in the first half of the twentieth century.

109. (a41) Twenty-fifth Jubilee banquet

Victory Reunion, June 20–22, 1946

The University held a reunion over commencement weekend to celebrate the end of World War II and to honor the alumni who served and died. The Martha Cook Building participated and sent invitations to alumnae which led to a great many fond responses but few attendees. A letter from Genevieve Goodman Johnson '26 was typical: "It is hard to express what Martha Cook has meant to me – the lasting friendships, the lovely associations and a feeling of affection for a dear home from which I still carry a residue of happiness."[13]

50th Anniversary, October 22–23, 1965

Under the direction of Chair Adele Huebner '54, the planning committee chose a non-football weekend for the Golden Jubilee and met several times to work out details. An updated address list was one of the first orders of business. The Ann Arbor women eventually typed five-part mailing labels, one of which became part of the Building's master file. Invitations were mailed to 1,655 alumnae.

The 500 who attended the weekend events began arriving at the Martha Cook Building on Friday, October 22.[14] Upon registering, each was given an anniversary booklet (these were unexpectedly held up at the printer and not delivered until the last minute), registration list, maps, and U-M literature. Early arrivals were welcome to attend Friday tea at the Building, and at 8 PM alumnae gathered in the Red Room for a slide presentation by the U-M Associate Director of Admissions on admissions policy. Sixty-five attended.

Saturday morning, Dr. Allan F. Smith, U-M Vice President of Academic Affairs, spoke in the Law Club Lounge to ninety alumnae on *Today's Faculty*. Bus tours took place from 11 AM until 1:30 PM, and a formal anniversary tea was held from 3 to 5 PM at the Building with residents and U-M officials invited. Retired Social Director Leona Diekema was among those in the receiving line (looking, according to Olive Chernow, "as beautiful, regal and charming as ever[15]) and 750 guests passed through.

The Michigan League Ballroom was again the banquet site, and the menu included fruit compote, breast of chicken a la Kiev, fried rice, cranberry relish, salad with chervil dressing, rolls, and eggnog rum chiffon pie.[16] The room must have been largely filled with women as the instructions for the Registration Committee had earlier stated, "Husbands are invited to all activities except the banquet .... Female guests at the banquet will be accepted by special arrangement."[17] Emilie Sargent '16, the first House President as well as the first alumna to sit on the Board of Governors, was mistress of ceremonies. U-M President Harlan Hatcher addressed the 385 in attendance. Special Regents Citations were presented to three women: Thelma James '20, Estefania Aldaba Lim PhD'42 and

Katayun Hormusji Cama MS'36, PhD'38.* Only Thelma was in attendance. Adele Huebner presented the Board of Governors with a formal letter stating the intention of the alumnae to give the Building a gift of a statue for the Garden.

The MCAAD had given the Building a silver tea set three days earlier, dedicating it at a Faculty Dinner on October 20, 1965.[18] Olive Chernow, then the President of the MCAAD, did the honors. The dinner was also attended by Adele Huebner and Governors Elizabeth Black Ross and Marguerite Chapin Maire. The tea set was placed on a small table in the dining room, covered by a white linen table cloth and after the meal, Chernow spoke and as she told it:

> I said that we wished to express our appreciation for the values and traditions we had learned and experienced while living there and we wished to add to their enjoyment .... I lifted the tablecloth. I was stunned. Everyone burst into laughter. Someone had tied a tiger's tail to the spigot. Adele quipped, "You've got a tiger in your tank, Olive." (That was the Pontiac Motor slogan that year.) I laughed, too. That's the way it is at Martha Cook – elegant, but not stuffy.[19]

60th Anniversary, April 3, 1976

The MCAAD asked Director Olive Chernow if they could hold their spring scholarship benefit tea at the Building in 1976. It was Miss Chernow's idea to celebrate MCB's sixtieth year. She

---

* Florentine Cook Heath handled recommendations for University of Michigan Regents Citations. Thelma James '20, professor of English at Wayne State University was noted for her expertise in folklore and her lectures on the Bible. She was also an intrepid MCB volunteer, heading up the Twenty-fifth Anniversary among other projects. Estefania J. Aldaba Lim PhD '42, was a Barbour Scholar, Director of the Institute for Human Relations at Philippine Women's University, member of the executive board of the World Federation of Mental Health, International Council of Psychologists and UNESCO. Katayun Hormusji Cama MS'36, PhD'38 was a Barbour Scholar, research consultant to the Bernard van Leer Foundation in the Netherlands, and was previously on the faculty of the Tata Institute of Social Science, Magistrate of the Juvenile court of Bombay, consultant to the UN and faculty chair of the International Institute of Social Studies at The Hague.

contacted the *University Record* and they ran an article, including photographs of a sit-down dinner and interviews with the residents receiving Anne E. Shipman Stevens Scholarships for the fall 1976, to publicize the event. She also contacted Ann Arbor historian Wystan Stevens, then the curator at Ann Arbor's Kempf House, to write a brochure for the Building, and she procured a new U-M flag to hang from the front of the Building. She described the day:

> Approximately 200 people attended. A tour of campus by bus was arranged for forty alumnae. The President of the Detroit Chapter, Mrs. Ann Hanson Perkins, presented an engraved silver punch bowl and ladle from the Detroit group .... Mrs. Connie Amick, President of the Ann Arbor Chapter, presented a check for $100 to be used for records for the stereo set .... Governor Veronica Smith donated two football tickets on the fifty yard line [as a door prize]. The scholarship recipients were announced and introduced .... It was a day for reminiscing and renewing friendships.[20]

75th Diamond Jubilee, October 26–28, 1990

The Seventy-fifth Anniversary weekend was, like the Fiftieth, a group effort between Building, residents, MCAA, and the Ann Arbor alumnae. Shirley Brown Vaughn '55 was the General Chairwoman and when she became ill, Elaine Macklin Didier '70, AMLS'71, PhD'82 stepped in to provide leadership.[21] A booklet briefly describing the Building and its residents was produced. MCAA members headed by Colleen Burns London '65 gathered information and dealt with printing, and Lynn Zimmerman Bloom '56 and Bernice Pericin Kostanecki '56 were the editors.

Registration began in June with a four page, double-sided invitation mailed to alumnae.[22] It included a call for sponsors to help defray expenses. Alumnae were encouraged to send either a business card or personal information to be designed into an advertisement and, for a donation, these were printed in the official program. Everyone was required to pay both the $3 registration fee and $5 dues for the MCAA fiscal year.

The weekend began with registration and a social mixer between 5 and 8 PM Friday, October 26. Saturday's events included late registration and bus tours of Central and North Campuses in the morning, followed by an afternoon tea at Martha Cook. There was music and a historical display of photos, articles and documents organized by Olive Chernow. Trudy Veneklasen Huebner '36, an alumna and former U-M Regent (1967–74), spoke and Margaret Yerkes Holden, House Board President in 1918, a former Governor and the oldest alumna at the Jubilee, re-dedicated *Portia*. She helped dedicate the statue when it was originally installed.

Alumnae gathered again for a 5:45 PM social hour at the Michigan League prior to the formal banquet. Honored guests included the present and former Governors and Building Directors, the chairwomen, MCAA President, resident leaders as well as U-M President and Mrs. James Duderstadt, former U-M Presidents Harlan Hatcher and Robben Fleming, Regent Deane Baker, and Interim VP for Student Services Mary Ann Swain. Elaine Didier welcomed everyone and introduced the honored guests. Veronica Latta Smith '48, a U-M Regent and former MCB Governor and MCAA President, introduced President Duderstadt who spoke briefly.

Following the traditional Roll Call of the Classes, Ann Bradford Cook, William Cook's great-niece and a former MCB Governor, regaled the audience with "Tales of William and Martha." She described Martha's plum pudding recipe, which brought a laugh from everyone as tastes had changed considerably in the years since the Building's namesake was last in a kitchen.

Dr. Penelope Pearl Russianoff '39, MCLPS '41, an alumna, clinical psychologist, professor, and author who "played herself" in the film *An Unmarried Woman*, was the featured speaker. Her theme was "The Feminine Advantage," and she recounted stories from her own years at MCB and changes in women's roles since her graduation. After songs performed by the residents' Cookie Chorale, led by Susan K. Duderstadt MD'93, MPH'94, and everyone joining in with *The Yellow and Blue*, the party broke up for the night.

Alumnae reconvened at the Building on Sunday for brunch and the Michigan historical marker dedication. The marker, installed in front of MCB, was the MCAA's anniversary gift. The Building became eligible for this official designation after being placed on the State Register of Historic Sites in October 1989.[23] Janet Kreger '72, who researched and filed the paperwork with the State Historical Commission, discussed the Building's architectural and historical features. Dr. Martha Bigelow, Director of the Bureau of History and Executive Secretary of the Michigan Historical Commission, spoke of the importance of preserving distinctive architectural sites. Margaret Holden, as the eldest alumna in attendance, dedicated the marker.

110. (mcb) Margaret Yerkes Holden '18

111. (mcb)

90th Anniversary Gala, September 23–25, 2005

The Martha Cook Building's Ninetieth Anniversary party was co-chaired by Sheila Davis '00, MBA '11 and Jennifer Munfakh Shaw '00, MSEE '01. Two hundred alumnae and approximately seventy guests converged on Ann Arbor for at least some of the events. They came from across the United States, Canada, the United Kingdom, and Palestine.[24] Registration began on Friday afternoon and alumnae gathered for tea, time to peruse the memorabilia boards, and a first look at *Edwina*, the new statue in the foyer.

"Built to Last"
Friendship • Home • Tradition

112. (bgm) Ninetieth logo

113. (wjd) Ninetieth attendees in the Gold Room.

Many alumnae and some spouses participated in the Decade Dinners that evening. Local alums from each decade made reservations at different local restaurants for attendees from their era. A wonderful time was had by everyone, and Decade Dinners may be a new Martha Cook reunion tradition. No one, however, ate dessert, but that had nothing to do with watching calorie intake; the next event provided a dessert buffet.

The Dessert Reception, held at the Gerald R. Ford Presidential Library on North Campus, was the weekend's formal kickoff event. It was an especially appropriate venue because not only had President Ford attended dinner at Martha Cook in 1977, but the Library Director was MCB alumna and former Governor Elaine Macklin Didier '70, AMLS'71, PhD'82. She was the evening's hostess and read a letter of welcome personally sent and signed by President Ford. Rousing entertainment was provided by the Friars, the U-M Men's Glee Club A Capella group. Over 150 attended.

Saturday featured a campus bus tour with MCB residents as guides. The sixty participants spontaneously sang *The Victors* as they passed Michigan Stadium. Attendees reconvened at MCB in the afternoon for the Tailgate Tea, a casual celebration free to all alumnae. Many alumnae wore maize and blue, and vintage Michigan apparel was encouraged. Awards were given for Most Spirited Attire, Oldest MCB T-shirt, and Oldest U-M T-shirt or Sweatshirt. The late 1970s group won the Decade Tea Cheer contest, a battle to devise the most clever Martha Cook pep cheer that pitted teams of alumnae, bonded by their graduation years' decade, against each other.

Everyone needed to find a place to change clothes for the formal banquet. Some went to hotel rooms, some changed in MCB bathrooms, others went to homes of nearby friends, and by dinner time, all were dressed up for the Gala Dinner, held as is now traditional in the Michigan League Ballroom. Each place setting featured a beautifully wrapped chocolate bar molded with the MCB logo. Introduced by her husband and fellow researcher, Professor Nicholas Steneck,

> Dr. Margaret Steneck gave the keynote address on the origins of the Martha Cook Building, sharing photos and historical insights that placed MCB's opening in historical context .... Dr. Steneck described Martha Cook women as sharing a ninety-year tradition of embracing change while maintaining tradition.[25]

Sunday was the traditional alumnae brunch at the Building. Following the sumptuous buffet, Cookies gathered in the Gold Room for the formal statue dedication by the artist, alumna Edwina Jaques '70, MFA'75. She was introduced by Dr. Diane Kilpatrick, a friend and her former U-M professor. Catherine Walsh Davis '70, '76, chair of the MCB Board of Governors, revealed the statue's name, *Edwina*.

As alumnae left the Martha Cook Building that afternoon, the conversations were about the wonderful time they had, the friends they met and anticipation for the 100th Anniversary in ten more years. Cookies have always relished returning to their college home and it is safe to say that when the celebration comes to a close at the end of the 100th Anniversary weekend October 23–25, 2015, the women who once lived in MCB will again look ahead to their next reunion.

As this book goes to press, maize and blue banners commemorating 100 years of community, friendship and service, hang from the Martha Cook Building façade and from lampposts on South University Avenue and State Street. They were in place to welcome residents on move-in day and will remain for the entire fall term.

114. (bgm) The Building is ready for its 100th anniversary

Postscript: The Future

What does the future hold for the Martha Cook Building? Will the Building look the same? Will the community still exist, and if it does, will it be the same as that envisioned by William Cook?

The Structure

MCB was built of the finest materials and the residents, staff, and Board of Governors have been excellent stewards. But, much of the Building's infrastructure is 100 years old and normal wear and tear and technological advances require some refitting.

Until final plans are drawn, financing obtained and everything is approved by the U-M Board of Regents, details regarding a renovation are mere speculation. But, to date, all surveys of the Building and discussion by the MCB Board of Governors have assumed that outwardly, this unique residence hall will continue to look as it does now, changes to the infrastructure will be opaque and the Building's historical integrity will be respected. It is logical to predict that the renovation will include new plumbing and electrical wiring, reconfigurations of bathrooms and some student rooms to make them handicapped accessible, reconstructed kitchen facilities, and an upgrade to the heating and cooling system, including the addition of air conditioning.

Past Building surveys are likely to be consulted as plans for the deep renovation are made. The kitchen and pantry areas have been problematic since the Building first opened and, as reported elsewhere in this book, the Governors sought advice from York and Sawyer in 1946.[1] In 1971, the U-M Department of Environmental Health and Safety surveyed the kitchen and recommended that it be modernized.[2] In 1998, University Housing Facilities Department surveyed the mechanical systems and noted that while all were adequate, they were nearing the end of their useful life.[3] In the following year, a larger survey financed by University Housing was performed on all residence halls, including MCB, by the ISES Corporation.[4] To better determine those areas of the Building which were of greatest historical significance and would therefore require special renovation techniques, architect Debra Ball Johnson '80, MArch'82 and historic preservationist Janet Kreger '72 recommended in 2000 that the Governors contract with Quinn Evans (QE), an Ann Arbor architecture firm which specializes in historic preservation, to assess MCB's historical relevance.[5] To lower the cost of the survey, Janet and Kathy Moberg '79, undertook the architectural inventory of the Building and provided the data to QE. The Martha Cook Alumnae Association volunteered to pay half the $10,000 cost of the survey. QE found, not surprisingly, that the most architecturally significant spaces were the high-visibility public spaces on the first floor. The most recent and most detailed survey of the Building was prepared by the firm of Lord Aeck Sargent in 2012 and provides the basic data from which architectural plans may be drawn closer to the time of the renovation.

The Community

In most years since 1997, the occupancy of the Martha Cook Building has been 100 percent of available beds and, often, there has been a waiting list of women seeking admission. This, along with the participation rates in house activities, bodes well for the future of the community. It is reasonable to assume that there will continue to be a large enough body of women seeking traditional living to ensure that MCB continues to exist in the future as a residence hall for women.

But will the community be as William Cook envisioned? The answer to that is a resounding yes and no. If the past is prologue, MCB will continue to be more than a residence hall, a home away from home, a place where tradition is valued, and it will continue to attract the "choicest spirits of the University," women of "character and womanly grace."[6] But, even during Cook's lifetime, the definitions of character and womanly grace were changing and the MCB community had moved beyond William Cook's ken. It was more diverse in terms of class year, ethnicity and citizenship, and schools and colleges than Cook preferred and, since his death, that trend has only continued. In a letter to House Treasurer Mack in 1922, Cook expressed, as he did many other times, his vision of the purpose of the Martha Cook Building as, "to gather together the choicest young women of the Senior Class and train them to exert a combined influence on each other and other young women in the University and on the University itself."[7] Expanding the diversity of the Building has allowed its residents an even greater opportunity to influence others in ways needed in today's global environment and so they have met his goal to an even greater extent than Cook hoped. If past history is an indicator, this inclusivity and the sense of family will only deepen as the years go by.

Other influences may also contribute to the Building's future. The Martha Cook community, although independent in its organization, is dependent upon interaction with the University of Michigan. As the past shows, the relationship between MCB and U-M has evolved over time and is not the same today as it was in Cook's time. It is likely that this relationship will continue to change, perhaps in ways not yet foreseen.

If Cook were alive today, would he be proud of his legacy? Yes, he would. The management of the Building has continued as he arranged, a Building run for women by women. As for the women who have lived at MCB as students—in that same letter to Mack, he wrote:

> the manners, dignity, daily conduct of life, views as to the future, and the ideals which all young people should have and do have if surrounded by the right environment—these things, constituting the wealth of womanhood, will depend largely on the management and the selection of the occupants. Women now have great power and should be trained to accept the corresponding responsibility of exercising that power with judgement and foresight.

I shall watch with great interest the results ....[8]

The results speak for themselves. For 100 years, the women of Martha Cook have fulfilled their benefactor's fondest dream and will hopefully continue to do so for the next century. How could William Cook argue with success?

115. (sc) To the Future!

Appendix A
Deed of Gift

Fourteen East Seventy-first Street

To the Regents

of the University of Michigan:

In memory of my mother, Martha Cook, I will build a Womans' Dormitory Building for the use of women exclusively (the building not to be used to furnish board except to the occupants thereof) on land now owned by you, on condition that the occupants shall have sole and exclusive charge of its income, expenses and management (subject to the approval of a woman or board of women appointed by the Regents); and on the further condition that the University shall at all times hereafter furnish heat, light and power for the building free of charge, and shall not derive any income from such building; and on the further condition that so much of the surplus income or profit from the building shall be used by the occupants for furniture, furnishings, works of art and improvements in or to the buildings as they deem best, and the remainder, if any, at the end of each year shall be set aside as a fund to be used in the following year to give lower or free rates in the building to such under-graduates or post graduates as the President of the University and the Dean of Women may designate from time to time.

New York, February 10th, 1914.

William W Cook

116. (bh1)

The original was typed on William W. Cook's personal letterhead with only his home address, Fourteen East Seventy-first Street, at the top.

Appendix B
Architecture and Furnishings

(I. Elbert Scrantom's essay on the MCB interior was originally published in the *Martha Cook Annual,* 1921)

There has been an oft-repeated request for some description of the architecture and furnishings of the Martha Cook Building, and, to satisfy the minds of those interested, this article is written, the intention being to add to the respect for this wonderful building.

The exterior of the building is pure Gothic in character, inspired by the best work at Cambridge and Oxford. One who is familiar with the buildings of these two great universities can at once picture its likeness in architecture to them. The pure Gothic entrance with the niche as a central feature is particularly beautiful, and the placing of the beautiful statue of Portia, portraying a woman of noble spirit and learning, is its crowning feature.

Upon entering the Vestibule one is confronted with the beautiful pierced screen of Tudor Gothic, and in the Entrance Lobby the surrounding work of paneled oak and ornamental modeled ceiling of a little later period, namely, Elizabethan, completes a dignified appearance. Beyond this Entrance is the Long Gallery which is certainly a noble site with its high groined Gothic ceiling reminding one so much of the ceilings as seen in Cloisters; this, combined with the high oak paneled walls of the Tudor period, lends itself admirably to a dignified setting for any gathering that might assemble there. At the end of this Gallery is the beautiful statue of the Venus de Milo, a perfect replica of the original in the Louvre. This statue was sculptured in Italy from the finest statuary marble and sent to Ann Arbor to adorn the end of this Gallery. The similarity of the setting of the beautiful statue, to that at the Louvre, is again impressive, both being first seen from a distance through a long gallery or corridor. The furniture of this Gallery is of Italian character of the Sixteenth Century with appropriate coverings of Verdure tapestry.

The Small Parlour, or Red Room, on the right of the Entrance has a vaulted ceiling and plaster frieze reproduced from the existing ceiling and frieze in the library of the Castleton Manor House,[*] built between the years 1603 and 1614 by Walter Jones, a merchant of whom it is said he was his own architect. The interior of this manner is considered to be amongst the most beautiful and quaintest of the period. The ceiling design is what is known as "Wagon Head Ceiling," being one of the most interesting features of the house. The woodwork of this room is in Butternut and designed in the same spirit as the ceiling, the mouldings and general details being reproduced from measured drawings of antique woodwork. The hangings are of red damask, being on an Italian design of the Sixteenth Century, and ending themselves admirably to the architecture.[†] The furniture is of the Jacobean period—the large sofas being taken from a detail of sofas still in existence in Lord Saxville's "Knole House" at Sevenoaks, England. The carved, caned-back arm chairs are exact copies of a fine example found at Astor Hall, Birmingham, England, which figured prominently in the days of Cromwell. The tapestry is of Flemish origin where some of the most famous tapestries were produced in the town of Arras—the Lords of Flanders having set up great works for the manufacture of tapestry in

---

[*] The original document incorrectly identified (or perhaps included a typographical error) the home from which the Red Room ceiling was modeled. Chastleton House near Moreton-in-Marsh, Oxfordshire, England is now a property of the UK National Trust and its website includes a photo of the original ceiling. <http://www.nationaltrust.org.uk/chastleton-house/> (July 4, 2015).

[†] The original hangings have since been replaced.

Arras. The works of the looms are often called "Arras," rather than our modern name of tapestry.

Adjoining the Small Parlour and connected with it by an alcove is what is known as the Large Parlour. The ceiling of this room was cast from original models of a ceiling in Sir Paul Pindar's house at Bishopgate, which now forms a part of the collection in the Victoria and Albert Museum at South Kensington. The ceiling is one of the best examples of plaster work of the period. The design and softness of the modeling of the ornament is delightful, and the concave treatment of the leaves is very characteristic of the purer and earlier work of the Sixteenth Century.

The woodwork of the room is constructed of Burma Teak, and is typical of the woodwork of the time. All the stiles and moulding, peggings, etc., are arranged and detailed according to measured drawings of woodwork executed by craftsmen of these days. The mantels are of particular interest with their arched head panellings, carvings and inlays typical of the period, and the impressive stone facings with Gothic arch. The three rugs, which cover the floor, made in the colors of the University, are of special Jacobean design and were manufactured in Donegal, Ireland.* The furnishings of the room are of Jacobean design with appropriate coverings of velvet and tapestries and the curtains of heavy velvet of typical design and coloring. The sundry bits Chinese pottery, it is interesting to know, were collected by a Chinese missionary in Central China, and are authentic bits of the old Chinese potters' art with their fine glazes.

In the Dining Hall one is at once impressed with the design of the beamed ceiling. This type of ceiling is inspired by the best Tudor work. The firred ceiling came into use in the Fifteenth Century in

---

* The rugs have been replaced several times. At least the most recent are of American manufacture and are a gold-toned Berber with a border design modeled after carvings on the mantel woodwork. Furniture upholstery and curtains have also been replaced more than once; the most notable change to the room occurred in 1962 when the Blue Room became the Gold Room.

both ecclesiastical and domestic work. This type of ceiling is the solution of the problem that the Gothic craftsmen had to solve to turn the purely utilitarian arrangement of rough hewn beams and posts into a thing of beauty. The panelling is laid out according to measured drawings taken of woodwork of the period. The ornament in the small panels above the mantel has no particular significance other than as an ornamental feature. The stone mantel with the arch opening is very characteristic of this type of room, and the motto inscribed in the stone, "Home the Nation's Safety," is of particular significance.

The furnishings of the room are of oak and are taken from pieces of the Jacobean period. The hangings at the window were selected in a neutral tone so as not to detract from the unusual and stately architecture of the room.[*]

The writer trusts that with these explanations of the origin of the designs, which inspired those whose pleasure it was to design and furnish the building, will provoke a desire for study and research in art and architecture to the great pleasure and benefit of the student.

I. Elbert Scrantom

---

[*] The original curtains have been replaced. The current window hangings are of navy and gold damask, chosen to honor U-M's colors of maize and blue, as well as to complement the woodwork.

Appendix C
Martha Cook Building Directors

117. (a23) From 1923 *Annual*

Gertrude Harper Beggs   **1915–1917**
BA 1893 (University of Denver), PhD 1904 (Yale University),
LLD (hon) 1914 (University of Denver)

    Dr. Beggs[1] was born in Pleasant Hill, Missouri, on February 27, 1874. She was a high school teacher in Denver prior to attending graduate school and, interrupting her studies, served one year as principal at Stanley Hall, Minneapolis. She was professor of Latin at the University of Denver from 1904–14. In 1914–15, she served as Dean of the Chicago Kindergarten Institute. She left MCB to become the Dean of Women and professor of Greek at the University of Minnesota, where she remained until 1919. Between 1920 and 1922, she was the principal of Tungchow American School, Tungchow, China.² From 1922–33, Dr. Beggs was professor of Latin at West Hampton College of the University of Richmond in Virginia. She authored *Four In Crete* in 1915. She died April 11, 1951, and is buried at Rolla Cemetery, Rolla, Missouri.³

Grace Greenwood 1917–1922
BA 1908, MA 1911 (both from Columbia University)

Grace Greenwood,⁴ was born in Milton, Kentucky. After teaching school in her native state, she entered Teacher's College, Columbia University. From 1908–17, she was the Social Director of Whittier Hall, a residence for women at Columbia. From there, Greenwood came to MCB. She raised a nephew and four nieces, two of whom, Barbara and Gretchen,⁵ were the only children to ever live at MCB. Greenwood was called GG by the residents who gave her a bridal shower just before she left Martha Cook to marry Albert Reeves on July 3, 1922.⁶ She lived in England for ten years, then returned to Ann Arbor, living in an apartment building on East University Street. She died in San Bernardino, California, on August 1, 1959.⁷

Zelma E. Clark 1922–1925
BA 1897 (University of Chicago), MA 1922 (Columbia University)⁸

Zelma Clark was born about 1875 in New York State.⁹ Prior to graduating from the University of Chicago she attended one year each at Wells College, Aurora, New York, and Bryn Mawr College, Bryn Mawr, Pennsylvania.¹⁰ She came to MCB from Columbia, where she had been an instructor of English. Clark authored *As a Girl Thinketh* and *Socialized English* and also edited Walter Scott's *Marmion* for Merrill and Company. In 1940, she was the hostess in a girls' residence in Chicago.

Elva Marcella Forncrook 1925–1928
BA 1903 (Oberlin College), MA 1927 (University of Michigan)[11]

Born about 1882 in Kansas,[12] Elva Forncrook taught at Hope, Western State Teachers (now Western Michigan University), and Smith Colleges.[13] Prior to coming to MCB, she was the Director of the Women's Division, Probation Department, Recorder's Court, Detroit.[14] She later worked for Associated Charities of Detroit, a forerunner of United Community Services. Miss Forncrook married Clinton B. Alexander on October 6, 1906, in Harrisburg, Pennsylvania,[15] but was divorced and using her maiden name in 1910.[16] She died at Baltimore, Maryland, in 1950.[17]

Ethel G. Dawbarn 1928–1929
BA (Barnard College), MA (Columbia University)[18]

A native of New York State, Ethel Dawbarn was born on August 10, 1897, and died in 1986.[19] Before coming to MCB, she had "been connected successively with the Institute of International Education, the McDowell Club, and the Open Road, Inc., all in New York City. After leaving the Building, she was with the Associated Glee Clubs of America, New York City."[20] She was later the Assistant Director of the Personnel Bureau of the New Jersey College for Women.

Margaret Ruth Smith 1929–1934
BA (Goucher College), MA (Columbia University), PhD 1937 (Columbia University)[21]

Prior to coming to MCB, Margaret Smith was Assistant Dean of Women at State Teacher's College, Westchester, Pennsylvania.[22] She was Director of Personnel for Women at Northwest Missouri State Teachers College, Marysville, from 1937–40.[23] She earned her PhD at Columbia University in 1937 where she was on staff in 1936–37. From there, she went to Wayne State University Detroit.

Kathleen Warner Codd 1934–1936

Kathleen Codd was the widow of George Pierre Codd, a U-M grad and Detroit attorney who served as mayor of Detroit, regent of U-M, circuit court judge, and representative to the US Congress.[24] The couple had three children.[25] Before coming to MCB, Codd was with the King Smith Studio School in Washington, DC, in 1931 and Kappa Delta at Michigan State College (now Michigan State University) in 1933–34.[26] Born on March 2, 1874, she died in October 1967.[27]

Mary E. Gleason 1936–1939
BA 1907 (Smith College)

Born March 26, 1885,[28] in McIndoes Falls, Vermont,[29] Mary Gleason held various secretarial positions both before and after spending two years in Europe and three years in Turkey. After working as a canteen worker and secretary for the YMCA in France, Germany, and Turkey, she spent her final two years overseas as a secretary at the US Embassy in Constantinople.[30] She described the latter as "one of the most exciting moments in that exciting land of Turkey."[31] After her return to the US in 1923, she held secretarial positions at Marble Collegiate Church, Near East Relief, International Institute of Teachers College, and the Encyclopedia of Social Sciences, all in New York City. After leaving Ann Arbor, she spent some time as the Alumni Secretary for the Cornell Medical School and in 1955, at age 70, married Luther Fowle.[32] She died March 27, 1977, in Barnstable, Massachusetts.[33]

Leona Belser Diekema 1939–1956
BA 1908 (University of Michigan)[34]

Leona Diekema was born November 11, 1885, in Ann Arbor and died May 19, 1972, in Carmel, California.[35] She was a member of Kappa Alpha Theta while a student at Michigan. In 1920, she married Gerrit J. Diekema who served as a representative to the Michigan

Legislature, US congressman from Holland, Michigan and US ambassador to the Netherlands. Prior to her marriage, she taught English in Holland, Michigan. After her husband's death in 1930, Diekema served as Social Director at Roblee Hall in Waukazoo, Michigan, and at Betsy Barbour Residence Hall at U-M. She held a similar position at Stanford from 1935 to 1936. At MCB, she directed a weekly current events seminar for residents and also held "a series of after dinner coffee hours, afternoon teas, and hors d'oeuvres hours in her room and thus made the rounds of the entire group living in the Building."[36]

Margaret Hingeley Blake   **1956–1959**

In 1919, Margaret Blake and her husband Edgar traveled to France to assist with reconstruction work of the Methodist Church Sunday Schools[37] and served many years as missionaries in Europe.[38] They had returned to the US by 1935 and settled near Gary, Indiana, where her husband was Superintendent of Methodist Hospital.[39] Immediately before coming to Martha Cook, Blake held positions as director and dietitian at Oberlin College, Oberlin, Ohio.[40] She was born about 1896.[41]

Isabel Kemp Quail   **1959–1969**
BA 1922 (University of Michigan)

Isabel Quail was born in Clinton, Michigan, on January 5, 1901.[42] She graduated from the University of Michigan School of Education in 1922 and married Kenneth Quail in Bad Axe, Michigan, on February 29, 1924. They had two daughters. Quail died on October 12, 1978. Prior to coming to Martha Cook, she was the Director of Couzens Hall at U-M.

Thelma Hanshaw Duffell   1969–1973

Thelma Duffell was born July 21, 1906, in Wisconsin.[43] She came to MCB from Gamma Phi Beta where she had been the housemother.[44] Prior to that, she was the Professional Director of Volunteers at Michael Reese Hospital in Chicago. She died April 28, 1999, in Ann Arbor.

Olive Chernow   1973–1979

BA 1947, MSW 1953 (both from University of Michigan)

Olive Chernow[45] is the only Building resident to serve as Director. After practicing social work for nine years, Chernow worked in personnel at General Motors from 1956 until she accepted the position of Director of the Martha Cook Building. She was the president of the Martha Cook Alumnae Association when the Building celebrated its Fiftieth Anniversary in 1965 and was part of the delegation that commissioned the statue for MCB's garden. In the early 2000s, she served on MCB's Fundraising Committee. She was born in Detroit on March 14, 1925, but grew up in Saginaw, Michigan, where she returned after leaving MCB, first managing a General Nutrition Center, then serving as an instructor of geriatric studies in the Home Health Care Companion Program at Delta College.[46] She died on September 14, 2007, in Saginaw.

Harriet Fenske Powers   Fall 1979

1949 (University of Michigan)

Harriet Powers was born in Michigan about 1928. She was a member of Wyvern, a junior academic society, while a student at U-M.[47]

Mary Josette Allan   1980–1981

MA 1982 (University of Michigan)

Josette Allan, who had previously been the Director of Oxford Housing,[48] served as MCB's Director while a graduate student. She resigned from the directorship to pursue a career in telecommunications.[49] She was the first Director to allow residents to call her by her first name.

Rosalie Moore   1981–1992
BA 1940 (University of Michigan)

Rosalie Moore[50] lived for many years in Birmingham, Michigan, and worked for Planned Parenthood before serving as MCB Director. Upon her retirement, she moved to Harbor Springs, Michigan, where she died April 25, 2014. She was the mother of two sons.

Gloria Picasso   1992–1997
BA 1969 (University of Michigan)

Gloria Picasso was originally from a small town in Texas.[51] Prior to coming to MCB, she served for three years as a cryptographic operator in the US Air Force and also worked as a real estate agent, travel agent, and office manager of the Medical School's Department of Psychology.

Marion Scher Law   1997–present

Marion Law[52] was born in Glasgow, Scotland, and became a US citizen in 1998. In 1965, shortly after Zambia became independent of Britain, she took a position in its government and lived there for more than twenty years. She moved to Ann Arbor in 1986. Prior to becoming Building Director in 1997, Marion worked as MCB's Office Manager for three years. She married David Law BS'67 in 2008 and they live in the Director's apartment. Some residents refer to Dave as "house dad." Their combined family includes three adult children.

Appendix D
Martha Cook Building Governors

118. (a36) Governors Florentine Heath, Vera Baits, and Grace Bruce, 1936

Forty-five women have sat on the MCB Board of Governors during the Building's first 100 years. Members of the Cook family are marked with an asterisk, and the names of MCB alumnae are in bold print. Only U-M degrees and graduation years are listed.

Anne E. Shipman Stevens: 1915–1932
Grace Grieve Millard 1897: 1915–1923
Louise Stock Cook: 1915–1921
Cora Strong Bulkley: 1921–1933
Emilie Gleason Sargent '16: 1923–1932
*****Florentine Cook Heath '17**: 1933–1938, 1945–1951, 1955–1961
Vera Burridge Baits 1915: 1933–1936
Grace Campbell Bruce: 1933–1941
*Jane Whitney Cook: 1939–1945
Marguerite Chapin Maire '20: 1937–1942, 1949–1952, 1961–1962
Daisy Chapin Jennings Murfin '49hon: 1941–1946
Elizabeth S. Brown Holbrook 1903: 1943–1949
Maxine Rust Muirhead '27: 1947–1949
Dora Vyn van den Berg Perrett '30: 1949–1946, 1957–1961
Janet MacIvor Lowrie '38: 1951–1957, 1965–1971

Muriel Bauman Mackey '20: 1952–1955
Viola Jeanette Chubb Perring '26: 1956–1959
Elizabeth Black Ross '29: 1959–1965
*Ann Bradford Cook '45: 1961–1969, 1975–1981
Margaret Yerkes Holden '18: 1967–1973
*Martha Cook Nash '40: 1969–1975, 1981–1984
Carrie Wismer Peebles '41:1971–1977, 1979–1985
Veronica Latta Smith'48: 1973–1979
Joan Semegen Iwasko '54: 1977–1979
Nancy Howe Bielby Sudia '56: 1979–1986, 1991–1994
*Sharon Warnock Nash, MD: 1984–1996
Catherine Walsh Davis '70, MM '76: 1986–1992, 2000–2006
Joyce Collins Tucker '54: 1985–1991
Janet Kreger '72: 1992–1995
Constance Butler Amick '57: 1994–2000
Elaine Macklin Didier '70, AMLS '71, PhD '82: 1995–2001
Mabelle Lengyel Chalfant Kirk '61, MA '68: 1996–2002, 2013–present
Dr. Susan Prakken Smith '57: 1997–1998
Elizabeth Yaros Johnston '90: 2001–2007
Kathryn Graneggen Moberg '79: 2002–2008
Maurita Peterson Holland BMUS '65, AMLS '66: 2005–2011
Anne Mills Greashaber '70, MA'76: 2006–2012
Sheila Davis '00, MBA '11: 2006–2012
Phyllis Valentine '65, MA '69, AMLS '77: 2007–2013
Nancy Short '03: 2008–2014
Carol Giacoletto '72: 2011–present
Jessica Roossien '10, BSN'11, MSN '14: 2012–2015
Margaret A. Leary, JD: 2012–present
Marie Fox Skrobola '95: 2014–present
Nina Cataldo '14: 2015–present

Appendix E
Martha Cook Building
Associate Directors

When MCB opened in 1915, two women lived at MCB and assisted the Social Director in the management of the Building. They were the House Director, responsible for the operation of the dining and housekeeping functions, and the Treasurer (Business Manager until 1921) who kept the books, accepted room and board payments, and paid the bills. In 1927, the two positions were combined under the title House Director. The title was changed to Dietitian in 1949 and to Associate Director in 1964. In 1973, direct management of dining and housekeeping services became the responsibility of non-live-in department managers and the assistant to the Director became a new yearly student staff position, the Assistant Resident Director.

F = fall term only   W = winter term only

House Treasurer (Business Manager)
1915–1927   Frances Mack

House Directors
1916–1918   Lulu F. Taylor
1918–1920   Clara L. Bigelow
1920–1922   Louise Roe
1922–1926   Mary Elizabeth Walton
1926–1928   Alice Graham
1928–1932   Alta B. Atkinson
1932–1949   Sara Louise Rowe

Dietitian
1949–1950   Betty Coleman

1950–1953	Shirley Remquist
	(Shirley Remquist Buslee after April 1953)
1953–1955	Barbara Child
1955–1956	Edna Garmene
1956–1957	Donna Stahl
1958–1959	Gertrude Metcalf
1959(F)	Shirley Cagle
1960(W)	Frances Watson
1960–1962	Margaret Funk
1962–1964	Ellen Scott
1978–1979	Margaret Bergren[*]

Associate Director

| 1964–1973 | Ellen Scott |

Assistant Resident Director

1973–1974	Martha Cook Nash
1974–1976	Linda Loving
1976–1977	Deborah Day
1977–1978	Deborah Ahern
1978–1980	Patti Duch[*]
1980–1982	Rebecca Shilit
1982–1983	Patrice Donovan
1983(F)	Christine Wantuck
1984(W)	Elaine Constand
1984–1985	Linda Pulley
1985–1986	Julie Urbonas
1986–1988	Kathy Coburn
1989–1990	Dena Ciolino
1990–1991	Phyllis Taylor
1991–1992	Phyllis Beels

---

[*] In 1978–79, instead of hiring an ARD, the Board of Governors required the dietitian (then called Food Service Supervisor) to live in the Building although she was not given all of the duties previously held by the ARD.[*] MCB Junior Patti Duch was hired as Student Service Assistant to coordinate the activities of the Front Desk. At the end of the year, Bergren requested to live outside the Building and Duch recommended, and the Governors accepted, the reinstatement of the ARD position. Bergren undertook some of the responsibilities of the Building Director for a brief time in fall 1980 following the resignation of Harriet Fenske Powers.

1992–1993	Kavita Ahluwalia
1993–1994	Judith Flynn
1994–1995	Christa Alessandri
1995–1996	Elizabeth Powers
1996–1997	Sangita Baxi
1997–1998	Sangita Baxi
1998–1999	Amy Bennett
1999–2000	Michelle Vogel
2000–2001	Leslie Calhoun
2001–2002	Antonia Henry
2002–2003	Allison Schwartz
2003–2004	Simone Welch
2004–2005	Sun Hee Kim
2005–2006	Londisa Halili
2006–2007	Kaitlyn Cheesebro
2007–2008	Jennifer Lowing
2008–2009	Lauren Humphrey
2009–2010	Maria Blood
2010–2011	Emma Lawton
2011–2012	Emma Lawton
2012–2013	Elaine Czech
2013–2014	Nina Cataldo
2014–2015	Eleni Kastanis
2015–2016	Elena Lorenzana

Appendix F
Martha Cook Building
House Presidents

One hundred four young women have served their fellow residents as President of the Martha Cook Student Organization, carrying out the position's leadership responsibilities in addition to their academic tasks as U-M full-time students.

F = fall term only   W = winter term only

1915–1916	Emilie Sargent
1916–1917	Helen Richey
1917–1918	Margaret Yerkes
1918–1919	Margaret Beckley
1919–1920	Gretchen Jones
1920–1921	Elizabeth Roberts
1921–1922	Juliet Peddle
1922–1923	Virginia Whitson
1923–1924	Lila Reynolds
1924–1925	Bernece Tomkins
1925–1926	Geraldine Knight
1926–1927	Edith Woollett
1927–1928	C. Janice Peck
1928–1929	Julia Ferguson
1929–1930	Margaret Sabom
1930–1931	Kathryn Van Zoeren
1931–1932	Elizabeth Lidy
1932–1933	Helen Hellmuth
1933–1934	Celia Guntrip
1934–1935	E. Lucille Alm
1935–1936	Dorothy McDonald
1936–1937	Mary Bennett
1937–1938	Sally Kenny
1938–1939	Catherine Sherman
1939–1940	Elizabeth Kimball

Appendix F: House Presidents

1940–1941	Marjorie Risk
1941–1942	Marion Chown
1942–1943	Virginia Capron
1943 (F)	Helen Speed
1944 (W)	Ruth Rodenbeck
1944–1945	Ann Terbrueggen
1945–1946	Martha Bradshaw
1946–1947	Harriet Risk
1947–1948	Pamela Wrinch
1948–1949	Georgiana Benesh
1949–1950	Audrey Riddell
1950–1951	Josephine Collins
1951 (F)	Ruth Dixon
1952 (W)	Patricia Wilcox
1952–1953	Nancy Hoddick
1953–1954	Vonda Genda
1954–1955	Shirley Boers
1955–1956	Clarissa Knaggs
1956–1957	Constance Butler
1957–1958	Kay Delle Smith
1958–1959	Julie Wasson
1959–1960	Emmagene Reisig
1960–1961	Ronnie Posner
1961–1962	Cecelie Goodrich
1962–1963	Luanne Cevala
1963–1964	Janet Zehnder
1964–1965	Elizabeth Meese
1965–1966	Cynthia Parry
1966–1967	Meril Penn
1967–1968	Susan Redlick
1968–1969	Vicki Bergsma
1969–1970	Elaine Macklin
1970–1971	Linda Rexer
1971 (F)	Joan Woodward
1972 (W)	Patricia Bucalo
1972–1973	Cheryl Porter
1973–1974	Gretchen Langschwager
1974–1975	Nancy Grace
1975–1976	Jeannell Mansur
1976–1977	Jean Coulter
1977–1978	Betsy Hooper

1978–1979	Debra Magolan
1979–1980	Mary Lisa Tanner
1980–1981	Kara Olson
1981–1982	Maia Bergman
1982–1983	Christine Wantuck
1983 (F)	Elaine Constand
1984 (W)	Barbara Middleton
1984 (F)	Mojdeh Khalili
1985 (W)	Kate Chapman
1985–1986	Deborah Eden
1986–1987	Jennifer Regan
1987–1988	Mary Tierney
1988–1989	Deveny Deck
1989–1990	Kimberly Steiner
1990–1991	Caroline Kosnik
1991–1992	Melissa Gedris
1992–1993	Beata Barci
1993–1994	Sina Lewis
1994–1995	Rebecca Dean
1995–1996	Tiffany Girard
1996–1997	Kathleen Barker
1997–1998	Nadja Hogg
1998 (F)	Courtney Fritz
1999 (W)	Sheila Davis
1999–2000	Sheila Davis
2000–2001	Emily Cloyd
2001–2002	Angela Bur
2002–2003	Rachel Green
2003–2004	Rachel Green
2004–2005	Tiffani Boss
2005–2006	Jodie Woznica
2006–2007	Christina Talamonti
2007–2008	Megan Beems
2008–2009	Megan Beems
2009–2010	Jessica Roossien
2010–2011	Kayla DeMarco
2011–2012	Megan Sajewski
2012–2013	Natalie Roxas
2013–2014	Alexandrea Garbus
2014–2015	Erin Bozek-Jarvis
2015–	Amy Pestenariu

Appendix G
Martha Cook Building
Outstanding Resident Award

The Martha Cook Alumnae Association began the tradition of formally honoring an exceptional senior in the spring of 1979. The recipient is announced at the Dinner for Graduating Seniors. She receives a small gift from the MCAA (originally engraved book ends, but it has since been a silver bowl, picture frame, and other objects) and her name is engraved on a commemorative plaque displayed in the Sparking Room. The first plaque was filled in 1999 and a second one was added. The Building Director and alumnae made the original selections, but it was later decided to allow residents to vote from the pool of graduating seniors who have lived in MCB two or more semesters.

1979	Debra Magolan
1980	Carol Cachey
1981	Kara Olson
1982	Ann M Sabty
1983	Jennifer L. Heusel
1984	Elaine S. Constand
1985	Mojden Khalili
1986	Debbie Eden
1987	Natalie Melnyczuk/Jill Campbell
1988	Becky Lawrence
1989	Emily Frydrych
1990	Christa Alessandri
1991	Caroline M.M. Kosnik
1992	Maria Tendero
1993	Beata Barci
1994	Judith Flynn
1995	Rebecca Dean
1996	Tiffany Troxel

Appendix F: Outstanding Resident Award

1997 Sharilee Turner
1998 Sangita Baxi
1999 Amy Bennett
2000 Sheila Davis
2001 Emily Cloyd
2002 Angela K. Bur
2003 Sonya Raisinghani
2004 Rachel Green
2005 Erin Whipkey
2006 Bonnie Grow
2007 Christina Talamonti
2008 Tara Whipkey
2009 Megan V. Beems
2010 Jessica Roossien
2011 Theresa Kennedy/Erika Valdivieso
2012 K.T. Michaelson
2013 Emma Bozek-Jarvis
2014 Nina Cataldo
2015 Eleni Kastanis

119. (dbj) The original Outstanding Resident Award plaque.

Appendix H
Martha Cook Women Who Served as U-M Regents

The Regents of the University of Michigan are elected by the people of the state of Michigan and form a board which, according to the State Constitution (Article 13, Section 8), has responsibility for "the general supervision of the university, and the direction and control of all expenditures from the university interest fund."

MCB Residents

Term as Regent	Years at MCB	
1958–1966	1918–1919	Irene Ellis Murphy MA'28
1967–1974	1934–1936	Gertrude Veneklasen Huebner '36
1985–1992	1945–1948	Veronica Latta Smith '48
		(also served as MCB Governor 1973–1979)

MCB Governor

Term as Regent	Term at MCB	
1943–1957	1933–1936	Vera Burridge Baits 1915

Notes

The Governors have accepted the authors' recommendation to move many of the materials stored at the Martha Cook Building to the Bentley Historical Library at the University of Michigan and this will be done in the near future. In these notes, references are cited at the location where the authors found them at the time of research.

ABBREVIATIONS USED IN NOTES
(Note: When the following reports are referred to by date in the text, they are not individually footnoted.)

AH *Minutes, All House Meeting*
 Martha Cook Building, Martha Cook Building Collection.

ANN *Martha Cook Annual* (Ann Arbor: Martha Cook Building). In most issues, pages are not numbered.
 1916–1920, 1923–1941, 1976, 1990–2015: Martha Cook Building, Martha Cook Building Collection
 1921, 1922: Bentley Historical Library, Martha Cook Building Publications, Box 1

DIR *Social Director's Reports*
 Undated–1956: Bentley Historical Library, Martha Cook Building Records, Box 2

GOV *Minutes of the Governors Meetings*
 1930–1973: Bentley Historical Library, Martha Cook Building Records, Box 1
 1974–2012: Martha Cook Building, Martha Cook Building Collection

HB *Minutes of the House Board of the Martha Cook Student Organization*
 1951–1991, 1994–95: Martha Cook Building, Martha Cook Building Collection
 1999–2006: Bentley Historical Library, Martha Cook Building Publications, Box 7

MCAA *Minutes of the Martha Cook Alumnae Association*
 1945–65 and 1988–91: Bentley Historical Library, Martha Cook Alumnae Association of Detroit Records, Box 1.
 1991–2004: Martha Cook Building, Martha Alumnae Association Collection

REG   Board of Regents, University of Michigan, *Proceedings*, 1837–2014
          <http://quod.lib.umich.edu/u/umregproc/>

The following abbreviations are also used in the notes.

ANC   <ancestry.com>
         Ancestry.com Operations Inc., 2004, Provo, UT

BHL   Bentley Historical Library

EGB   Elizabeth Gaspar Brown Papers
         Bentley Historical Library

HBH   Harry Burns Hutchings Papers
         Bentley Historical Library

MCB 1   Martha Cook Building Collection
         Martha Cook Building

MCB 2   Martha Cook Papers
         Bentley Historical Library

WHS   Walter Hulme Sawyer Papers
         Bentley Historical Library

Introduction

[1] *Michiganensian, 1916* (Ann Arbor: The Senior Classes of the University of Michigan, 1916).
[2] University of Michigan, Housing Facilities Department, *Martha Cook Renewal and Capital Improvements: An Overview for Near and Medium Term (<10 Years) Planning, 1998, p 5.*
[3] Slemons, Marion. *A Booklet of the Martha Cook Building at the University of Michigan* (Ann Arbor: Board of Governors of the Martha Cook Building, 1936).

Chapter One

[1] Shirley Wheeler Smith, *Harry Burns and the University of Michigan* (Ann Arbor: University of Michigan Press, 1951), pp 304-5, n7.
[2] Margaret Leary. *Giving It All Away: The Story of William W. Cook & his Michigan Law Quadrangle.* (Ann Arbor: The University of Michigan Press, 2011).
[3] Leary, p 134.
[4] Except where specifically noted, information in this section was obtained from Leary, pp 17-28, 37, 39, 42-57, 63-64, 67, 71, 80-81,92, 99-101,153,194-205, 222.
[5] Ilene H. Forsyth. *The Use of Medieval Metaphor in the Michigan Law Quadrangle.* (Ann Arbor: The University of Michigan Press, 1993), p8.

[6] Forsyth, pp 7-8.
[7] Leary, p 61.
[8] Leary, p 57.
[9] *William W. Cook's Written Work,* <http://www.law.umich.edu/library/info/cook/Pages/cookwritings.aspx> (Sep 23, 2014).
[10] State of North Dakota, County of Richland, District Court, 4th Judicial District, *Ida C. Cook, Plaintiff v. William W. Cook, Defendant, Decree, June 9, 1898* (copy), Bentley Historical Library, U-M Law School, Box 67.
[11] For details of the Cooks' courtship, marriage, and divorce, see Leary, pp 42-54, 63-64. For further information on the lawsuit, see pp 194-205.
[12] Elizabeth Gaspar Brown, *Memorandum, Brown to Sandlow,* June 23, 1982, EGB, Box 1.
[13] State of North Dakota.
[14] *1900 United States Federal Census,* ANC (Nov 20, 2013).
[15] Elizabeth Gaspar Brown, *Memorandum to the Law Faculty,* September 29, 1959, EGB, Box 1.
[16] Smith, p 306.
[17] Brown, September 29, 1959.
[18] *Martha Cook Building to Schwartz Floral Company, Port Chester, NY,* Jun 4, 1930. MCB 1.
[19] *Martha Cook Building to Family of Mr. William Cook, Port Chester, NY,* Jun 4, 1930. MCB 1.
[20] *Harry Burns Hutchins to Olen Templin,* Jul 17, 1911. HBH, Box 3.
[21] *Hutchins to Otto Kirchner,* Nov 13, 1911. HBH, Box 3.
[22] Leary, pp 79-80.
[23] *William Cook to Walter Sawyer,* HBH, Box 1.
[24] Leary, p 92.
[25] *Hutchins to Cook,* June 1, 1910, HBH, Box 1.
[26] *Cook to Hutchins,* June 5, 1910, HBH, Box 3.
[27] *Hutchins to Myrtle White,* Nov 7, 1910, HBH, Box 3.
[28] "Interview Catches W. W. Cook's Attention," *The Michigan Alumnus,* Vol 36, No 35, Aug 16, 1930.
[29] *White to Hutchins,* Jan 16, 1911, BHL, Hussey Family Papers, Box 7.
[30] *Hutchins to Cook,* Feb 10, 1911, HBH, Box 2.
[31] *Hutchins to White,* Feb 10, 1911, HBH, Box 2.
[32] *Hutchins to Cook,* June 1, 1911, HBH, Box 3.
[33] *Cook to Hutchins,* June 5, 1911, HBH, Box 3.
[34] *Hutchins to Cook,* June 5, 1911, HBH, Box 3.
[35] *Cook to Frances Mauck,* February 20, 1912, BHL, Law School Records, Box 67.
[36] Leary, p 90.
[37] Smith, p 161.
[38] Smith, p 161.
[39] *The University of Michigan, An Encyclopedic Survey,* (Walter A. Donnelly, Wilfrid B. Shaw, Ruth W. Gjelsness, ed.) (Ann Arbor: University of Michigan Press, 1958), p 1793.
[40] *The University of Michigan* (Donnelly, et al., ed.), p 1793.
[41] *The University of Michigan,* (Donnelly, et al., ed.), p 1794.

[42] *The University of Michigan,* (Donnelly, et al., ed.), p 1795.
[43] Forsyth, p 25.
[44] *Last Will and Testament, William W. Cook,* Executed Nov 13, 1924, State of New York, County of New York, p3. Digital copy provided to the authors by Margaret Leary, Jul 8, 2013.
[45] *Shipping Notices,* Nov 5, 1930 (needlework) and Nov 8, 1930 (piano). MCB 1.
[46] "Law School Now World's Richest," *Washington Star,* June 11, 1930.
[47] *William W. Cook, Law School Benefactor,* <http://www.law.umich.edu/library/info/cook/Pages/default.aspx> (Jan 10, 2014).

Chapter Two

[1] *Edward P. York to Cook,* Nov 4, 1915, MCB 2, Box 1.
[2] *Hutchins to Chauncey Cook,* July 30, 1912, HBH, Box 5.
[3] *Hutchins to Chauncey Cook,* March 6, 1913, HBH, Box 5.
[4] *Hutchins to Chauncey Cook,* May 17, 1913, HBH, Box 6.
[5] *Hutchins to Chauncey Cook,* Jun 30, 1913, HBH, Box 6.
[6] Margaret A Leary, "William W. Cook and his Architects: Edward York and Philip Sawyer," *Law Quadrangle Notes* (Ann Arbor: The University of Michigan Law School, Vol 45, No 3, Fall/Winter 2003).
[7] Philip Sawyer, *"Edward Palmer York: Personal Reminiscences by his Friend and Partner* (Stonington, NY: Privately Printed, 1951), p 29.
[8] Royal Cortissoz, "Biographical Sketch," introduction to P. Sawyer, "p 12.
[9] P. Sawyer, p 38.
[10] P. Sawyer, pp 23-24.
[11] Debra McMillan, "Architect's Corner," *Martha Cook Building Annual Report, 2003.*
[12] *Scrantom to Cook,* June 21, 1915, MCB 1.
[13] *Cook to York and Sawyer,* Dec 1, 1913, MCB 2, Box 1.
[14] *York to Cook,* Jan 31, 1914, MCB 2, Box 1.
[15] *Seven Ways to Compute the Relative Value of a US Dollar - 1774 to the Present,* <http://www.measuringworth.com/uscompare/> (Jun 7, 2015).
[16] Seven Ways ... *Relative Value of a US Dollar,* (Jun 7, 2015).
[17] Cook to York and Sawyer, Jun 10, 1914, MCB 2, Box 1.
[18] *York and Sawyer to Cook,* Jul 13, 1914, MCB 2, Box 1.
[19] *Cook to George A. Fuller Company,* Oct 6, 1914, MCB 1.
[20] *Cook to I. Elbert Scrantom,* Jun 23, 1915, MCB 1.
[21] *Scrantom to Cook,* Jul 13, 1915, MCB 1.
[22] *Cook to Scrantom,* Jul 19, 1915, MCB 1.
[23] *Scrantom to Cook,* Aug 19, 1915, MCB 1.
[24] *Scrantom to Cook,* Sep 2, 1915, MCB 1.
[25] *Cook to Scrantom,* Sep 29, 1915 and *Letter, Edward F. Caldwell & Co. to Cook,* Nov 20, 1915, MCB 1.
[26] *Scrantom to Cook,* Sep 2, 1915, MCB 1.
[27] "Magnificent Home for Girls Opens in Ann Arbor," *Detroit Saturday Night,* October 2, 1915.

[28] "Dormitory, Martha Cook Building, University of Michigan, York and Sawyer, *The Brickbuilder: An Architectural Monthly,* Jan 1916, p 42, <books.google.com> (May 10, 2015).
[29] *York to Cook,* Nov 4, 1915, MCB 2, Box 1.
[30] *Hutchins to Cook,* Oct 2, 1915, HBH, Box 10.
[31] *Hutchins to Cook,* Oct 4, 1915, HBH, Box 10.
[32] *Woodbridge N. Ferris to Hutchins,* Oct 11, 1915, HBH, Box 10.
[33] *York to Cook,* Nov 4, 1915, MCB 2, Box 1.
[34] *York to Cook,* Nov 4, 1915, MCB 2, Box 1.

Chapter Three

[1] I. Elbert Scrantom, "Architecture and Furnishings," *The Martha Cook Annual 1921,* ANN.
[2] *Cook to Scrantom,* Feb 13, 1915, MCB 1.
[3] *Scrantom to Cook,* Mar 19, 1915, MCB 1.
[4] *Scrantom to Cook,* Mar 23, 1915, MCB 1.
[5] *Cook to Scrantom,* Oct 4, 1915, MCB 2, Box 1.
[6] *Cook to Scrantom,* October 29, 1918, MCB 1.
[7] *Michigan Stained Glass Census,* <michiganstainedglass.org> (May 29, 2015).
[8] Brown, September 29, 1959.
[9] ANN 1933
[10] DIR, Apr 1934.
[11] GOV, Jan 8, 1944, MCB 2, Box 1.
[12] HB, Dec 17, 1957, MCB 1.
[13] Chernow, pp 28-29.
[14] *Olive Chernow to Josette Allen,* May 12, 1980, MCB 1.
[15] HB, April 25, 1955, MCB 1.
[16] HB, Feb 1, 1967, MCB 1.
[17] *Law to Evan H. Caminker,* Nov 16, 2007, MCB 1.
[18] *Cook to Scrantom,* July 27, 1915, MCB 1.
[19] Slemons.
[20] Slemons.
[21] *Frank J. Connell to Sara Rowe,* Sep 16, 1936, MCB 1.
[22] *Cook to York and Sawyer,* Aug 1, 1917, MCB 2, Box 1.

Chapter Four

[1] Wilfred Shaw, General Secretary of the Alumni Association and Editor of the Michigan Alumnus, in his book, *The University of Michigan* (New York: Harcourt, Brace and Howe, 1920), p 292.
[2] *Scrantom to Cook,* Apr 6, 1916, MCB 1.
[3] *Cook to Scrantom,* April 7, 1916, MCB 1.
[4] GOV, Sep 12, 1992.
[5] GOV, Dec 21, 1995, 16, 1996, June 3, 1997.
[6] Slemons
[7] *Theodore Spicer-Simpson to Scrantom,* Oct 5, 1916, MCB 1.
[8] *Scrantom to Cook,* Nov 18, 1916, MCB 1.

[9] *"The Art of Portraiture,"* Henry Caro-Delvaille, ANN 1921
[10] "A Portrait of Martha Cook," *Michigan Alumnus*, Vol 23, 1916-1917, (Ann Arbor: May 1917), pp 453-455, <hathitrust.org.>, (July 17, 2015)
[11] *Guest Book*, MCB 1.
[12] *Misc. Papers (1)*, MCB 2, Box 4.
[13] *Scrantom to Cook,* Aug 23, 1916, MCB 1.
[14] *Scrantom to Cook,* Feb 6, 1917, MCB 1.
[15] *Scrantom to Cook,* May 8, 1917, MCB 1.
[16] *Scrantom to Cook*, May 15, 1917, MCB 1
[17] *Cook to York and Sawyer*, Jun 29, 1917, MCB 2, Box 1.
[18] *York and Sawyer to Cook*, May 10, 1917, MCB 2, Box 1
[19] *York and Sawyer to Cook*, June 20, 1917, MCB 2, Box 1.
[20] *Cook to York and Sawyer,* June 29, 1917, MCB 2, Box 1.
[21] *Cook to York & Sawyer,* Aug 1 1917, MCB 2, Box 1.
[22] *Samuel Parsons to Cook*, Dec 19, 1917, MCB 2, Box 4.
[23] *Furio Piccirilli to Samuel Parsons, Feb 20, 1918*, Box 4.
[24] *Furio Piccirilli to Cook, Jun 20, 1918*, MCB 2, Box 4.
[25] "Portia," *The Michigan Alumnus*, Vol. XXV, No. 238, November 1918, p 73, <hathitrust.org.>, (July 17, 2015).
[26] *Cook to York and Sawyer,* June 29, 1917, MCB 2, Box 1.
[27] Leary, pp 234-242.
[28] *Scrantom to Cook,* Jul 16, 1919, MCB 1.
[29] *Cook to Scrantom,* Jul 18, 1919, MCB 1.
[30] *Scrantom to Grace Greenwood,* Sep 27, 1919, MCB 1.
[31] "Martha Cook Steinway– Not Your Ordinary Grand Piano," *Washtenaw Impressions* (Washtenaw County Historical Society), Oct 1996, MCB 1.
[32] Leary, pp 105 – 110.
[33] *Washtenaw Impressions.*
[34] *The Hayden Co. to Martha Cook Dormitory*, Nov 8, 1930, MCB 1.
[35] DIR, Nov 1 – Dec 1, 1930.
[36] "Martha Cook's Piano: A Grand Tale." *University Record*, Mar 27, 2000, <http://www.ur.umich.edu/9900/Mar27_00/6.htm> (July 17, 2015).
[37] Chernow, pp 52-23.
[38] GOV, Jun 9, 1993, Nov 8, 1995, March 13, 1996.
[39] "Regents Consider Many Items," *The Michigan Alumnus*, Vol. 37, 1930, p 573, <hathitrust.org.>, (July 17, 2015).
[40] *Adele Huebner to MCB Alumnae*, 50th Anniversary Report, 1965, MCB 2, Box 4.
[41] Chernow, p 5.
[42] Chernow, p 5.
[43] Chernow, p 5.
[44] GOV, June 27, 1966.
[45] *University of Michigan Transfer Voucher*, Dec 20, 1967, Misc. files, MCB 1.
[46] Chernow, p 5.
[47] Chernow, p 6.
[48] "The Lady of the Garden," *President's Advisory Committee on Public Art*, <http://www.public-art.umich.edu/the_collection/campus/central/93>, (July 17, 2015).
[49] Chernow, pp 30-31.

[50] *Martha Cook Building Alumnae Newsletter*, Spring 2005.
[51] GOV, Executive Session, Apr 2, 2004.
[52] *Martha Cook Building Annual Report*, 2007, MCB 1.

Chapter Five

[1] Samuel Parsons, "Martha Cook Lawn," ANN 1921.
[2] REG, Feb 21, 1918, pp 162-164, (May 15, 2015).
[3] REG, Nov 16, 1917, p 63, (May 15, 2015).
[4] Slemons.
[5] *Cook to York and Sawyer,* Aug 9, 1915, MCB 2, Box 1.
[6] *York to Cook,* Nov 4, 1915, MCB 2, Box 1.
[7] *Condon Family Papers,* Bentley Historical Library.
[8] *Cook to Scrantom,* June 27, 1918, MCB 1.
[9] *Scrantom to Cook,* Jul 18, 1918, MCB 1.
[10] *Scrantom to Cook,* Jun 13, 1918, MCB 1.
[11] *Gisela M. Richter to York and Sawyer,* Jul 22, 1918, MCB 2, Box 1.
[12] *Scrantom to Cook,* Jun 13, 1918, MCB 1.
[13] Leary, p 95.
[14] Parsons, Samuel. *Blueprint, Martha Cook Building Garden, undated,* MCB 1.
[15] *Cook to Frances Mack,* Mar 6, 1923, MCB 2, Box 1.
[16] *Cook to E. C. Pardon,* Feb 15, 1921, MCB 2, Box 1.
[17] *Cook to Mack,* Mar 6, 1923, MCB 2, Box 1.
[18] *Cook to Chauncey Cook,* Nov 28, 1918, MCB 2, Box 1.
[19] *Cook to Pardon,* Jul 19, 1927, BHL, Walter Sawyer Papers, Box 4.
[20] *Lorch Hall,* http://umhistory.dc.umich.edu/mort/central/south%20of%20south%20U/Lorch%20Hall/index, (May 25, 2015).
[21] Parsons, "Martha Cook Lawn."

Chapter Six

[1] "Aesthetically Speaking," ANN 1926, p 41.
[2] *Detroit Saturday Night,* October 2, 1915.
[3] *Cook to York and Sawyer,* Dec 1, 1913 and *York to Cook,* Dec 23, 1913, MCB 2, Box 1.
[4] *Hutchins to Olen Templin,* July 17, 1911 and *Otto Kirchener,* Nov 13, 1911, HBH, Box 3.
[5] *Hutchins to Robert L. Kelly,* Nov 25, 1914, HBH, Box 8.
[6] York and Sawyer, *Architectural Drawings, Martha Cook Building,* April 27, 1914, revised May 12 and May 25, MCB 1.
[7] *List of Girls 1915/16.* MCB 2, Box 4.
[8] *Martha Cook Building Handbook, 1931,* BHL, Housing Division Records, Box 3.
[9] *Florentine Cook Heath to Alexander G. Ruthven,* August 20, 1945, MCB 2, Box 1.
[10] *Housing Bulletin,* March 12, 1990. (Ann Arbor: University of Michigan).
[11] *Social Director's Report, Sep 20-Nov 1, 1936.* Bentley Historical Library, Martha Cook Building Papers, Box 2.
[12] DIR, Sep 17-Sep 30, 1939.
[13] *Leona B. Diekema to MCB Alumnae,* Jan 23, 1947. Attached to DIR, Jan 1947.

[14] *Ruthven to Heath,* August 14, 1945, MCB 2, Box 1.
[15] *Heath to Ruthven,* August 20, 1945, MCB 2, Box 1.
[16] *Diekema to MCB Alumnae,* Jan 23, 1947. Attached to DIR, Jan 1947.
[17] DIR, Jun 28-Sep 30, 1950.
[18] DIR, Feb 1949.
[19] *Monthly Salary and Wage Schedule,* 1946-47, MCB 2, Box 1.
[20] AH, May 7, 1956.
[21] Room lists, Winter 1929—Spring 1936, MCB 1 and DIR, Oct 24-Nov 30, 1943.
[22] GOV, Nov 9, 1933, May 5, 1934, Sep 28, 1934, Jan 26, 1935.
[23] *Martha Cook Building Alumnae Newsletter,* Fall 2008.
[24] Leona Diekema, *History of the TV Room,* undated, MCB 2, Box 4.
[25] DIR, Oct 1-31, 1941.
[26] HB, May 3, 1956.
[27] GOV, Oct 25, 1969.
[28] Chernow. pp 37-38.
[29] GOV, Apr 8, 2011.
[30] HB, Oct 25, 1979.
[31] *Mack to W. Sawyer,* Nov 23, 1915, BHL, Walter Sawyer Papers, Box 3.
[32] *Alta Atkinson to Anne E. Shipman Stevens,* March 3, 1930, MCB 2, Box 4.
[33] *The University of Michigan,* (Donnelly, et al., ed.), p 1723.
[34] Kirner, Nancy. "Result of Food Service Survey Conducted Feb 4, 1971 at Martha Cook," *Memo,* Feb 5, 1971.
[35] GOV, Jan 7, 1984 and Mar 10, 1984.
[36] *Dining Services Report,* GOV, Nov 9, 2005.
[37] GOV, Nov 9, 2005.
[38] *Chauncey Cook to J. H. Marks,* Sep 27, 1915, MCB 2, Box 1.
[39] *Room List,* Second Semester, 1928-29, MCB 1.
[40] *Room Lists,* First and Second Semesters, 1929-1930, MCB 1.
[41] HB, Sep 22, 1960.
[42] HB, Apr 19, 1974.
[43] GOV, Apr 2, 1963.
[44] AH, Oct 27, 1963.
[45] Myers, Jane. "Martha Cook's Switchboard Moves to Hot l Baltimore," *The Ann Arbor News,* July 4, 1975, MCB 2, Box 1.
[46] GOV, May 22, 1996.
[47] *Finding Aid for the Computing Center (University of Michigan, History,* BHL), <http://quod.lib.umich.edu/b/bhlead/umich-bhl-9551?byte=154949042; focusrgn=bioghist;subview=standard;view=reslist≥> (Jul 15, 2014).
[48] *Jeff Odgen to Rosalie Moore,* Jan 18, 1986 and *Work Order,* Nov 15, 1985.
[49] GOV, May 22, 1996 and DIR, Jun 12, 1996.
[50] GOV, May 22, 1996.
[51] GOV, Apr 12, 2010.
[52] *Cost Quote from Haughton Elevator & Machine Company, Toledo, OH,* June 8, 1927. MCB 1.
[53] *Rules, September 1937,* DIR.
[54] *F. C. Shiel to Diekema,* March 15, 1956. MCB 1.
[55] *J. N. Ockun to Mr. Bryant,* Jan 24, 1958. MCB 1.
[56] Chernow, p 62.

[57] HB, Nov 2, 1970.
[58] Jim Vibbart, *Review and Report on the Elevator at Martha Cook Dormitory,* (University of Michigan, Plant Department, Elevator Shop, June 3, 1997), MCB 1.
[59] *Minutes, Martha Cook 1997-98 Planning Retreat (Governors and House Board),* Sep 21, 1997, MCB 1.
[60] GOV, Jul 29, 1998.
[61] GOV, May 26, 1998.
[62] *Law to Davis,* Email, Jun 25, 2015.
[63] GOV, Oct 7, 1992.
[64] GOV, Apr 7, 1993.
[65] *Martha Cook Alumnae Association International Newsletter,* Spring 1994.
[66] GOV, Mar 2, 1994.
[67] *Martha Cook Alumnae Association Newsletter,* Fall 1995.
[68] *Board of Governors to James Duderstadt,* Feb 23, 1996, GOV.
[69] *Martha Cook Alumnae Newsletter,* Fall 1996, p2.
[70] DIR, Oct 1950.
[71] DIR, Oct 1951.
[72] Chernow, pp 13, 62, 91.
[73] Chernow, p 35.
[74] GOV, Jul 29, 1998.
[75] *MCAA Newsletter,* fall 2000, p 4.
[76] *Martha Cook Building Annual Report,* 2013.
[77] Chernow, pp 14-15.
[78] *Director's Summer Letter,* GOV, July 2007.
[79] GOV, Feb 8, 1995.
[80] *Facilities Report,* GOV, Feb 8, 2008 and March 13, 2008.
[81] GOV, Apr 5, 2005.
[82] *Facilities Report,* GOV, March 13, 2008.
[83] GOV, Apr 8 2011.
[84] *Martha Cook Building Alumnae Newsletter,* Spring 2008, p 1.
[85] Trudy Zedeker-Witte, *Martha Cook Roof Update,* June 13, 2008, GOV.
[86] Trudy Zedeker-Witte, *Martha Cook Roof Update,* Feb 8, 2008, GOV.
[87] *Martha Cook Building Alumnae Newsletter,* Fall 2008, p 1.
[88] *Facilities Report,* GOV, Oct 13, 1997.
[89] *The University of Michigan* (Donnelly, et al., ed), p 1722.
[90] DIR, June 28-Sep 1950.
[91] *Deed of Gift,* Cook to the Regents of the University of Michigan, Feb 10, 1914. MCB 2, Box 2.
[92] Slemons.
[93] *York to Cook,* Mar 27, 1918, MCB 1.
[94] Chernow, p 35.
[95] GOV, Nov 12, 1998.

Chapter Seven

[1] Price Waterhouse & Co., *Martha Cook Building, Report and Accounts,* Jun 30, 1927, MCB 2, Box 2.
[2] *Financial Statement at Close of Year 1924-25.* MCB 2, Box 2.

[3] *Cook to Chauncey F. Cook,* January 5, 1918, MCB 2, Box 1.
[4] *Cook to Mack,* Oct 12, 1922, MCB 2, Box 1.
[5] *Cook to Mack,* Sep 22, 1925, MCB 2, Box 1.
[6] *Mack to Walter Sawyer,* November 23, 1915. BHL, Walter Hume Sawyer Papers, Box 3.
[7] *Martha Cook Building Financial Statement for ... 1915-1916,* MCB 2, Box 2.
[8] *Folder of Letters Regarding Depression Payments,* MCB 1.
[9] GOV, Mar 14, 1933.
[10] GOV, Apr 27, 1933.
[11] *Herbert G. Watkins to Mrs. Delos P. Heath,* July 8, 1946, MCB 2, Box 1.
[12] GOV, Sep 21, 1946.
[13] GOV, Nov 22, 1946.
[14] *R. P. Briggs to Board of Governors,* Oct 11, 1948, MCB 2, Box 1.
[15] GOV, Sep 21, 1946.
[16] GOV, May 12, 1947.
[17] GOV, Oct 6, 1949.
[18] GOV, Feb 8, 1995.
[19] GOV, Mar 3, 1993.
[20] *Martha Cook Alumnae Association International Newsletter,* Spring 1994, p 3.
[21] *Cook to Marion Burton,* July 14, 1923, BHL, Walter Hume Sawyer Papers, Box 3.
[22] *Cook to Mack,* Mar 11, 1924, MCB 1.
[23] *Cook to the Board of Regents of the University of Michigan,* Jan 11, 1929, REG, Jan 11, 1929 (Mar 29, 2015).
[24] *Martha Cook Building Bylaws (Revised 8-14-08),* MCB 1.
[25] *Herbert G. Watkins to Mrs. Jane W. Cook,* Mar 13, 1944, DIR, Mar 1944.
[26] Chernow, p 130.
[27] *Financial Statement for Year 1915-1916,* MCB 2, Box 2.
[28] Seven Ways ... *Relative Value of a US Dollar,* (Jun 7, 2015).
[29] *Marion Law to Davis,* Email, Jun 15, 2015, Private collection of Catherine Davis.
[30] GOV, Aug 29, 2000.
[31] Yearly Budget Forecast, June of each year, GOV.
[32] *Revenues and Expenses 2014* (for each expendable gift fund) *and Fund Statement 2013* (for each endowed fund). MCB 1.

Chapter Eight

[1] *Last Will and Testament, William W. Cook,* Article 10.
[2] *DIR,* Dec 1949-Jan 1950.
[3] MCAA, Apr 11, 1949.
[4] *Constitution of the MCAA,* Revised 1977, MCB 2, Box 3.
[5] GOV, Jul 14, 1993.
[6] *Martha Cook Alumnae Newsletter,* Spring 1994.
[7] *Martha Cook Alumnae Newsletter,* Fall 1994.
[8] GOV, Nov 9, 1994.
[9] GOV, Nov 9, 1994.
[10] GOV, Nov 9, 1994.
[11] GOV, Apr 5, 2005.
[12] *Director's Report,* GOV, Nov 7, 1996.

[13] GOV, Apr 14, 1998.
[14] *Minutes, Fundraising Committee Meeting, Jun 13, 1998.* MCB 1.
[15] MCAA, Sep 14, 1998.
[16] GOV, Nov 12, 1998.
[17] MCAA, Oct 11, 1999.
[18] MCAA, Feb 2, 2000.
[19] *Martha Cook Alumnae Association Newsletter,* Fall 2000.
[20] *Martha Cook Alumnae Association Newsletter,* Spring 2000.
[21] *Martha Cook Building Alumnae Newsletter,* Fall 2005.
[22] *Martha Cook Alumnae Association Newsletter,* Fall 2000.
[23] *Martha Cook Building Preservation Fund Update,* Fall 2001.
[24] *Martha Cook Building Alumnae Newsletter,* Spring 2007.
[25] *Martha Cook Alumnae Association Newsletter,* Spring 2002
[26] *Board of Governors to Alumnae,* September 2015, MCB 1.
[27] *Martha Cook Building Alumnae Newsletter,* Spring 2005.
[28] *Martha Cook Building Alumnae Newsletter,* Spring 2005.
[29] *Martha Cook Building Alumnae Newsletter,* Fall 2005.
[30] *Martha Cook Building Annual Report of Gift Funds,* Fall 2004 (Ann Arbor: Regents of the University of Michigan, Fall 2004).
[31] *Martha Cook Building Annual Report 2009* (Ann Arbor: Regents of the University of Michigan, 2009).
[32] *Martha Cook Building Alumnae Newsletter,* Spring/Summer 2013.
[33] *Martha Cook Building Annual Report 2008* (Ann Arbor: Regents of the University of Michigan, 2008).
[34] *Martha Cook Building Annual Report 2010* (Ann Arbor: Regents of the University of Michigan, 2010).
[35] *Rob Yallop to Phyllis Valentine,* April 7, 2014. MCB 1.
[36] *Martha Cook Building Annual Report 2013* (Ann Arbor: Regents of the University of Michigan, 2013).
[37] *MCB Board of Governors to Individual Alumnae,* Email, Aug 12, 2014.

Chapter Nine

[1] *Cook to Walter Sawyer,* May 5, 1925, MCB 1.
[2] *Martha Cook Building Bylaws,* revised Aug 18, 2004, MCB 1.
[3] GOV, May 4, 1994.
[4] REG (1929-1932), April 30, 1931, p 606, (June 25, 2015).
[5] REG (1945 – 1948), Dec 27, 1946, p 645, (June 25, 2015).
[6] *Heath to Alexander G. Ruthven,* Aug 20, 1945, MCB 2, Box 1.
[7] *Cook to Walter Sawyer,* June 30, 1920, BHL, Walter Hume Sawyer Collection, Box 3.
[8] *Walter Sawyer to Cook,* July 2, 1920, BHL, Walter Hume Sawyer Collection, Box 3.
[9] *Cook to Walter Sawyer,* July 15, 1920, BHL, Walter Hume Sawyer Collection, Box 3.
[10] *Sawyer to Cook,* Aug 16, 1920, BHL, Walter Hume Sawyer Collection, Box 3.
[11] REG, (1920-1923), January 7, 1921, p 106.
[12] Leary, p 165

[13] *Report, Christmas Breakfast,* Dec 15, 1938, MCB 2, Box 3.
[14] *Jubilee Bells*, October 12, 1940, MCB 2, Box 4.
[15] *Walter Sawyer to Cook*, April 28, 1924, MCB 1.
[16] *Cook to Walter Sawyer,* Aug 25, 1920, BHL, Walter Hume Sawyer Collection, Box 3.
[17] *Heath to C. W. Edmunds*, May 11, 1938, MCB 2, Box 1.
[18] *Cook to Marion L. Burton,* Jul 14, 1923, BHL, Walter Hume Sawyer Collection, Box 3.
[19] *Cook to Walter Sawyer*, May 5, 1925, MCB 1.
[20] GOV, Jun 10, 1946.
[21] GOV, Aug 29, Sep 13 and Oct 3, 2000.
[22] GOV, April 25, 1997.
[23] HB, Sep 29, 1962 and Apr 20, 1962.
[24] GOV, Sep 12, 1992.
[25] GOV, Apr 20, 1996.
[26] *Martha Cook Building Bylaws*, revised Aug 18, 2004, MCB 1.
[27] *Cook to Grover C. Grismore,* Sep 20, 1927, BHL, Walter Hume Sawyer Collection, Box 4.

Chapter Ten

[1] Lynn Zimmerman Bloom and Bernice Pericin Kostanecki, ed., *The Martha Cook Building, Seventy-Fifth Anniversary, 1915-1990* (Ann Arbor, Martha Cook Alumnae Association, 1990).
[2] *Cook to Dr. Walter Sawyer,* Aug 25, 1920. BHL, Walter Hume Sawyer Papers, Box 3.
[3] Slemons.
[4] GOV, May 12, 1947 and Oct 6, 1949, and *Heath to R. P. Briggs,* undated, MCB 2, Box 1.
[5] *DIR,,* Dec 1949-Jan 1950.
[6] *Governors Announcement,* Nov 12, 2003, MCB 1.
[7] This function is mentioned in several of Mrs. Diekema's Reports, DIR.
[8] See, for example, ANN, 1940, p 8.
[9] Chernow, p 30.
[10] GOV, Jun 21, 1976.
[11] *Cook to Stevens,* July 8, 1925, MCB 1.
[12] *House Director's Notebook,* MCB 2, Box 2.
[13] Bloom and Kostenecki, ed.
[14] GOV, Oct 2, 1975.
[15] GOV, Aug 29, 2000.
[16] GOV, Feb 7, 2001 and Mar 28, 2001.
[17] GOV, Mar 28, 2001.
[18] *F. C. Shiel to Robert Briggs,* Mar 29, 1949. MCB 1.
[19] GOV, Sep 15, 1973.
[20] Chernow. p 117.
[21] ANN, 1940, p 9.
[22] *"To Mr. Nissle,* undated, MCB 2, Box 4.
[23] Chernow. p 20.

²⁴ Chernow, p 61.
²⁵ Chernow, p 118.
²⁶ Chernow, pp 135-136.
²⁷ GOV, Nov 8, 1995.
²⁸ GOV, Apr 24, 1995.
²⁹ *Student Wages,* September 28, 1934, MCB 1.
³⁰ Slemons.
³¹ *Notebook of House Director,* MCB 2. Box 2.
³² Bloom, and Kostenecki,
³³ *Analysis of Night Chaperone's Duties,* Apr 7, 1936, DIR.
³⁴ DIR, Jan 1955.
³⁵ *Notebook of House Director,* MCB 2, Box 2.

Chapter Eleven

¹ *Joan Woodward to New Residents,* Jul 25, 1971, MCB 1.
² *Cook to the Young Women of the Martha Cook Building,* Sep 15, 1923, MCB 1.
³ *Cook to Walter Sawyer,* May 5, 1925, MCB 1.
⁴ REG, Feb 1915, pp 118-119, (Jun 23, 2015).
⁵ DIR, June 1931.
⁶ DIR, May 1938.
⁷ *House President's Report (1946-1947).* MCB 2, Box 2.
⁸ *Martha Cook House Board,* <http://cookies.studentorgs.umich.edu/houseboard.html> (Jun 21, 2015).
⁹ *President's Report, 1936-1937.* MCB 2, Box 2.
¹⁰ AH, Sep 14, 1971.
¹¹ HB, Feb 16, 1961.
¹² *Secretary's Reports,* MCB 2, Box 3.
¹³ *President's Report, 1942-1943.* MCB 2, Box 2.
¹⁴ DIR, December 1943.
¹⁵ AH, Mar 14, 1955, Apr 18, 1955.
¹⁶ AH, Mar 20, 1961.
¹⁷ GOV, Mar 14, 1970.
¹⁸ *Law to Davis,* Email, Jul 13, 2015, private collection of Catherine Davis.
¹⁹ *Cook to Stevens,* Jul 8, 1925. MCB 2, Box 1.
²⁰ *Cook to Stevens,* Jul 8, 1925. MCB 2, Box 1.
²¹ *Cook to Cornelia Skinner Blodget,* Aug 2, 1929, as quoted in *Cook to the Governors, Officers, and Residents of the Martha Cook Building,* Dec 25, 1929, MCB 2, Box 1.
²² ANN 1921.
²³ *House Director's Report 1930-31.* DIR.
²⁴ DIR, Sep 20-Nov 1, 1936.
²⁵ DIR, Feb 1940.
²⁶ Chernow, pp 75, 101-103 and HB, Mar 6, 1989.
²⁷ Chernow, pp 104-106.
²⁸ Deborah Day Jansen to Moberg, Email, May 4, 2015.
²⁹ HB, Jan 9, 1984.
³⁰ HB, Feb 4, 1985.

[31] Except where noted, all dates from DIR, Sep 18–Nov 1, 1933, Nov 1933, Jan 1936, Feb 1941, May 1941, Jun 1941, Mar 1942, Dec 1942, Oct 23-Nov 30, 1945, May 1953.
[32] ANN, 1931.
[33] Chernow, p 53.
[34] *Martha Cook Building Annual Report, 2013.*
[35] *Martha Cook Building Alumnae Newsletter,* Spring 2014.
[36] DIR, Nov 1941.
[37] *Martha Cook Building Alumnae Newsletter,* Spring 2014.
[38] *Martha Cook Building Alumnae Newsletter,* Spring 2006.
[39] ANN 1923 and DIR, Apr 1930.
[40] *President's Report, 1935-36.* MCB 2, Box 2.
[41] DIR, May 1941.
[42] *The Michigan Memorial Phoenix Project,* <http://energy.umich.edu/about-us/phoenix-project>, (May 27, 2014).
[43] *Martha Cook Alumnae Newsletter, Fall 2007.*
[44] DIR Feb 1948, Sep 1955 and *Martha Cook Building Annual Report,* 2009.
[45] *Martha Cook Building Alumnae Newsletter,* Spring 2014.
[46] HB, Dec 2, 1985, Jan 26, 1988, Oct 24, 1988, Oct 23, 1989.
[47] *HB, Feb 16, 1988, Jan 30, 1989* and *Martha Cook Alumnae Newsletter,* Spring 2012.
[48] *Martha Cook Building Annual Report,* 2013 and Facebook post, Nov 17, 2013 at *CookieNet* (Jun 4, 2014).
[49] DIR, Feb 1942.
[50] DIR, May 1943.
[51] DIR, May 1943.
[52] DIR, Apr 1943, Mar 1944, May 1945.
[53] DIR, Jun 1944.
[54] DIR, Oct 24-Nov 30, 1944.
[55] DIR, Feb 1942.
[56] Bloom and Kostenecki (ed.).

Chapter Twelve

[1] *MCB Annual,* 1921
[2] *MCB Annual,* 1927
[3] *MCAA of Detroit Newsletter,* Spring 1989.
[4] MCAA, Feb 23, 1952.
[5] *Carrie Peebles to Board Members,* May 29, 1969, MCB 1.
[6] *Minutes,* June 9, 1984, BHL, Martha Cook Alumnae Association of Ann Arbor Records, Box 1.
[7] *Mrs. Ross to Mrs. Amick,* Ap. 8, 1964, BHL, Martha Cook Alumnae Association of Ann Arbor Records, Box 1.
[8] Chernow, pp 47–48.
[9] *Margaret Smith to Stevens,* June 5, 1931, MCB 2, Box 1.
[10] *Mrs. Kenneth H. Quail to Alums,* Ap. 1963, MCB 1.
[11] *Director's Report,* GOV, Oct 7, 1992, MCB 1, and MCAA, Sep 13, 1993.
[12] MCAA, Oct 9, 1950.

[13] DIR, Mar 1951.
[14] *Connie Amick to Olive Chernow*, Aug 17, 1977, MCB 1.
[15] GOV, Sep 25, 1967; Apr 15, 1968.
[16] GOV, Mar 11, 1978; Oct 29, 1978; Apr 22, 1979.
[17] Chernow, p 139.
[18] *Annual Report – Membership 1985*, MCAA.
[19] *Membership Report*, Oct 3, 1988, MCAA.
[20] *The Martha Cook Directory*, Susan Walsh, Chair, (Grigg Graphic Services: Detroit, MI, 1990).
[21] *Martha Cook Alumnae Newsletter, Spring 2001.*
[22] *Martha Cook Alumnae Newsletter, Spring 2001.*
[23] *Martha Cook Alumnae Newsletter*, Fall 2003.
[24] MCAA, Oct 26, 1998; Mar 15, 1999.
[25] *Martha Cook Alumnae Newsletter*, Spring 2015.
[26] *Martha Cook Building Alumnae Newsletter*, Fall 2007.
[27] "Society News," *Detroit News*, Dec 3, 1934.
[28] *Christmas Breakfast Candle Ceremony*, Dec 10, 1988, MCB 1.

Chapter Thirteen

[1] Yang, Shui Chin. *A Farewell to my American Friends*, ANN, 1928.
[2] *Cook to Stevens*, July 8, 1925, MCB 1.
[3] *Cook to Stevens*, July 8, 1925, MCB 1.
[4] Brown, September 29, 1959.
[5] *Cook to. Stevens*, August 25, 1925, MCB 2, Box 1.
[6] Leary, p 233.
[7] *Heath to Dr. C. W. Edmunds*, May 11, 1938, MCB 2, Box 1.
[8] ANN, 1919.
[9] *Cook to the Young Women of the Martha Cook Building*, Sep 15, 1923, MCB 1.
[10] DIR, March 1950.
[11] ANN, 1920.
[12] *Ethel Dawbarn to Emilie Sargent*, Apr 4, 1929, MCB 2, Box 4.
[13] *MCB Board of Governors to Ethel Dawbarn*, Apr 17, 1929, MCB 2, Box 2.
[14] *Cook to Heath*, Mar 25, 1926. MCB 2, Box 1.
[15] DIR, Oct 24 – Nov 30, 1943 and Oct 23-Nov 30, 1945.
[16] GOV, Feb 5, 1972.
[17] *Heath to Edmunds*, May 11, 1938, MCB 2, Box 1.
[18] "General Information, June 1929," *Social Director's Notebook*, DIR.
[19] "Sorority Policy, Sep 29, 1939," *Social Director's Notebook*, DIR.
[20] "Sorority Policy, 1937-38," *Social Director's Notebook*, DIR.
[21] DIR, March 1948.
[22] HB, Feb 13, 1958.
[23] DIR, March 1948.
[24] *Application Form*, MCB 2, Box 4.
[25] "Interviews," *House Director's* Notebook, MCB 2, Box 2.
[26] *Catherine Walsh to Isabel K. Quail*, Winter, 1968, Private Collection of Catherine Davis.
[27] Chernow. p 138.

[28] "Selection of Residents, June 1929", *Social Director's Notebook,* MCB 2, Box 2.
[29] "Selection of Residents, June 1934", *Social Director's Notebook,* MCB 2, Box 2.
[30] ANN, 1919.
[31] Photos, ANN, 1921 and 1922.
[32] Slemons.
[33] ANN, 1928.
[34] Peckham, Howard H. *The Making of the University of Michigan 1817-1992*, edited and updated by Margaret L. Steneck and Nicholas H. Steneck (Ann Arbor: University of Michigan, Bentley Historical Library, 1994), p 201.
[35] Peckham, Steneck, and Steneck, p 190.
[36] Peckham, Steneck, and Steneck, p 241.
[37] DIR, March 1950.
[38] GOV, Jan 26, 1994.
[39] GOV, Jan 12, 1994.
[40] GOV, Jan 12, 1994, Jan 26, 1995.
[41] GOV, Nov 8, 1995.
[42] *Director's Report,* GOV, Feb 29, 1996.
[43] *Cook to Mack,* Feb 8, 1923. MCB2, Box 2.
[44] *Cook to Stephens,* July 8, 1925, MCB 1.
[45] GOV, Nov 7, 2000.
[46] See, for example, *Cook to Elsie Beck,* Mar 10, 1927, MCB 2, Box 2 or *The Martha Cook Alumnae Association International Newsletter,* Fall 1993.
[47] See, for example, the clipping attached to DIR, March 1950.
[48] *Application Information,* <cookies.studentorgs.umich.edu/how-to-apply.html>, (Feb 13, 2015).

Chapter Fourteen

[1] "Rules 1937," *Social Director's Notebook,* DIR.
[2] Dorothy Gies McGuigan, *A Dangerous Experiment: 100 Years of Women at the University of Michigan* (Ann Arbor: Center for Continuing Education of Women, University of Michigan, 1970), pp 62-68.
[3] *Uniform House Rules for Fall, 1916.* MCB 2, Box 4.
[4] *Etiquette Suggestions 1933-1934* and *Etiquette Suggestions 1934-1935,* MCB 2, Box 4.
[5] <http://cookies.studentorgs.umich.edu/handbook.html>, (June 27, 2015).
[6] Donnelly, Shaw, Gjelsness, ed., Part 8, p 1835.
[7] Donnelly, Shaw, Gjelsness, ed., Part 8, p 1836.
[8] HB, Nov 22, 1958.
[9] *Regulations, Constitution and By-Laws of Martha Cook Building.* (Ann Arbor: The University of Michigan, 1969), p 6.
[10] "Lateness Penalties," undated, *Social Director's Notebook,* DIR.
[11] "Permissions." June 1929, *Social Director's Notebook,* DIR.
[12] "Lateness Penalties," undated, *Social Director's Notebook,* DIR.
[13] *Night Receptionist Duties,* undated document, MCB 2, Box 4.
[14] AH, April 29, 1957.
[15] *Lateness Rules,* undated document, MCB 2, Box 4.
[16] HB, Oct 2, 1962.

[17] HB, Sep 14, Sep 29, Oct 2, Nov 3, Nov 7, Nov 14, Dec 16,1962 and Jan 9, Feb 19, Feb 26, May 2, May 6, 1963.
[18] HB, Nov 7, 1962.
[19] HB, Apr 13, Apr 26, Aug 31, Sep 15, Sep 21, Sep 28, 1964.
[20] HB, Aug 31, 1964.
[21] HB, Sep 28, 1964.
[22] *The End of 'Hours,'* <http://heritage.umich.edu/story/end-of-hours/#>, (Feb 14, 2014).
[23] GOV, Oct 3, 1970.
[24] Chernow, p 8.
[25] *House Rules for Undergraduate Women.* MCB 2, Box 4.
[26] Donnelly, Shaw, Gjelsness, ed., Part 8, p 1792.
[27] Slemons.
[28] AH, Apr 24, 1954.
[29] HB, Sep 14, 1954.
[30] AH, Oct 27, 1963.
[31] HB, Apr 1, 1965.
[32] *The Regents Rule,* <http://heritage.umich.edu/story/end-of-hours/#the-regents-rule>, (Feb 14, 2014).
[33] HB, Feb 12, 1968.
[34] HB, Sep 3, 1968.
[35] HB, Oct 2, 1968.
[36] HB, Jan 22, 1969.
[37] AH, Sep 15, 1969.
[38] HB, Sep 28, 1970.
[39] GOV, Apr 12, 1975.
[40] HB, Apr 10, 1974.
[41] HB, Nov 3, 1975.
[42] GOV, Mar 11, 1978.
[43] GOV, Mar 27, 1978.
[44] http://cookies.studentorgs.umich.edu/handbook.html (Jun 27, 2015).
[45] "Policy Concerning Necking," *Social Director's Notebook*, DIR.
[46] Untitled, Undated List of Rules, MCB 2, Box 4.
[47] DIR, April 1949.
[48] Chernow, p 9.
[49] HB, Oct 9, 1952.
[50] Rubin, Gayle S. and Miller, Karen. "Revisioning Ann Arbor's Radical Past: An Interview with Gayle S. Rubin," *Michigan Feminist Studies,* Vol 12, 1997-1998 (Ann Arbor: M Publishing, University of Michigan Library, <http://hdl.handle.net/2027/spo.ark5583.0012, (Mar 24, 2014).
[51] GOV, Mar 14, 1970.
[52] Chernow, p 9.
[53] HB, Jan 22, 1973.
[54] < http://cookies.studentorgs.umich.edu/handbook.html> (Feb 8, 2014).
[55] AH, Sep 9, 1968.
[56] National Education Association of the United States, American Normal School Association, National Association of School Superintendents, National Teachers' Association (U.S.), Central College Association (U.S.), *Addresses and Proceedings*

of the Fifty-seventh Annual Meeting held at Milwaukee, Wisconsin June 28-July 5 1919 (Washington, DC: National Education Association of the United States, 1919), VOLUME LVII, p 425, <www.googlebooks.com>, (Aug 2, 2010).
[57] Chernow. *Op. Cit.,* p 96.
[58] *Cook to Stevens,* July 8, 1925, MCB 1.

Chapter Fifteen

[1] GOV, Nov 29, 1935.
[2] GOV, Apr 27, 1933.
[3] *Alice Lloyd to Heath,* May 10, 1935, MCB 2, Box 1.
[4] *Ethel Dawbarn to Stevens,* Dc 12, 1928, MCB 2, Box 4.
[5] *Mary Gleason to Grace Campbell Bruce,* Jan 13, 1939, MCB 2, Box 1.
[6] *Leona B. Diekema to Frank Robbins, Chair,* December 1, 1939, MCB 1.
[7] GOV, Apr 16, 1956.
[8] Chernow, p 26.
[9] *Rosalie Moore to MCB Residents,* Memo, Oct 8, 1985, MCB 1.
[10] "General Information," DIR, Jun 1929, MCB 2, Box 2.
[11] *Alta Atkinson to Stevens,* March 3, 1930 MCB 2, Box 4.
[12] *Heath to Shirley Smith,* Oct 8, 1935, MCB 2 Box 1.
[13] Margaret Smith to Vera Baits, May 3, 1933, MCB 2, Box 1.
[14] HB, Oct 9, 1958, MCB 1.
[15] "Unique University Living at the Martha Cook Building", *University of Michigan News Service Press Release,* Sep 29, 1965, MCB 1.
[16] DIR, Jan 1951.
[17] REG (1936-1939), June 18, 1937, p 278, (Jun 29, 2015).
[18] *Marguerite Chapin Maire to MCB Alumnae,* Mar 15, 1939, MCB 2, Box 1.
[19] GOV, Nov 16, 1939.
[20] GOV, Apr 18, 1970.
[21] *Heath to Lloyd,* Oct 1, 1946, BHL, Housing Division Records, Box 3.
[22] DIR, Jun 1950.
[23] *Martha Cook Building Preservation Fund Update,* Fall 2001.
[24] Chernow, p 25.
[25] Miscellaneous Papers, 1977, MCB 1.
[26] *Martha Cook Alumnae Association of Ann Arbor to Alumnae,* Winter 1987, BHL, Martha Cook Alumnae Association of Detroit Records, Box 1.
[27] *Betty Bishop and Maurita Holland to Beth Johnston and Kathy Moberg,* June 2, 2007, and *Holland to Johnston and Moberg, June 7, 2007,* GOV, June 2007.; MCB Student Handbook 2006, MCB 1.

Chapter Sixteen

[1] *President's Report,* 1947-48, MCB 2, Box 2.
[2] *Margaret Blake to MCB Residents,* Summer 1957, MCB 2, Box 4.
[3] GOV, Feb 1, 1960.
[4] DIR, Mar 1943.
[5] Chernow, p 97.
[6] GOV, Sep 5, 2001.

[7] *Gertrude Beggs to Grace Greenwood,* undated, MCB 2, Box 4.
[8] DIR, Jan 1956.
[9] GOV, Jul 29, 1998.
[10] GOV, Aug 7, 2001.
[11] GOV, Jan 26, 1935.
[12] GOV, Mar 3, 1993.
[13] Email messages between Nancy Sudia, Mabelle Kirk, Catherine Davis and Kathy Moberg, June 29 and 30, 2015, Private Collection of Kathy Moberg.
[14] HB, Nov 16, 1964.
[15] Chernow, p 56.
[16] Chernow, p 49.
[17] *Martha Cook Building Alumnae Newsletter,* Spring 2015.
[18] DIR, Oct 1942 and Oct 1950.
[19] *President's Report* 1929-1930, MCB 2, Box 2.
[20] "H D Job at MCB," Sara Rowe, undated (Misc. Papers 2), MCB 2, Box 4.

Chapter Seventeen

[1] ANN, 1927, p 16.
[2] ANN, 1932, p 42.
[3] ANN, 1924.
[4] ANN, 1930, p 38.
[5] ANN, 1931, p 50.
[6] ANN, 1932, p 40.
[7] DIR, Dec 1944.
[8] DIR, Apr 1944.
[9] *Vice President's Report,* 1933–43, MCB 2, Box 2.
[10] *Vice President's Report,* 1937–38, MCB 2, Box 2.
[11] ANN, 1929, p 34.
[12] Spring 2007 MCAA newsletter, KGM's files
[13] *BTN Tailgate, Episode 48 - Michigan,* broadcast Oct 19, 2012, <http://vimeo.com/user6834654/review/52121503/692cede1a8>, (Nov 7, 2012).
[14] *Dawbarn to Cora Strong Bulkley,* Apr 29, 1929, MCB 2, Box 4.
[15] *Garden Party Report,* May 11, 1946, May 3, 1947, MCB 2, Box 4.
[16] DIR, May 1938.
[17] *Report of Reception for Kathleen Codd,* Nov 11, 1934, MCB 2, Box 4.
[18] *International Chairwoman's Report,* 1959-60, MCB 2, Box 3.
[19] DIR, Nov 1947.
[20] HB, Oct 3, 1983.
[21] HB, Jan 15, 1990.
[22] Henry James, *Portrait of a Lady,* (New York: Penguin Books, 2003) p 59. (Work originally published in *The Atlantic Monthly,* 1880-81.

Chapter Eighteen

[1] <http://www.merriam-webster.com/dictionary/tradition> (accessed May 27, 2015).
[2] *Certificate of Copyright,* Apr 3, 1916, MCB 1.

[3] Doughty, Edna R., Ed, *Martha Cook Songs* (Ann Arbor: Ann Arbor Press, 1922) p 8, <Hathitrust.org> (Nov 2, 2014).
[4] *Martha Cook Cookbook*, (Ann Arbor: Martha Cook Building, 1989), unnumbered page.
[5] *Messiah Dinner Program*, Dec 5, 2004, private collection of Kathy Moberg.
[6] *Chorister's Report*, 1935-36, MCB 2, Box 3.
[7] Slemons.
[8] GOV, Feb 2015, per email from Mabelle Kirk to Kathy Moberg Jul 7, 2015, Private Collection of Kathy Moberg.
[9] *Martha Cook Building Alumnae Newsletter*, Spring 2015.
[10] Series of letters between Cook and Scrantom, March 4 - June 13, 1919, MCB 1.
[11] GOV, Dec 20, 1934.
[12] GOV, May 1, 1936.
[13] *Vice President's Report*, 1938, MCB 2, Box 2.
[14] DIR, Feb 1942.
[15] *Frances Osborn Gibson to Sara Rowe*, May 28, 1946, MCB 2, Box 4.
[16] *Martha Cook Cookbook*, (Ann Arbor: Martha Cook Building, 1980).
[17] *Martha Cook Cookbook*, (Ann Arbor: Martha Cook Building, 2003).
[18] Michigan Alumnae Club of Ann Arbor, *Blue Book of Cooking: a collection of favorite recipes of University of Michigan alumnae throughout the United States* (Ann Arbor: The Alumnae Club, 1938, 2nd ed. 1941, <hathitrust.org>, (May 27, 2015).
[19] *MCAA International Newsletter*, Fall 1992.
[20] *MCAA International Newsletter*, Spring 1993.
[21] HB, May 8, 1962.
[22] *Regulations, Constitution and By-Laws of Martha Cook Building.* (Ann Arbor, The University of Michigan, 1969), p 1.
[23] *The Martha Cook Building Handbook,* 2013, p 6. http://cookies.studentorgs.umich.edu/handbook.html (accessed Feb 8, 2014).
[24] *Law to Moberg,* Email, May 11, 2015, private collection of Kathy Moberg.
[25] *Martha Cook Cookbook*, Ann Arbor: Martha Cook Building, 1989), unnumbered page.

Chapter Nineteen

[1] ANN, 1941, p 7.
[2] ANN, 1916.
[3] DIR, Sep 1950.
[4] "CookieNet," *Facebook,* Social Media, Jun 8, 2013.
[5] *Dance Report*, Spring 1955, MCB 2, Box 4.
[6] DIR, Nov 1943.
[7] *Report of the Spring Formal,* May 8, 1959, MCB 2, Box 4.
[8] House Board Files 1990 - 2015, MCB 1.
[9] *Orientation Square Dance,* Sep 26, 1958, MCB 2, Box 3.
[10] *Vice President's Report,* Spring 1960, MCB 2, Box 2.
[11] ANN, 1938, p 15.
[12] Elva Forncrook, "Christmas Morning Breakfast", June 1929, *Social Director's Notebook,* MCB 2, Box 2.

[13] Forncrook, "Year End Report", June 1929, *Social Director's Notebook*, MCB 2, Box 2.
[14] "Christmas Morning Breakfast," *Social Director's Notebook*, June 1931, MCB 2, Box 2.
[15] *Forncrook to Cook*, Jan 14, 1928, MCB 2, Box 1.
[16] "Social Report 1935 – 1936", Dec 20, MCB 2, Box 3; DIR, Dec 1–Dec 18, 1936.
[17] *1938 Christmas Breakfast at Michigan Women's Dorm*, <https://www.youtube.com/watch?v=o8Db22OYV5U>, (July 20, 2015).
[18] Slemons.
[19] *Vice President's Report*, Sep 1930 – June 1931, MCB 2, Box 2; *Christmas Party for Mothers Report*, 1935, MCB 2, Box 4; ANN 1930.
[20] ANN, 1937, p 22.
[21] *Vice President's Report*, Spring 1930-31, MCB 2, Box 2.
[22] President's Report 1935 – 1936", *Social Director's Notebook*, MCB 2, Box 2.
[23] *Report of the Christmas Breakfast*, Dec 18, 1941, MCB 2, Box 3.
[24] *Christmas Breakfast Report*, Dec 1942, MCB 2, Box 3.
[25] *Christmas Breakfast Report*, Dec 1942, MCB 2, Box 3.
[26] DIR, Dec 1945.
[27] DIR, Dec 1948.
[28] *Reports of the Christmas Breakfast*, 1954 – 1962, MCB 2, Box 3.
[29] *Reports of the Christmas Breakfast*, 1954 – 1962, MCB 2, Box 3.
[30] Chernow, p 65.
[31] ANN, 1931, p 55.
[32] DIR, Mar 1943.
[33] *Cookie Press*, Mar 15, 1946.
[34] *Faculty Dinner Report*, Winter 1977, MCB 2, Box 7.
[35] DIR, Apr 1951.
[36] "Initiation Service," *Social Director's Notebook*, June 1929, MCB 1.
[37] "House President's Speech, First Formal Dinner," 1931 – 32, *Social Director's Notebook*, MCB 2, Box 2.
[38] "Initiation Service," Sep 1934, *Social Director's Notebook*, MCB 2, Box 2.
[39] DIR, Oct 1950.
[40] HB, Sep 29, 1960.
[41] *Reports of Senior Dinner*, various years, MCB 2, Box 4.
[42] GOV, Apr 7, 1993.
[43] *Reports of Senior Dinner*, various years, MCB 2, Box 4.
[44] ANN, 1916.
[45] DIR, Nov 1950.
[46] DIR, Nov 1954.
[47] HB, Mar 17, 1958.
[48] *Reports of Birthday Dinners*, various years, MCB 2, Box 3.
[49] *Birthday Dinner Report*, Mar 1974, MCB 2, Box 7.
[50] *Birthday Dinner Report*, April, 1975, MCB 2, Box 7.
[51] HB, Mar 29, 1988.
[52] DIR, May 1941.
[53] DIR, Dec 1948.
[54] *Vice President's Report*, Spring 1960, MCB 2, Box 2.
[55] DIR, Dec 1948.

[56] *Messiah Dinner Report,* 1964, MCB 2, Box 3.
[57] *MCAA Newsletter,* Spring 2000.
[58] *Rosalie Moore to MCB Residents,* undated, MCB 1.
[59] HB, Apr 14, 1965.

Chapter Twenty

[1] Slemons.
[2] DIR, Dec 1944.
[3] HB, Nov 5, Nov 10 and Dec 1, 1955.
[4] *G. G. Millard to unknown,* undated, MCB 2, Box 4.
[5] GOV, May 10, 1935.
[6] Slemons.
[7] ANN, 1918.
[8] *Vesper Service,* MCB 2, Box 4.
[9] ANN, 1917.
[10] Slemons.
[11] DIR, Apr 1944.
[12] DIR, Mar 1945.
[13] DIR, Mar 1949.
[14] DIR, May 1949.
[15] *Activities Chairwoman's Report,* 1950, MCB 2, Box 4.
[16] DIR, May 1955 and *Senior Dinner Reports,* 1955, 1956, 1958, MCB 2, Box 4.
[17] GOV, Mar 5, 1968.
[18] DIR, Dec 1–Dec 16, 1939.
[19] DIR, Dec 1944.
[20] *Martha Cook Alumnae Newsletter,* Spring 2001.
[21] *Sara Rowe to Maire,* Oct 10 1938, MCB 2, Box 1.
[22] Slemons.
[23] "President's Report," *Social Director's Notebook,* MCB 2, Box 2.
[24] DIR, Sep–Oct 1942.
[25] ANN, 1927.
[26] HB, Apr 19, 1961.
[27] DIR, Oct 1951.
[28] HB, Dec 5, 1957, Oct 27, 1963, Nov 2, 1964.
[29] "International Dinner Report," Feb 18, 1976, MCB 2, Box 7.
[30] Chernow, p 17.

Chapter Twenty One

[1] ANN, 1926.
[2] ANN, 1920.
[3] Shaw, Wilfred, *The University of Michigan, An Encyclopedic Survey,* (Ann Arbor: University of Michigan Press, 1941), p 1865.
[4] *President's Report,* 1932-33, MCB 2, Box 2.
[5] *Vice President's Report,* 1938, MCB 2, Box 2.
[6] *President's Report,* 1937-38, MCB 2, Box 2.
[7] *President's Report,* 1946, MCB 2, Box 4.

[8] *Twenty-Fifth Anniversary Tea,* Oct 12, 1940, MCB 1.
[9] ANN, 1941.
[10] ANN, 1941.
[11] *Silver Jubilee Program,* Oct 12, 1940, MCB 1.
[12] *Jubilee Bells,* Oct 12, 1940, MCB 1.
[13] Victory Reunion Responses, MCB 2, Box 4.
[14] Chernow, p 4.
[15] Chernow, p 3.
[16] *Menu, 50th Reunion Banquet,* Oct 23, 1965, MCB 2, Box 4.
[17] *Instructions for Registration Committee,* 50th Anniversary, MCB 1.
[18] *MCAA of D President's Report 1965 66,* MCB 2, Box 2.
[19] Chernow, p 3.
[20] Chernow, p 80.
[21] *Martha Cook 75th Anniversary Report* by Shirley Vaughn, BHL, MCAA of D Records, Box 1.
[22] *75th Anniversary Jubilee Communication,* June 1, 1990, MCB 1.
[23] *Martha M. Bigelow to Board of Governors c/o Rosalie Moore,* Oct 24, 1989, MCB 1.
[24] *MCAA Newsletter,* Fall 1995.
[25] *MCAA Newsletter,* Fall 1995.

Postscript

[1] GOV, Jun 10, 1946.
[2] Nancy Kirner, *Result of Food Service Survey Conducted Feb 4, 1971 at Martha Cook, Memo,* Feb 5, 1971.
[3] University of Michigan Housing Facilities Department. *Martha Cook Renewal and Capital Improvements: An Overview for Near and Medium Term (<10 Years) Planning,* (Ann Arbor: Fall 1998).
[4] ISES Corporation. *The University of Michigan, Facility Condition Analysis, Martha Cook Residence* (Stone Mountain, GA, 1999).
[5] Quinn Evans|Architects. *Martha Cook Building, Ann Arbor, Michigan: Interior Building Assessment,* (Ann Arbor: Feb 2001).
[6] *Cook to the Young Women of the Martha Cook Building,* Sep 15, 1923, MCB 1.
[7] *Cook to Mack,* Oct 12, 1922, MCB 2, Box 1.
[8] *Cook to Mack,* Oct 12, 1922, MCB 2, Box 1.

Appendix C

[1] *The Arrow of Pi Beta Phi,* Vol 21, 1904, pp 76-77, <googlebooks.com>, (Jul 8, 2015).
[2] *Jubilee Bells,* Oct 12, 1940. MCB 2, Box 4.
[3] <findagrave.com>, (Jan 11, 2015).
[4] Slemons.
[5] ANN, 1922.
[6] ANN 1922.
[7] *California, Death Index, 1940-1997,* <familysearch.org> (January 11 2015).
[8] Slemons

[9] *United States Census, 1940,* <familysearch.org> (Nov 30, 2014),
[10] Slemons.
[11] *The Michigan Alumnus,* (Ann Arbor: University of Michigan Alumnae Association, Vol 58, May 10, 1952) p 371, <googlebooks.com>, (Dec 2, 2014).
[12] *United States Census, 1910,* <familysearch.org> (Dec 1, 2014).
[13] Slemons.
[14] Elva M. Forncrook, "Probation for Women," *Journal of Criminal Law and Criminology,* (Evanston, IL, Northwestern University, Vol. 14, Issue 4, Article 10, 1924.)
[15] *Pennsylvania, County Marriages, 1885-1950,* <familysearch.org> (Dec 1, 2014).
[16] *United States Census, 1910,* <familysearch.org>, (Dec 1, 2014).
[17] *The Michigan Alumnus,* Vol 58, May 10, 1952) p 371, *(Dec 2, 2014).*
[18] Slemons.
[19] *United States Social Security Death Index,* <familysearch.org> (Dec 1, 2014).
[20] Slemons.
[21] *Jubilee Bells,* Oct 12, 1940. MCB 2, Box 4.
[22] Slemons.
[23] *Jubilee Bells,* Oct 12, 1940. MCB 2, Box 4.
[24] Slemons.
[25] <http://en.wikipedia.org/wiki/George_P._Codd,> (Dec 4, 2014).
[26] Slemons.
[27] *United States Social Security Death Index,* <familysearch.org>, (Dec 4, 2014).
[28] *Vermont, Vital Records, 1760-1954,* <familysearch.org>, (12 July 2015).
[29] *Luther Fowles to Dear Friends,* Jan 5, 1959, Smith College Archives (Northampton, MA), Box 1746.
[30] *Class of 1909 Reunion Booklet,* 1924, Smith College Archives, Box 1745.
[31] *Class of 1909 Reunion Booklet,* 1924, Smith College Archives, Box 1745.
[32] *Mary Fowle to Smith College Class Secretary,* Feb 4, 1959 and *Luther Fowles to Dear Friends,* Jan 5, 1959, both from Smith College Archives, Box 1746.
[33] *Massachusetts, Death Index, 1970-2003,* <familysearch.org>, (July12, 2015).
[34] *Michigan Alumnus,* 1960, vol 67, p 120. <googlebooks.com>, (Jan 8, 2015).
[35] *Michigan Obituaries, 1820-2006,* <familysearch.org> (January 8, 2015).
[36] DIR, January 1941.
[37] *US Passport Applications, 1795-1925,* application for Margaret Hingeley Blake, 1919, ANC (Jul 7, 2015).
[38] Multiple passport applications and ships rosters at ANC (Jul 7, 2015).
[39] *Us Census, 1940,* ANC (Jul 7, 2015).
[40] "Locke Announces Plan for Assuming Post at Grad House, *Oberlin Review,* vol 76, no. 45, April 16, 1948, p1, <http://dcollections.oberlin.edu/cdm/ref/collection/p15963coll9/id/29164>, (Jan 27, 2015).
[41] *Illinois, Cook County Marriages, 1871-1920,"* <familysearch.org> (January 27, 2015).
[42] "Obituary, Isabel K. Quail," *Ann Arbor News, Oct 12, 1978.*
[43] *United States Social Security Death Index,* <familysearch.org> (January 9, 2015).
[44] *MCAA Newsletter,* Feb 9, 1970, MCB 2, Box 4.
[45] Chernow, pp2-3, 5-6.
[46] *The University Record,* Feb 1, 2008, <http://www.ur.umich.edu/0708/Jan28_08/obits.shtml>, (Jan 11, 2015).

[47] *The Michigan Alumnus,* Vol 53, June 14, 1947, p 397, <googlebooks.com>, (Jan 30, 2015).
[48] University of Michigan. *The President's Report to the Board of Regents for the Fiscal Year,* (Ann Arbor: U-M Libraries, 1979) Vol 2, p 66, <googlebooks.com>, (Jan 30, 2015).
[49] GOV, June 24, 1981.
[50] *Martha Cook Building Alumnae Newsletter,* Fall 2014.
[51] *Martha Cook Alumnae Association International Newsletter,* Fall 1992.
[52] *Martha Cook Alumnae Association Newsletter,* Fall 1997.

Photo Credits

a03	Martha Cook Annual 2003
a05	Martha Cook Annual 2005
a06	Martha Cook Annual 2006
a19	Martha Cook Annual 1919
a20	Martha Cook Annual 1920
a23	Martha Cook Annual 1923
a25	Martha Cook Annual 1925
a28	Martha Cook Annual 1928
a29	Martha Cook Annual 1929
a31	Martha Cook Annual 1931
a33	Martha Cook Annual 1933
a34	Martha Cook Annual 1934
a36	Martha Cook Annual 1936
a37	Martha Cook Annual 1937
a40	Martha Cook Annual 1940
a41	Martha Cook Annual 1941
a76	Martha Cook Annual 1976
a90	Martha Cook Annual 1990
as	Adriana Saroki
avr	Abigail Rogers
bgm	Bert Moberg
bh1	Bentley Historical Library, Martha Cook Building records (Bimu F17 2) Box 1
bh5	Bentley Historical Library, Martha Cook Building records (Bimu F17 2) Box 5
bh6	Bentley Historical Library, Martha Cook Building records (Bimu F17 2) Box 6
bhc	Bentley Historical Library, Ann Bradford Cook papers (2014021 Aa2)
bhi	Bentley Historical Library, Bentley Image Bank
cjd	Catherine J. Walsh Davis
clr	Carolyn L. Romzick
dbj	Debra Ball Johnson
fty	Marion L. Slemons, *A Booklet of the Martha Cook Building: A History of the First Twenty Years*
jm	Joan Hornbach Masters
ke	Kim Essenburg
kgm	Kathy Moberg
mbs	Margaret Bergren Schwartz

Photo Credits

mcb	Martha Cook Building collection*
mz	Michelle Zaydlin
rpj	Ruth Pew Jaynes
sc	Sarah Cravens
sfa	Martha Cook Building Seventy-fifth Anniversary booklet
tw	Tessa Wiles
twd	Thomas W. Davis
wjd	William J. Davis

1. (mcb) William W. Cook 2
2. (fty) Martha Wolford Cook 3
3. (bh1) Architects' sketch of the proposed Martha Cook Building, from the garden. 15
4. (bhi) The bricks were laid in the Flemish Diagonal Bond pattern. 16
5. (cjd) Arched windows and buttresses, shown here along the Terrace, reflect the medieval influence on the Building's architecture. 16
6. (kgm) Turrets and crenellations are among the Building's medieval features. 17
7. (mcb) Marginalia from a letter to Cook from Scrantom, June 21, 1915 18
8. (kgm) Chimera 18
9. (mcb) The Flemish Bond pattern of the brick is easily discernable in this photo of the portal, ca 1915–1917, before the installation of the statue of *Portia*. 19
10. (bgm) The corridor with *Venus* 21
11. (bhc) By October 1914, the walls were beginning to rise. 23
12. (a23) Sketch of the Dining Room fireplace motto by Catherine Heller '22 24
13. (mcb) Corridor with the grandfather clock, before *Venus* 30
14. (kgm) The decorative plaster work of the Red Room ceiling, with its barrel vault or "wagon head" shape, is a replica of a ceiling in the early seventeenth century Chastleton Manor House in Oxfordshire, England. 31
15. (kgm) Foyer ceiling 32
16. (kgm) Stained-glass lamp of knowledge in the Red Room 33
17. (bh6) The elegance of the architectural details and furnishings are evident in this early picture of the Blue Room. 35
18. (kgm) Carving from the Red Room wall paneling 36
19. (bh1) Sketch drawn by the artist while visiting MCB in 1916. The finished portrait can be seen in Chapter 18. 39
20. (bgm) The Martha Cook *Venus* 43
21. (bgm) *Portia* 46
22. (sfa) MCB's seventeenth century Flemish verdure tapestry 48
23. (a41) Art Case Steinway piano, 1941 50
24. (bgm) Bust of William W. Cook 52
25. (bgm) *Eve* in the garden 55
26. (bgm) *Edwina* 57
27. (a30) Tennis court by Dorothy Wilson '31 62
28. (bhi) The Condon garden, 1915 63
29. (bhi) Parson's garden, June 1921 64
30. (a33) Parsons' garden, ca 1930 65

---

* Most of the collection currently in the Martha Cook Building will be moved to the Bentley Historical Library

The Martha Cook Building's First 100 Years · 375

31. (cjd) Softball in the garden, spring 1969 67
32. (a40) Fourth floor sewing room, 1940 74
33. (a40) Phone in the cloak room, 1940.. 76
34. (a19) Drawing by Juliet Peddle '22 80
35. (kgm) Barrier-free access 83
36. (bh6) This early photo shows that women of the past, like their modern counterparts, opened windows on cold days to offset the Building's excess heat. 88
37. (a17) Frances C. Mack 92
38. (a33) Sara Rowe 94
39. (kgm) Resident using wi-fi to study in the Sparking Room. 100
40. (cjd) Mailing party in the Red Room, 2003 106
41. (bgm) Room plaque... 109
42. (wjd) Edwina Jaques with *Edwina* at the 2005 dedication. 110
43. (a19) Grace Grieve Millard 115
44. (a19) Louise Stock Cook... 116
45. (a19) Anne E. Shipman Stevens.. 117
46. (a17) Gertrude Beggs, first Social Director 126
47. (a41) Leona Diekema, 1941 128
48. (a05) Olive Chernow, Marion Law, and Rosalie Moore, Messiah Dinner 2005 . 129
49. (a76) Vivian Jones, 1976... 131
50. (a34) MCB Staff, 1934.. 132
51. (a41) Mr. Nissle 133
52. (bgm) Office assistant, 2014 135
53. (mbs) MCB busmen, 1979 136
54. (avr) Maize and blue Cookies, 2013.. 140
55. (a17) House Board, 1917 141
56. (a37) House Board on the terrace, 1937... 142
57. (a20) A sketch by Juliet Peddle '22 reveals the solution to overly-long meetings. 144
58. (a06) Welcome Week, 2006.. 146
59. (clr) President Gerald R. Ford in the Gold Room, 1977................................. 148
60. (a30) Intramural hockey team, 1930 150
61. (jm) Intramural football, 1981 151
62. (a28) Alumnae meeting in the Blue Room, 1928 157
63. (cjd) Golden Alumnae (fifty or more years as Cookies) were honored in 2000. . 166
64. (ke) A 21st century Spring Tea 167
65. (a25) Illustration of Returning Alumnae by Dorothy Eggert '25 168
66. (a19) Freshmen residents, 1919... 173
67. (a34) Graduate students and Barbour Scholars, 1934..................................... 178
68. (a25) Dorothy Eggert's 1925 Sparking Room sketch celebrates MCB diversity. 179
69. (as) "New Women," at the dinner in their honor, 2011 184
70. (a36) Whoa! The lawyers did not observe the same curtain rules as MCB. (1936) 187
71. (a41) More than "three feet on the floor": Residents and guests play bridge in a student room during a 1940-41 open house... 192
72. (a28) Three feet on the floor? (Sketch by Anne Schell '29)............................ 196
73. (mcb) A 1960s tea in the Gold Room.. 199
74. (a19) Mock tea, 1919 200
75. (mcb) Students were expected to keep their rooms neat and tidy.................... 201
76. (kgm) *The Scholar*, portal of Martha Cook Building 210

77. (cjd) Fall AESS Scholarship recipients during Welcome Week, 2011 214
78. (a23) Standing in the "bread line," 1923 220
79. (a25) Sketch by Dorothy Eggert '25 223
80. (a24) From the *Martha Cook Annual,* 1924 (artist unknown) 224
81. (a24) From the *Martha Cook Annual,* 1924 (artist unknown) 224
82. (bh6) Dining Room, ca 1915 226
83. (as) A sit-down dinner, 2011 227
84. (a24) From the *Martha Cook Annual,* 1924 (artist unknown) 232
85. (a41) Tea in the corridor, 1941 233
86. (tw) Cookies welcome U-M President Mark Schlissel to tea September 26, 2014. 235
87. (mcb) Garden Party Tea, ca 1928–30 236
88. (mcb) Old English Festival costumes, ca 1928-1930 237
89. (a05) International Tea, 2005 239
90. (a90) Booth at International Tea, 1990 240
91. (avr) Silver teapots and china cups and saucers are still used regularly. 241
92. (kgm) "Cookies" with cookies, 1979 251
93. (rpj) The Ghost of Martha at Spring Tea, 2015 255
94. (a29) The 1928 Halloween costume contest was won by this line of Cookie convicts. 259
95. (kgm) Bar-B-Q on tennis court for Welcome Week, ca 1999 261
96. (a90) Welcome Week 1989 included croquet in the Garden. 262
97. (kgm) Bounce house on the lawn, 2013 263
98. (a18) Sketch by Helen Osband '19 264
99. (bh6) Spring formal with the traditional lantern lighting, 1935 265
100. (mbs) Holiday Breakfast procession, 1979 267
101. (kgm) Christmas Breakfast, 1978 270
102. (a90) New residents with their roses, 1989 274
103. (a90) UMS President Ken Fischer, Messiah Dinner, 1989. 281
104. (a90) 1989 Musicale 282
105. (jm) Waitresses just before the 1981 Messiah Dinner 284
106. (a17) The first Scholarship Dinner, 1917 292
107. (a28) *Bridge* by Anne Schell '29 295
108. (a37) Flowers for the Ruthvens, 1937 296
109. (a41) Twenty-fifth Jubilee banquet 305
110. (mcb) Margaret Yerkes Holden '18 310
111. (mcb) 310
112. (bgm) Ninetieth logo 311
113. (wjd) Ninetieth attendees in the Gold Room. 311
114. (bgm) The Building is ready for its 100th anniversary 314
115. (sc) To the Future! 318
116. (bh1) 319
117. (a23) From 1923 *Annual* 325
118. (a36) Governors Florentine Heath, Vera Baits, and Grace Bruce, 1936 333
119. (dbj) The original Outstanding Resident Award plaque. 344
120. (twd) Catherine Walsh Davis 382
121. (bgm) Kathy Graneggen Moberg 383

Index

Ahern, Deborah, 134, 336
Alessandri, Christa, 105, 337, 343
Allan, Mary Josette, 208, 331, 351
Altman, Robert, 148
Amick, Constance Butler, 105, 159, 163, 308, 334, 360, 361
Angell, James B., 27
Asha Latika Haldar, 178
Atkinson, Alta, 75, 209, 335, 354, 364
Baits, Vera Burridge, 122, 210, 333, 345, 364
Baker, Deane, 309
Barbour Scholars, 178, 307
Barrier-Free Access, 82
Beggs, Gertrude Harper, 160, 222, 224, 228, 325, 365
Berardi, Alexandra, 284
Bergren, Margaret, 134, 336
Bergsma, Vicki, 194, 340
Berndt, Joan Gassaway, 251
Birthday Dinner, 254, 278–280, 367
Blake, Margaret Hingeley, 126, 175, 329, 364, 370
Bloom, Lynn Zimmerman, 153, 308, 358
Blue/Gold Room, ii, 2, 27, 30, 32, 34, 49, 51–53, 100, 105, 131, 143, 148, 149, 198, 199, 201, 226, 231, 232, 235, 238, 241, 245, 260–263, 265, 268, 269, 271, 274, 275, 277, 281, 283, 284, 287, 290, 291, 293, 295, 296, 298, 313, 323
Board of Governors, i, ii, 3, 6, 10, 26, 27, 31, 34, 35, 51, 52, 54, 56, 58, 65, 66, 71, 72, 74, 78, 79, 81, 82, 84, 87, 91, 92, 94–99, 101, 105–107, 111–115, 118–130, 133, 134, 141, 144, 145, 148, 158, 159, 162, 164, 167, 169, 170–174, 177, 181, 182, 190, 192, 193, 195, 196, 198, 199, 202, 205–209, 211–214, 216, 223, 225, 233, 238, 247, 248, 250, 252, 253, 257, 261, 268, 275, 280, 281, 283, 285, 290, 303, 306, 307, 309, 313, 315, 316, 333, 336, 347, 348, 355–359, 361, 369, 384
Board of Regents, v, 7, 8, 13, 27, 52, 61, 66, 95, 96, 98, 100, 108, 112, 114, 115, 117–119, 124, 141, 185, 193, 212, 281, 306, 307, 315, 345, 352, 355–357, 363, 371
Boice, Gratia, 261
Bollinger, Lee, 123, 235
Bridge Tournaments, 295
Burnson, Kimberly Lingenfelter, 167
Business Manager/Treasurer, 24, 91, 92, 125, 130, 131, 317, 335
Buslee, Roger, 72
Buslee, Shirley Remquist, 72, 336
Calhoun, Leslie, 284, 337
Cama, Katayun Hormusji, 307
Caro-Delvaille, Henri, 30, 39
Cevala, Luanne, 252, 340
Chernow, Olive, 38, 50, 53, 54, 56, 84, 128, 131, 134, 159, 161, 176, 195, 198, 208, 215, 221, 267, 271, 298, 306, 307, 309, 330, 351, 352, 354–356, 358–361, 363–365, 367–370
Chinese Vases, 37
Christmas/Holiday Breakfast, 122, 151, 165, 215, 257, 264, 267, 269–271, 291, 358, 361, 367
Clark, Zelma E., 210, 326
Codd, Kathleen Warner, 328
Communications, 118, 160–164, 167, 365, 385
Computers, 78, 79, 122, 124, 162
Cook, Ann Bradford, 120, 309, 334
Cook, Chauncey, 3, 13, 14, 61, 66, 91, 113, 116, 119, 141, 350, 353, 354, 356
Cook, Jane Whitney, 119, 333
Cook, John Potter, 3, 40
Cook, Louise Stock, 27, 114, 116, 333

Cook, Martha Wolford, 27, 39, 254, 255, 279, 290
Cook, William Wilson, i, iii, v, vi, 1–14, 17, 18, 20, 22–27, 29–31, 34, 35, 37–42, 44, 45, 47, 49, 50, 52, 53, 58, 59, 61–64, 66, 68, 69, 71, 74, 75, 77, 88, 91–93, 96–100, 103, 109, 112, 113, 115–120, 123, 124, 126, 129, 130, 134, 135, 139, 141, 143, 146, 147, 153–156, 161, 163, 165, 169–174, 177, 179, 180, 182, 185–187, 189, 198, 202, 205, 206, 209–212, 217, 223, 236, 243–245, 247, 251, 252, 254, 263, 268, 275, 291, 296, 301, 305, 307, 309, 313, 315, 317–319, 333, 348–353, 355–359, 361, 362, 364, 366, 367, 369, 370
Cornell, Bernice, 245, 301, 328
Crawford, Jean, 246
Curie, Eve, 148
Dances and Mixers, 234, 235, 240, 241, 248, 263, 264–266, 280, 284, 297, 298, 309
Davis, Catherine Walsh, 214, 313, 334, 356, 359, 361, 365, 384
Davis, Sheila, 284, 311, 334, 341, 344
Dawbarn, Ethel G., 173, 177, 196, 197, 327, 361, 364, 365
Dean of Women, 7, 94, 115, 118–120, 122, 127, 137, 185, 188, 191, 193, 205–208, 212, 269, 270, 325, 327
DeBeliso, Patrick, 51
Dessert for New Women, 277, 278
Didier, Elaine Macklin, 82, 308, 309, 312, 334
Diekema, Leona Belser, 71–73, 84, 104, 128, 129, 145, 148, 150, 153, 161, 162, 172, 175, 180, 181, 192, 197, 198, 200, 202, 208, 213, 215, 222, 227, 233, 234, 237, 239, 250, 253, 260, 261, 264, 270, 272, 278–280, 282, 292, 293, 295, 297, 303, 304, 306, 328, 353, 354, 358, 364
Dining Facilities, 24, 29, 32, 75, 121, 219, 226, 235, 238, 246, 262, 275, 276, 281, 284, 286, 298

Dinner for Graduating Women, 140, 199, 215, 275, 276, 367, 368
Dinner for New Women, 140, 199, 273
Duch, Patricia, 134, 336
Duderstadt, James, 84, 309, 355
Duderstadt, Susan K., 310
Duffell, Thelma Hanshaw, 38, 133, 330
Edwina, statue, 35, 56, 58, 59, 110, 311, 313
Elevator, 32, 80–82, 100, 105, 131, 132, 136, 152, 261, 291, 303
Etiquette, rules, 128, 187
Eve (Girl in the Garden), statue, 35, 53–55, 59, 65, 148
Exam Snacks, 143, 222, 286
Fire Alarm, 84, 85, 98, 100, 107, 108, 266
Fire Suppression System, 85, 99, 101, 107, 111
Fischman, Quinn, 264
Fleming, Robben, 309
Ford, Gerald R., 148, 312
Forncrook, Elva Marcella, 157, 170, 171, 238, 268, 327, 366, 367, 370
Fresh Air Camp Picnic, 297
Freshman admissions, 171, 174, 183, 186, 188, 260
Fundraising Committee, 107–109, 123, 159, 163, 167, 330, 357, 384, 385
Garden, 17, 21, 44, 53, 54, 61, 62, 64–67, 87, 167, 265, 280, 287, 330
Giacoletto, Carol, 109, 334
Gibson, Frances Osborn, 303, 366
Gift Funds
    Anne E. Shipman Stevens Fund (see Scholarships)
    Annual Fund, iii, 58, 93, 107, 109, 110, 112
    Historic Preservation Fund, 93, 105–108, 111
    Martha Cook Alumnae Memorial Fund, 51, 100, 104, 105, 159, 211, 215, 216
    Pressler Fund, 106
Gleason, Mary E., iii, 191, 207, 238, 260, 269, 328, 333, 364

Glover, Grace, 245
Grace, 146, 155, 165, 226, 243
Great Depression, 5, 92, 93, 233, 247, 303, 356
Greenwood, Grace, 49, 64, 200–202, 220, 222, 250, 277, 326, 352, 365
Grijalva, Bob, 49, 51
Hager, Adele, 245
Hagerty, Hilda, 243
Halloween, 58, 140, 255, 258, 259, 264, 279, 290
Harper, E. Royster, 58, 110, 123
Harry Potter Week, 287
Hatcher, Harlan, 306, 309
Heath, Florentine Cook, 2, 5, 6, 71, 75, 115, 119, 120, 122, 170, 206, 209, 211, 213, 248, 307, 333, 353, 354, 356–358, 361, 364
Hockman, Meredith, 284
Hoilen, Genevieve, 137
Holden, Margaret Yerkes, 46, 309, 334, 339
Holland, Maurita Peterson, 162, 163, 334, 364
Hours, Lateness, Permission, 41, 73, 78, 124, 137, 143, 153, 185, 187–191, 193–196, 222, 225, 241, 280, 329, 363
House Board, 34, 46, 78, 79, 81, 105, 107, 120, 123, 124, 135, 139, 141–146, 148, 151, 156, 162, 164, 165, 167, 175, 188–193, 195, 198, 199, 206, 224, 228, 232, 234, 238–240, 246, 249, 252, 254, 261, 266, 267, 273–280, 285, 290, 292, 297, 303, 309, 355, 359, 366
House Director, 71, 72, 75, 77, 91, 93, 95, 121, 125, 127, 130, 182, 197, 209, 220, 228, 260, 297, 335, 358, 359, 361
Huebner, Adele, 53, 54, 305, 307, 352
Huebner, Trudy Veneklasen, 309
Hurst, Margaret, 258
Hutchins, Harry Burns, i, v, 7–9, 13, 26, 27, 70, 71, 113, 141, 291, 349–351, 353
Ivy Day, 293

James, Thelma, 118, 303, 304, 306, 307
Jaques, Edwina, 56, 110, 313
Johnson, Beth Yaros, 167, 214, 334
Johnson, Debra Ball McMillan, ii, iii, 107, 316
Johnson, Genevieve Goodman, 305
Jones, Vivian, 131
Keys, 86, 137, 189, 190, 191, 277
Knitting, 297
Knutson, Nina Jean, 205
Kostanecki, Bernice Pericin, 308, 358
Kreger, Janet, iii, 107, 310, 316, 334
Law, David, 72, 331
Law, Marion Scher, ii, iii, 57, 73, 121, 129, 254, 331, 356
Leary, Margaret A., iii, 1, 8, 10, 12, 49, 64, 120, 171, 254, 334, 348–350, 352, 353, 357, 361
Lim, Estefania Aldaba, 306, 307
Livingston, Virginia Capron, 144, 340
London, Colleen Burns, 308
Lotteries
  Football Game, 295
Mack, Frances, 24, 71, 75, 92, 93, 97, 130, 182, 317, 318, 335, 353, 354, 356, 362, 369
Main Corridor, 21, 26, 30, 34, 42, 54, 56, 83, 145, 219, 322
Male Visitation, 124, 184, 191–196
Marisa Szabo, 105
Martha Cook Alumnae Association
  Ann Arbor, 159
  Detroit (MCAAD), 104, 158, 307, 364
Martha Cook Alumnae Association (MCAA), ii, vi, 38, 51, 53, 74, 79, 100, 104–107, 111, 123, 155, 156, 158–168, 174, 206, 208, 211, 214–216, 246, 251, 281, 294, 308–310, 316, 330, 343, 355–358, 360–362, 364–366, 368–371, 384, 385
Mass Notification System, 99
Mathews, Rachel, 245
May Day Flower Basket, 296
McKnight, Beatrice, 258
Meals, 219

Al Fresco, 280
Brunch & Lunch, 225, 280
Cafeteria Meals, 219
Sunday Breakfast, 96, 224
Sunday Tea, 143, 225, 228, 275
Mehta, Nancy Kovacs, 34
Mehta, Zubin, 34, 148
Messiah Dinner, 133, 245, 247, 264, 280–285, 293, 366, 368, 384, 385
Milk & Cookies Tea, 167
Millard, Grace Grieve, 114, 115, 121, 333, 368
Moberg, Kathy Graneggen, 214, 316, 364–366, 385
Moore, Rosalie, 79, 128, 129, 208, 255, 285, 331, 354, 364, 368, 369
Munson, Elizabeth, 51
Munson, Marguerite, 34
Nash, Martha Cook, 120, 134, 334, 336
Open Houses, 191, 222, 294, 295
Open-opens, 192–195
Osborn, Barbara Osborne, 107
Outstanding Resident Award, 41, 159, 276, 343
Panchuk, Helen Lightfoot, 51
Parsons, Samuel, 17, 27, 45, 61, 62, 352, 353
Payne, Elizabeth, 53
Perkins, Ann Hanson, 308
Piano, Steinway, 11, 37, 49
Picasso, Gloria, 38, 83, 105, 174, 182, 276, 331
Plumbing, 87, 299, 315
Portia, statue, ii, 18, 30, 39, 44–47, 53, 59, 244, 301, 309, 321, 352
Powers, Harriet Fenske, 247, 330, 336, 337
Pressler, Louise, 105
Public Display of Affection, 197
Putnam, Pauline, 191, 234
Quail, Isabel Kemp, 128, 129, 161, 190, 275, 283, 329, 360, 361, 370
Ramseyer, Carrie, 247
Renovation, 75, 76, 84, 88, 89, 93, 101, 105, 109, 111, 112, 127, 152, 285, 315
Reunions
 1919, 301
 25th Anniversary, 118, 199, 200, 248, 303–305, 307
 50th Anniversary, 53, 54, 65, 159, 162, 166, 305, 330
 60th Anniversary, 248, 307
 75th Anniversary, 46, 102, 125, 154, 159, 161, 162, 308, 309
 90th Anniversary, 58, 108, 110, 159, 311
 100th Anniversary, i, 123, 276, 313
 Alumnae Weekends, 302
 U-M Victory Reunion, 305, 369
Roof, 17, 86, 87, 101, 107, 111, 152, 298, 304
Room Inspections, 200
Roosevelt, Eleanor, 148
Ross, Elizabeth Black, 53, 159, 307, 334, 360
Rowe, Sara, 72, 93, 95, 121, 127, 197, 221, 249, 250, 260, 270, 283, 294, 297, 335, 351, 365, 366, 368
Russianoff, Penelope Pearl, 309
Ruthven, Alexander G., 71, 74, 115, 122
Safety and Security, 84, 86, 100, 188
Sahn, Lenore Libby, 65, 66
Sargent, Emilie, 27, 120, 306, 339, 361
Sawyer, Philip, 14, 27, 39, 62, 350
Sawyer, Walter, i, 6, 8, 13, 93, 116, 117, 349, 353, 354, 356–359
Scholarship Dinner, 291, 292
Scholarships
 Anne E. Shipman Stevens Fund, 108, 112, 213
 Loans, 209, 210
 Minority Merit, 159, 211, 216
 Recipients, 178, 206
Scott, Ellen, 130, 133, 336
Scrantom, I. Elbert, 14, 18, 24, 29, 30–32, 38, 39, 41, 42, 47, 49, 62, 63, 247, 321, 324, 350–353, 366
Shaw, Jennifer Munfakh, 311
Skinner, Cornelia Otis, 5, 147, 359
Skrobola, Marie Fox, 123, 164, 334
Slemons, Marion, vi, 26, 27, 248, 289, 293, 295, 296, 348, 351, 353, 355, 358, 359, 362, 363, 366–370
Smith, Margaret Ruth, 210, 327

Smith, Shirley Wheeler, 1, 6, 10, 209, 348, 364
Smith, Veronica Latta, 308, 309, 334, 345
Songs, 243
Spicer-Simpson, Theodore, 39, 45, 351
Stevens, Anne E. Shipman, 54, 93, 95, 104, 114, 117, 118, 122, 129, 146, 157, 161, 165, 170, 183, 207, 209–213, 244, 265, 267–269, 271, 276, 291, 302, 304, 308, 333, 354, 358–361, 364
Stevens, Wystan, 308
Student Employment, 77, 120, 130, 133–137, 143, 182, 208, 220, 223, 226, 254, 335, 336, 359
Sudia, Nancy Howe Bielby, 105, 334, 365
Suttman, Paul, 53, 54, 55
Sutton, LaTonya, 182
Swain, Mary Ann, 309
Takai, Stephanie, 245, 256
Talent Show, 298
Teas
    Daily Tea, 232
    International Tea, 133, 150, 238–240, 254
    Special Teas, 146, 232, 234

Spring Tea, 52, 107, 159, 167, 199, 247, 254, 298
Tedesco, Lisa, 123
Terrace, 66
The Hayden Company, v, 6, 14, 24, 29, 41, 47, 49, 63, 352
Thompson, Elizabeth, 108, 213
Tinker, Mary Ann, 108
Turnover Dinner, 140, 275, 277
U-M Alumni Association, 163
Vaughn, Shirley Brown, 308, 369
Venus de Milo, statue, 21, 30, 41, 321
Vespers, 291
Welcome Week, 146, 258–262, 286
White, Myrtle, v, 7–10, 14, 349
Wine Tasting Parties, 297
World War I, 39, 41, 71, 152, 153, 180, 221, 234, 236, 269, 291, 305
World War II, 71, 152, 153, 180, 221, 234, 236, 269, 291, 305
Wreath, Martha Cook's Grave, 290
Wright, Katherine, 245
York and Sawyer (architects), v, 5, 13–15, 17, 20, 22, 24, 25, 42, 44, 45, 70, 73–75, 316, 350–353
York, Edward Palmer, 13, 14, 20, 25, 27, 62, 350
Zehnder, Jan, 193, 340

About the Authors

Catherine Walsh Davis '70, MM'76

Catherine lived at MCB during her junior and senior year while earning her BA in mathematics with a minor in journalism. She earned her Master of Management from U-M while working as a health record analyst at the Commission on Professional and Hospital Activities in Ann Arbor. She "retired" as the Manager of CPHA's Data Research and Statistics department to be a stay at home mom to two children. Her daughter is also a Cookie.

120. (twd) Catherine Walsh Davis

As a resident of the Martha Cook Building, Catherine served as chair of the Messiah Dinner and other committees. As an alumna she has twice served on the Building's Board of Governors. She has also been President of the Martha Cook Alumnae Association and Chair of MCB's Fundraising Committee.

She and husband Bill Davis '69, MM '76 are avid amateur genealogists.

Kathy Graneggen Moberg '79

Kathy majored in English and Honors History and lived in MCB the entire time she was at U-M. As a resident her activities included Cookie Corner chair, Messiah Dinner co-chair, office assistant, and tour guide. She earned a Masters in Historic Preservation from Eastern Michigan University in 1982.

121. (bgm) Kathy Graneggen Moberg

Kathy joined the MCAA Board in the mid-1990s and was newsletter editor for several years. She is still the "Cookie Crumbs" editor and writes regularly for the newsletter. She has also served MCB as a Governor and Fundraising Committee member.

The mother of three (and aunt to one Cookie), she is Volunteer Coordinator for the Friends of her local library and helps run their used book shop. Her hobbies include reading mystery novels, attending theater, and traveling with her husband, Bert Moberg '76.